ANGLO-AMERICAN INSANITY DEFENCE REFORM

Anglo-American Insanity Defence Reform

The war between law and medicine

FAYE BOLAND, BCL (N.U.I.), PhD
Lecturer in Law
The University of Liverpool

Ashgate

DARTMOUTH

Aldershot • Brookfield USA • Singapore • Sydney

Published by
Dartmouth Publishing Company Limited
Ashgate Publishing Ltd
Gower House
Croft Road
Aldershot
Hants GU11 3HR
England

Ashgate Publishing Company
Old Post Road
Brookfield
Vermont 05036
USA

British Library Cataloguing in Publication Data
Boland, Faye
  Anglo-American insanity defence reform : the war between
  law and medicine
  1.Law reform 2.Insanity - Jurisprudence
  I.Title
340.3

Library of Congress Cataloging-in-Publication Data
Boland, Faye.
    Anglo-American insanity defence reform : the war
between law and medicine / Faye Boland.
        p.   cm.
    Includes bibliographical references and index.
    ISBN 1-84014-716-4 (hc.)
    1. Insanity--Jurisprudence--United States--History.
2. Criminal liability--United States--History. 3. Law
reform--United States--History. I. Title.
KF9242.B65 1998
345.73'04--dc21   98-36009
                                                       CIP

ISBN 1 84014 716 4

Printed and bound by Athenaeum Press, Ltd.,
Gateshead, Tyne & Wear.

Contents

Preface

Insanity defence reform in England, Ireland and the United States has been plagued by controversy. Chapters 1 to 4 of this book explore the extent of the polemic surrounding the insanity defence, the source of the controversy and the view of many commentators that all reformulations of the insanity defence are doomed to failure. Chapters 5 and 6 examine the origin and operation of the English diminished responsibility defence, introduced in 1957, as a partial defence to murder. This book is an examination of the degree to which the diminished defence has abated the controversy over the insanity defence and resolved the medico-legal conflict at the heart of this polemic.

The first three years of studying insanity defence reform were made possible thanks to the generosity of my parents who supported me financially whilst a PhD student at the University of Leeds. This book would never have been possible without them. Nor would it have been possible without the support and guidance of Mr Alan Reed at the University of Leeds. The encouragement and support of colleagues at the University of Liverpool was invaluable in ensuring the completion of this project: particular thanks are due to Professor Dominic McGoldrick, Dr Judy Laing, Ms Kirsty Keywood, Mr Steve Cooper, Mrs Marie Ball and Ms Janet Hughes.

Finally, a big thank you is due to Steve Culshaw for reading parts of this book and producing camera ready copy, a task which I could never have completed on my own.

Table of Statutes

Table of Cases

1 The McNaghten Rules

McNaghten's case

In approaching the issue of Anglo-American insanity defence reform I intend to take as my starting point the McNaghten Rules. The McNaghten Rules form the test of insanity in both England and Ireland and at some point or another have comprised the basis of the insanity defence in almost every State of the United States.[1] They are considered to be *"the* point of reference for the insanity plea's history",[2] pre-McNaghten authorities being long-since regarded as mere "antiquarian curiosities".[3] Indeed it has been said that "there is abundant authority for treating the McNaghten rules as independent of earlier authority, as if they were a new code of the law of insanity".[4]

The Rules arose out of the highly controversial acquittal[5] on the grounds of insanity of Daniel McNaghten, for the murder of Sir Robert Peel's private secretary. McNaghten, a paranoiac, believed that he was being persecuted by the Tories for voting against them in an election. He decided to kill Sir Robert Peel, the Prime Minister, but mistaking Sir Robert Peel's private secretary, Drummond, for Peel himself, McNaghten shot and killed Drummond. McNaghten was acquitted by reason of his insanity, leading to a public furore. As a result,[6] on March 13 1843 the House of Lords took the unusual (though not unprecedented)[7] step of formulating a series of questions for the consideration of the judges of England. Lord Brougham's stated reason for putting the questions to the assembly of judges was his belief that their answers

> Would lead to more uniformity in the language they used on future occasions in charging and directing juries on this most delicate and important subject...They would no longer indulge in that variety of phrase which only served to perplex others, if it did not also tend to bewilder themselves, as he supposed it sometimes did; but they would use one constant phrase, which the public and all persons concerned would be able to understand.[8]

Following a debate in the House of Lords[9] the judges were asked the following questions:-

1. What is the law respecting alleged crimes committed by persons afflicted with insane delusion, in respect of one or more particular subjects or persons; as, for instance, where at the time of the commission of the alleged crime, the accused knew he was acting contrary to law, but did the act complained of with a view, under the influence of insane delusion, of redressing or revenging some supposed grievance or injury or of producing some supposed public benefit?
2. What are the proper questions to be submitted to the jury when a person alleged to be afflicted with insane delusion respecting one or more particular subjects or persons, is charged with the commission of a crime (murder, for example), and insanity is set up as a defence?
3. In what terms ought the question to be left to the jury, as to the prisoner's state of mind at the time when the act was committed?
4. If a person under an insane delusion as to existing facts commits an offence in consequence thereof, is he thereby excused?[10]

The answers given,[11] are known as the McNaghten Rules and they have been applied ever since in determining the criminal responsibility of insane offenders. They are:-

Assuming that your Lordships' inquiries are confined to those persons who labour under such partial delusions only, and are not in other respects insane, we are of opinion that notwithstanding the party accused did the act complained of with a view, under the influence of insane delusion, of redressing or revenging some supposed grievance or injury, or of producing some public benefit, he is nevertheless punishable according to the nature of the crime committed, if he knew at the time of committing such crime that he was acting contrary to law; by which expression we understand your Lordships to mean the law of the land

The answer to question 1 can be read in conjunction with the answer to question 4 which also dealt with delusions.

The answer must of course depend on the nature of the delusion: but, making the same assumption as we did before, namely, that he labours under such partial delusion only and is not in other respects insane, we think he must be considered in the same situation as to responsibility as if the facts with respect to which the delusion exists were real. For example if under the influence of his delusion he supposes another man to be in the act of attempting to take away his life, and he kills that man, as he supposes, in self defence, he would be exempt from punishment. If the delusion was that the deceased had inflicted a serious injury to his character and fortune, and he killed him in revenge for such supposed injury, he would be liable to punishment.

Question 2 and question 3 were answered together and have come to be regarded as the heart of the Rules[12]:-

...the jurors ought to be told in all cases that every man is to be presumed to be sane, and to possess a sufficient degree of reason to be responsible for his crimes, until the contrary be proved to their satisfaction; and that to establish a defence on the ground of insanity, it must be clearly proved that, at the time of the committing of the act, the party accused was labouring under such a defect of reason from disease of the mind, as not to know the nature and quality of the act he was doing; or if he did know it, that he did not know he was doing what was wrong. This mode of putting the latter part of the question to the jury on these occasions has generally been, whether the accused at the time of doing the act knew the difference between right and wrong: which mode, though rarely, if ever, leading to any mistake with the jury, is not, as we conceive, so accurate when put generally and in the abstract, as when put with reference to the party's knowledge of right and wrong in respect to the very act with which he is charged. If the question were to be put as to the knowledge of the accused solely and exclusively with reference to the law of the land, it might tend to confound the jury, by inducing them to believe that an actual knowledge of the law of the land was essential in order to lead to a conviction; whereas the law is administered upon the principle that everyone must be taken conclusively to know it, without proof that he does know it. If the accused was conscious that the act was one which he ought not to do, and if that act was at the same time contrary to the law of the land, he is punishable; and the usual course therefore has been to leave the question to the jury, whether the party accused had a sufficient degree of reason to know that he was doing an act that was wrong: and this course we think is correct accompanied with such observations and explanations as the circumstances of each particular case may require.

It is worth noting that questions 1, 2 and 4 were framed with reference to delusions and that the judges answers were also confined to "[t]hose who labour under such partial delusions only". The judges' view was that to establish a successful plea of insanity it must be proved that the accused at the time of the act, was labouring under such *defect of reason from disease of the mind that he did not know the nature and quality of his act and if he did know this, he did not know that it was wrong.*[13] Interestingly, if this test had been applied at the trial McNaghten would not have been found insane.[14]

The meaning of these key words has been settled by precedent. In *R v Clarke*[15] a moment of absentmindedness brought on by depression led the defendant to transfer some items from a supermarket shopping basket to her bag without paying for them. The Court of Appeal held that "defect of reason" does not include mere failure to exercise reasoning powers which are still intact. The assistant recorder was therefore wrong in ruling that her defence amounted to a defence of insanity.

"Disease of the mind" has a legal rather than a medical meaning[16] and has been construed broadly so as to include mental disorders which are functional or organic, permanent or transient and intermittent or whose source is physiological, provided that the disorder has impaired the mental faculties of "reason memory and understanding".[17] In *Bratty v A.G. for Northern Ireland,*[18] Lord Denning went so far as to say that "any mental disorder which has manifested itself in violence and is prone to recur is a disease of the mind". It now appears that absence of the danger of recurrence is not a reason for saying that an abnormal condition cannot be a disease of the mind,[19] provided that its cause can be considered "internal" to the defendant rather than "external".[20] This interpretation, which has led to an absurd result for epileptics, hyperglycaemics and sleep-walkers, will be discussed further *below*. The meaning of "nature and quality" of the act has been defined as an understanding of the physical nature of the act in *Codère's case*[21] and *R v Windle*[22] held that "wrong" implies knowledge of the illegality of the act. Windle's wife was always talking about suicide and to relieve her of her suffering he gave her a fatal dose of 100 aspirin tablets. He later told the police that he supposed he would be hanged for it. Because he knew the illegality of his act the Court of Criminal Appeal held that the insanity defence was not open to him and that Devlin J. had been right to withdraw the case from the jury.

In the United States it has been said that "conflict of opinion exists..regarding almost every word of the famous Opinion of the Judges and its numerous and motley progeny".[23]   Thus although lack of knowledge of the nature and quality of the act and lack of knowledge of wrongfulness are required disjunctively in the Rules, in some decisions these have been put conjunctively and in many decisions "and" and "or" have been used indiscriminately.[24] By the late 1960's few courts had adopted the strict approach of their English counterparts (discussed *below*) in interpreting the knowledge requirement[25] and it has been said that the United States courts have generally avoided the interpretation of wrong as legally wrong.[26]

The above interpretations have been subject to a great deal of criticism in the considerable body of literature which has grown up around the Rules. By drawing on this literature I hope to show why the Rules caused as much controversy as they did. This will enable me to examine in later Chapters, the adequacy of reforms of the insanity defence in Ireland and the United States, in terms of resolving the controversy over the McNaghten Rules.

Criticism of the Rules

Criticism of the Rules commenced in the House of Lords itself.[27] Maule J. protested that the questions were put without reference to the facts of any particular case, that there had been no debate on them and that the answers given might embarrass the administration of justice.[28] Tindal C.J. protested that

> they deemed it at once impracticable, and at the same time dangerous to the administration of justice, if it were practicable, to attempt to make minute application of the principles involved in the Answers.[29]

As Glueck has commented[30] this suggests that the judges felt that the law as they had stated it applied to the hypothetical facts of the questions submitted and that it was too narrow to cover all possible conditions of insanity.

Although the status of the Rules was questionable, there is no doubt that they have acquired authority through repeated reference to them.[31] However, their extension in *R v Windle* to cover all cases of insanity (and not just delusion) has been most controversial,[32] as the questions and answers were framed solely with reference to delusions.

The most incisive criticism of the Rules has probably been the fact some insane offenders went to the gallows because the tests were too narrow a criterion of responsibility.[33] This criticism still applies to those United States that maintain the death penalty. Although the death penalty has long been abolished in England and Ireland, the McNaghten Rules continue to wreak fierce injustice. As the Butler Committee noted in 1975 the interpretation of "wrong" as meaning knowledge of the legal wrongness of the act[34] greatly narrows the scope of the insanity plea since even grossly disturbed persons generally know that murder, for example, is a crime.[35] Surprisingly, Mackay's research has found that it is this particular limb which is most commonly used to secure a special verdict.[36] This suggests that judges or juries may be ignoring the meaning of wrong, stated in *Windle*.

The correctness of the interpretation of wrong as meaning legal wrongness is, in fact, questionable in light of the judges' statement in *McNaghten* that

> If the question were to be put as to the knowledge of the accused solely and exclusively with reference to the law of the land, it might tend to confound the jury, by inducing them to believe that an actual knowledge of the law of the land was essential in order to lead to a conviction; whereas the law is administered upon the principle that every one must be taken conclusively to know it, without proof that he does know it. If the accused was conscious that the act was one which he ought not to do, and if that act was at the same time contrary to the law of the land, he is punishable.[37]

The scope of the Rules was restricted by the interpretation of "nature and quality" to mean the physical quality of an act.[38] This excludes the offender who knows what he is doing but does not appreciate the impact of his act or its consequences. Stephen argued that knowledge required a deeper level of understanding than "mere knowledge",[39] but the courts have not required an appreciation or understanding of the nature, quality or wrongness of an act, thereby excluding a vast number of medically insane offenders from the ambit of the insanity plea.

The broadness with which "disease of the mind" is interpreted (requiring simply that the disease be internal to the defendant)[40] has led to epileptics,[41] diabetics (in a state of hyperglycaemia)[42] and sleep-walkers[43] being classified as insane. This widening of the concept of disease of the mind in the McNaghten Rules in the interest of public protection, has resulted in a restriction of the defence of automatism, which leads to an outright acquittal in the case of unconscious involuntary acts not attributable to disease of the mind within the Rules.

The widening of "disease of the mind" began with *R v Kemp*[44] where Lord Devlin ruled that arteriosclerosis (which in this case had not yet caused degeneration of the brain cells) was a disease of the mind as a disease of the mind was not restricted to a disease of the brain, and insofar as the accused's condition affected the ordinary mental faculties of "reason, memory and understanding".[45] This case was in marked contrast to the earlier approach of Barry J. in *Charlson*[46] who allowed the jury to consider whether a brain tumour in the defendant caused a state of automatism, after he had hit his son on the head with a hammer and thrown him out of a window causing him serious injury.

Then in *Bratty v A.G. for Northern Ireland*[47] Lord Denning disclosed the public protection role of the insanity defence, asserting that "any mental disorder which has manifested itself in violence and is prone to recur is a disease of the mind. At any rate it is the sort of disease for which a person should be detained in hospital rather than be given an unqualified acquittal".[48] It appeared likely from this *dictum* that a mental condition would not qualify as McNaghten madness if it was not likely to recur, but the Court of Appeal in *Burgess*[49] has stated that absence of the danger of recurrence will not prevent a finding of disease of the mind within the McNaghten Rules.

Another criterion for distinguishing automatism from insanity has emerged out of the Court of Appeal decision in *R v Quick and Paddison*.[50] There the first named defendant was tried for assault occasioning actual bodily harm on a patient in the hospital where he worked as a nurse. The trial judge ruled that his condition of hypoglycaemia (brought on by food abstinence and alcohol following an injection of insulin to treat his diabetes) could only support the defence of insanity and not automatism.

Presumably this is because *Quick* had previously suffered several hypoglycaemic episodes, some of which had issued in violence. The Court of Appeal held that disease of the mind within the McNaghten Rules did not include a malfunctioning of the mind of transitory effect caused by the application to the body of some *external* factor such as violence, drugs, anaesthetics, alcohol, hypnotic influences or insulin and that accordingly, the issue of automatism should have been left to the jury.

It should be noted that the Court of Appeal stated who were not to be treated as suffering from disease of the mind and did not suggest that the converse of this principle was an infallible indication of those who were suffering from a disease of the mind.[51] "To say that the presence of an external cause of mental trouble saves a man from the imputation of madness does not imply that the absence of an external cause necessarily means that he is mad".[52]

Sleep-walking and Epilepsy

However the Court of Appeal has recently confirmed in *Burgess* that there *is* an internal/external cause doctrine by ruling that the defendant's sleep-walking amounted to insanity because it arose from an internal cause and had manifested itself in violence, although it was unlikely to recur in the form of serious violence. Burgess had spent the evening watching video tapes at the flat of a female friend. The friend fell asleep, during which time the appellant hit her over the head with a bottle and the video recorder and then grasped her around the throat. When she cried out the defendant appeared to come to his senses and showed great anxiety over his deeds. After calling for an ambulance for the victim, who was severely cut on the head, he ran away from the scene. At his trial for wounding with intent he argued unsuccessfully that he lacked *mens rea* at the time he attacked the victim because he was sleepwalking and was suffering from automatism. The Court of Appeal dismissed his appeal.

Although the extension of disease of the mind to cover sleep-walking had been anticipated,[53] it is a difficult proposition to accept in view of the fact that for years sleep-walking has been cited as a self-evident illustration of automatism. An example is Stephen J. in *Tolson's* case[54] who asked "Can anyone doubt that a man who, though he might be perfectly sane, committed what would otherwise be a crime in a state of somnambulism would be entitled to be acquitted? And why is this? Simply because he would not know what he was doing".[55] In *Bratty* both Lord Denning[56] and Lord Morris of Borth-Y-Gest[57] referred to sleep-walking as an example of automatism.

Furthermore, a defence of automatism based on evidence of sleep-walking has succeeded in several earlier English cases. In 1936 *Stone* was acquitted of an offence against a girl who lived in his house, on the grounds that he was asleep.[58] In 1949 a soldier, *Price*, attacked his corporal with a bayonet while awaking from a dream and was acquitted.[59] In 1951 *Paltridge*, who tried to strangle his wife and then hit her with an axe while asleep, was acquitted after a mere ten minutes deliberation by the jury.[60] More significantly, Sergeant *Boshears* was acquitted of the murder of a young girl on the grounds of automatism caused by sleep-walking.[61] As late as 1978 *Hughes* was acquitted on the same grounds after she had risen in the night while still asleep, to fetch a knife to peel potatoes and then stabbed her husband with it.[62]

Another objection to the decision in *Burgess* is that the fundamental requirement that the defect of reason be caused by disease of the mind was not satisfied. The defendant's consciousness and therefore his faculty of reason was suspended when he fell asleep and hence his defect of reason was caused by sleep, a natural condition, and not by sleep-walking which was classified as a pathological or internal condition.[63] This is the approach which was taken by the Ontario Court of Appeal in *R v Parks*,[64] approving the trial judge's ruling that "it would not seem consonant with sound criminal law policy to force into the notion "disease of the mind", and hence legal insanity, and the stigmatization and confinement associated with a special verdict, a person who suffers from a sleep disorder whose behaviour whilst in an awakened state is otherwise socially acceptable".[65]

Notwithstanding the English Court of Appeal's decision in *Burgess*, which was decided in the interim between the decision of the Ontario Court of Appeal and that of the Supreme Court, the Supreme Court of Canada upheld *Parks'* acquittal on the grounds of automatism,[66] the majority following the Court of Appeal's line of reasoning. The minority (consisting of LaForest and five concurring judges) was of the opinion that somnambulism is a condition that is not well-suited to analysis under either of the "continuing danger" or "internal cause" theories and that the court may also have to look to certain additional policy considerations such as whether the condition is easily feigned and whether the recognition of the condition as non-insane automatism would open the floodgates. The minority found that none of these factors suggested that somnambulism should be considered a disease of the mind and that accordingly, there were no compelling policy factors to preclude a finding that the accused's condition in this case was one of non-insane automatism.

It appears that the House of Lords may have *sub silentio* adopted the internal/external cause distinction in the earlier case of *R v Sullivan*.[67] There the appellant, a man of blameless reputation, was charged with inflicting grievous bodily harm in the final stage of recovering from a minor epileptic seizure. He pleaded guilty to the lesser charge of assault occasioning actual bodily harm, after the trial judge ruled that his condition amounted to insanity and not automatism. The House of Lords conceded that an external factor such as a blow to the head causing concussion or the administration of an anaesthetic for therapeutic purposes might warrant a finding of automatism. However if, as in this case, there was impairment of the defendant's faculties of reason, memory and understanding, it did not matter whether this impairment was organic, as in epilepsy, or functional or permanent or transient and intermittent provided that it subsisted at the time of the commission of the act.

As with sleep-walking, epilepsy was presumed for many years to be a paradigmatic example of automatism. Barry J. in *Charlson* was of the view that a criminal act committed by an epileptic would warrant an acquittal "because the actions of an epileptic are automatic and unconscious and his will or consciousness is not applied to what he is doing",[68] while Lord Denning in *Bratty* described automatism as "an act which is done by the muscles without any control by the mind, such as a spasm, a reflex action or a convulsion".[69] It is interesting to note the Law Commission's decision to include "a reflex, spasm or convulsion" in the Draft Criminal Code's definition of automatism.[70]

In the course of this endeavour to protect the public, the courts have clearly eschewed all logic in the classification of conditions as insane.[71] On a commonsense understanding of the term insanity (and the Court of Appeal in *Quick* did, after all, stress that the issue of insanity should be approached "in a commonsense way")[72] neither the epileptic nor the sleep-walker can be classified as insane. The test in *Quick* is capable of leading to very arbitrary results. Although sleep-walking will be treated as a disease of the mind, if caused by eating cheese it will qualify for the defence of automatism as cheese[73] would probably be considered to be an external cause.[74] Under the internal/external factor doctrine it matters whether the accused's automatism was the result of a failure to take insulin or a failure to take the proper amount.[75] Whilst the latter diabetic will receive an outright acquittal, the former has, until recently, received automatic indefinite incarceration and the stigma of an insanity label. Avoidance of this fate was obviously the primary consideration of *Sullivan* and *Quick*, both of whom pleaded guilty after hearing that his condition amounted to insanity. Contrary to the popular assumption, it is interesting to note Mackay's finding that hospitalisation has not always followed a finding of not guilty by reason of insanity and that the majority of those acquitted by reason of insanity have been sent to local hospitals where in some instances they were released within a mere matter of months.[76]

The situation has been ameliorated in England by the Criminal Procedure (Insanity and Unfitness to Plead) Act, 1991 which provides for discretionary disposal of the criminally insane except in the case of offences carrying a fixed penalty. The inapplicability of the 1991 Act to insane murderers however, signifies a continuing need for the discretionary disposal consequences which accompany the diminished responsibility defence, to protect the epileptic, the diabetic and the sleep-walker[77] who kill, from the "double-edged acquittal"[78] which follows a finding of insanity in the case of murder. The merits of this defence will be discussed further in Chapter Six.

Psychological Blow

Whether a dissociative state resulting from a psychological blow can give rise to a defence of automatism, has yet to be decided by the English Courts, although a number of Canadian cases have accepted that a psychological blow may be viewed as an external cause leading to an acquittal on the grounds of automatism.[79] However, the Ontario Court of Appeal in *Rabey*[80] has since held that a dissociative state arising from a psychological blow is not an external cause for the purposes of automatism. Holding that "the ordinary stresses and disappointments of life which are the common lot of mankind do not constitute an external cause constituting an explanation for a malfunctioning of the mind which takes it out of the category of a 'disease of the mind'", the Court of Appeal left open the question whether a dissociative state resulting from an emotional shock that might be presumed to affect the average normal person can amount to an external cause.

The facts of *Rabey* are of interest as an illustration of the circumstances that can give rise to a dissociative state. The defendant, a university student who was emotionally attached to the victim, discovered in a letter she had written that she regarded him as a "nothing". The next day the defendant met the victim by chance and hit her with a rock which he had taken from the geology lab to study. He then began to choke her. A witness who saw the defendant shortly afterwards, described him as very pale, sweating, glassy-eyed and as having a frightened expression. The defendant testified that he could not remember striking the victim. A psychiatrist called by the defence testified that the accused had entered into a complete dissociative state after conversing with the victim, in which he was capable of performing physical actions but without consciousness of such action. The dissociative state, which was comparable to that produced by a physical blow, was caused by a psychological blow. A psychiatrist called by the defence testified that this was not a disease of the mind, that he could find no evidence that the accused had suffered from any pathological condition and that there was only a slight possibility of recurrence. The trial judge accepted the evidence of the defence psychiatrist and the defendant was acquitted. The Crown then successfully appealed to the Ontario Court of Appeal. The Canadian Supreme Court affirmed the finding of the Court of Appeal.

The minority view that in the absence of psychiatric disorder, or the likelihood of recurrence, *Rabey's* dissociative state should not have been branded with the label of insanity, has received support from academic commentators.[81] However, in view of the increasingly visible public protection role of the insanity defence and the recent unsatisfactory developments with regard to sleep-walking and epilepsy, it is likely that *Rabey* will be followed by the English Courts. The English Court of Appeal has already held in *Hennessy*[82] that ordinary stresses and strains do not amount to an external cause for the purpose of a defence of automatism. However a distinction might legitimately be made between Rabey who dissociated before committing a crime and a defendant like Hennessy who committed a crime without dissociating.

In the recent Crown Court decision of *R v T.*,[83] the defendant was acquitted on the grounds of automatism of charges of robbery and actual bodily harm, after medical evidence was led that being the victim of a rape three days prior to the offences had led to post traumatic stress disorder in the defendant. The psychiatrist testified that at the time of the offence she had entered a dissociative state and that the offences had been committed during a psychogenic fugue so that she was not acting with a conscious mind or will. In deciding that the rape was an external cause for the purposes of automatism the judge found that "such an incident could have an appalling effect on any young woman, however well-balanced normally".[84] The decision falls squarely within the exceptional circumstances which would affect the average person, envisaged in *Rabey*, but the availability or not of the defence of automatism where a dissociative state is induced by the "ordinary stresses and disappointments of life" has yet to be decided by the English Court of Appeal. No argument is needed to show that the indefinite confinement of the above-named classes of offenders, who on a common sense interpretation of the word could not possibly be considered insane, is unjust (although the situation in England has been ameliorated somewhat by the discretionary disposal consequences introduced by the Criminal Procedure (Insanity and Unfitness to Plead) Act, 1991 where the offence does not carry a fixed sentence). Furthermore, in deciding that a condition is a "disease of the mind" for the purposes of the Rules, the courts need not take account of the fact that the condition will not recur.[85] It is *dicta* like these which have provoked the criticism that the Rules "have been interpreted with all the clinical detachment of a tax statute".[86] Another criticism is that the Rules were never intended to deal with involuntary action, for which the automatism defence was developed.[87]

It is also likely that the McNaghten Rules are in breach of Article 5(1)(e) of the European Convention on Human Rights. In order to conform with Article 5(1)(e), hospitalisation following an acquittal of criminal charges must be a "lawful detention" of a person "of unsound mind".[88] Public policy or perceived dangerousness are not criteria which justify deprivation of liberty under the European Convention. However in *Burgess*[89] these appear to be the factors that led to the application of McNaghten. *Sullivan*[90] pleaded guilty to avoid a finding of insanity and consequent indefinite committal.

Section 1(1) of the Criminal Procedure (Insanity and Unfitness to Plead) Act, 1991 lays down that the jury must hear medical evidence from at least two medical practitioners before returning an insanity verdict, one of whom must be "duly approved" by the Secretary of State under section 12(2) of the Mental Health Act, 1983 "as having special experience in the diagnosis or treatment of mental disorder". At first glance this appears to bring the McNaghten Rules within the terms of Article 5(1)(e), which has been interpreted as requiring psychiatric evidence of mental illness and of the need for compulsory confinement.[91] In reality however, the necessary medical evidence under section 1(1) lacks any binding force[92] and so the Rules continue to be in breach of the European Convention, at least in murder cases where indefinite hospitalisation remains the only possible disposal, and in the case of other offences, where the chosen method of disposal involves the deprivation of liberty.

In recent years Lord Brougham's aspiration of a clear definition of legal insanity has not been realised and "[i]t is doubtful whether there is any field of law in which there has been as much confusion and variation in interpreting the very same words of a seemingly simple legal formula as there has been in the court-room operation of the McNaghten rules".[93] The vast majority of witnesses who gave evidence to the Royal Commission on Capital Punishment (1949-53) were of the view that the Rules were now more liberally interpreted by judges, some going so far as to say that "interpretation" might occasionally mean that the words were twisted into a meaning that could not reasonably be put on them, or even that the Rules might be ignored altogether.[94] That this might be the position today is lent weight by Mackay's finding that despite the Butler Committee's view of the narrowness of legal wrongness, it is this particular limb which is most commonly used to secure a special verdict[95] and that in many cases there is little attempt made to distinguish between lack of knowledge of legal wrong and unawareness of moral wrong.[96] Mowat commented that judges *and* juries interpret the Rules with some elasticity, often to the extent of paying only lip-service to them.[97] The complicated requirements of the McNaghten Rules create a real risk that the minds of the jury may become confused.[98] Indeed the Scottish Lord Justice General, Lord Cooper, told the Royal Commission on Capital Punishment of 1949-53 that however much the jury were charged as to the McNaghten Rules or any other test, when they retired they simply asked themselves "Is the man mad or is he not?".[99] However this opinion may be far-fetched as Simon's research on jury deliberations in insanity cases suggests that the jury recognises the distinction between a clinical diagnosis and the application of a moral legal criterion and that this is what they must apply in deciding the case[100] and that juries are by and large conscientious in performing their task.[101] However whether the jury understands the moral legal criterion *itself* is a different matter.[102] Mr Justice Frankfurter was highly critical of the practice of by-passing the Rules, in his evidence to the Royal Commission:[103]

> If you find rules that are, broadly speaking, discredited by those who have to administer them, which is, I think, the real situation, certainly with us - they are honoured in the breach and not in the observance - then I think the law serves its best interests by trying to be more honest about it..I think that to have rules which cannot rationally be justified except by a process of interpretation which distorts and often practically nullifies them, and to say the corrective process comes by having the Governor of a State charged with the responsibility of deciding when the consequences of the Rule should not be enforced, is not a desirable system..I am a great believer in being as candid as possible about my institutions. They are in large measure abandoned in practice, and therefore I think the M'Naghten Rules are in large measure shams.

The Medical Critique

The main criticism of the McNaghten Rules from a medical point of view is that they over-emphasise the cognitive aspect of mental functioning and ignore the affective and conative aspects.[104]

> The modern science of psychology..does not conceive that there is a separate little man in the top of one's head called reason whose function it is to guide another unruly little man called instinct, emotion, or impulse in the way he should go. The tendency of psychiatry is to regard what ordinary men call reasoning as a rationalization of behaviour rather than the real cause of behaviour.[105]

The Rules are founded on the now "half scientific, half fantastic"[106] doctrine of phrenology, first put forward by Franz Gall, a Viennese physician, at the turn of the 18th century. Phrenology divides the mind into separate compartments and assumes that each aspect of mental functioning can operate independently of the others. Gall was of the view that there were at least thirty four such faculties and that their degree of development could be discovered by examining the corresponding bump on the skull.[107] This doctrine has long been totally discredited.[108] The Rules have been criticised for assuming that although one region of the brain may be diseased e.g. volition, the mind may be sound in all its other aspects and that reason or understanding may function perfectly.[109] In fact one critic goes so far as to say that the judges' stipulation - "assuming that your Lordships' inquiries are confined to those persons who labour under such partial delusions only, and are not in other respects insane", vitiates any credibility that the Rules might have as criteria of responsibility as "this is a class of offender that does not exist and never has existed".[110]

The judges' treatment of delusion (questions 1. and 4.) has been much criticised, especially their assumption that a deluded man can reason as a sane man and should be judged by the same standard.[111] This in effect, makes the courts pick and choose between delusions.[112] According to Stephen, to a sane man, the belief that his finger was made of glass "would supply no reason for taking any particular view about murder, but if a man is mad and such a belief is a symptom of his madness, there may be a connection between the delusion and the crime as insane as the delusion itself".[113] Fortunately this objection is of less practical importance today since the scenario of the deluded offender in question 1 is now governed by the knowledge tests.[114] Another valid criticism is that by focusing entirely on knowledge of the nature and quality of the act and its wrongness, the court is apt to lose sight of what should be the central issue:- a defect of reason caused by disease of the mind.[115] Sutherland and Gearty assert that the courts have traditionally attached only limited significance to medical opinion regarding mental abnormality[116] and McAuley speaks of "the relatively neglected notion of 'disease of the mind'".[117]

The Rules are framed in such a way that psychiatric testimony is limited to an account of the accused's cognitive powers.[118] The fact that psychiatrists cannot give an overall account of the accused's condition, which would paint a much more realistic picture than snippets of information do, has provoked strong dissatisfaction amongst the medical profession.[119] Goldstein, however, claims that there is virtually no support in law for the view that McNaghten is responsible for inhibiting the flow of testimony on the insanity issue[120] but that prolonged criticism of the Rules has convinced psychiatrists that they cannot give a full account of the accused's mental life and that the critics have in fact "created the very devil they were trying to exorcise".[121]

On the other hand there are some staunch defenders of the Rules. As Baron Bramwell said in his evidence before the Select Committee on the Homicide Law (Amendment) Bill in 1874[122]

> I think that although the present law lays down such a definition of madness, that nobody is hardly ever really mad enough to be within it yet it is a logical and good definition.

Lady Wooton has praised the intellectualist quality of the McNaghten formula which, she says, makes it "a model of clarity and precision".[123] In the light of the defence of irresistible impulse, discussed in Chapter Two, she praises the McNaghten Rules, saying

> The state of a man's intellect or knowledge is much more easily tested by such court procedures as cross-examination, than is say, the state of the will.[124]

The Rules have also been commended on the grounds that they are in harmony with the law's fundamental doctrine of *mens rea*. Lord Devlin has commented

[A]s part of the doctrine of *mens rea* it ensures that a man who does an injurious act without appreciation of its consequences does not forfeit the protection of the law. But the failure to appreciate must be total, for, if he has an appreciation in some degree, he is rightly made answerable to the law.[125]

Later Lord Devlin says

There is something logical - it may be astringently logical, but it is logical - in selecting as the test of responsibility to the law, reason and reason alone. It is reason which makes a man responsible to the law. It is reason which gives him sovereignty over animate and inanimate things. It is what distinguishes him from the animals, which emotional disorder does not; it is what makes him man; it is what makes him subject to the law. So it is fitting that nothing other than a defect of reason should give him complete absolution.[126]

McNaghten's critics on the other hand, argue that *mens rea* requires volition[127] and also requires a guilty *healthy* mind.[128] The view that impairment of knowledge is more readily demonstrable than impairment of will, will be examined further in Chapter Six.

As the above discussion reveals, much ink has been spent criticising the McNaghten Rules. The majority of this ink has come from the pens of psychiatrists who advocated a more medicalised defence of insanity. The judges have resisted this pressure and repeatedly asserted that the law's conception of insanity is not the same as medicine's. This tension has often been revealed in the judgments. For example in *Burgess* Lord Lane CJ commented that "What the law regards as insanity for the purpose of these enactments may be far removed from what would be regarded as insanity by a psychiatrist".[129]

Many of the critics have advocated different tests of insanity. Of these the irresistible impulse test has gathered the most supporters. The debate over whether irresistible impulses should be regarded as a species of insanity marked the highpoint of the medico-legal tension over the insanity defence in England and Ireland. I will now examine the history of the debate and attempt to discover why, in light of McNaghten's inadequacies, this test of insanity failed to win acceptance in English law.

Notes

1 Report of the Royal Commission on Capital Punishment (1949-53) Cmd.8932 (London, 1953) para.300
2 R.Smith *Trial by Medicine* (Edinburgh, 1981) p.3
3 J.Fitzjames Stephen *A History of the Criminal Law of England* Vol.ii (London, 1883) p.150
4 J.L.Montrose "The McNaghten Rules" (1955) 18 M.L.R.505 p.506
5 N.Walker *Crime and Insanity in England* Vol.1 (Edinburgh, 1968) p.95
6 R.D.Mackay *Mental Condition Defences* (Oxford, 1995) p.95
7 N.Walker op cit p.96
8 Hansard's Debates (1843) Vol.LXVII 714 pp.732 & 733
9 ibid
10 The 5th question is not relevant to this discussion.
11 10 Cl.& Fin.200
12 N.Walker op cit p.100
13 P.Devlin "Responsibility and Punishment: Functions of Judge and Jury" [1954] Crim.L.R.661 pp. 678 & 679 says that the first requirement, that the accused did not know the nature and quality of his act, is practically obsolete as anyone who does not know the nature and quality of his act is mad in the popular sense and so will be found unfit to plead at all.
14 N.Walker op cit p.102
15 [1972] 1 All.E.R.219
16 Smith and Hogan *Criminal Law* (7th ed) (London, 1993) p.197
17 *R v Kemp* [1956] 3 All.E.R.249; *R v Sullivan* [1983] 2 All.E.R.673
18 [1961] 3 All.E.R.523 p.534
19 *R v Burgess* [1991] 2 All.E.R.769
20 This doctrine was introduced into English law by *R v Quick and Paddison* [1973] 3 All.E.R.347
21 *R v Codère* [1916] 12 Cr.App.R.21
22 *R v Windle* [1952] 2 All.E.R.1
23 S.Glueck *Mental Disorder and the Criminal Law* (Boston, 1925) p.226
24 ibid
25 A.Goldstein *The Insanity Defense* (New Haven, 1967) p.49
26 N.Morris "Wrong in the M'Naghten Rules" [1953] 16 M.L.R.435 p.438
27 H. Barnes "A Century of the McNaghten Rules" [1944] 8 C.L.J.300 p.308
28 *R v McNaghten* 10 Cl.& Fin.200 p.204
29 ibid p.208
30 S.Glueck op cit p.180
31 H.Barnes op cit p.302
32 S.Glueck op cit pp.168,180 & 426.
33 Report of the Committee on Insanity and Crime Cmd 2005 (London 1923) p.293
34 *R v Windle* [1952] 2 All.E.R.1
35 Report of the (Butler) Committee on Mentally Abnormal Offenders Cmnd 6244 (London, 1975) para.18.8

36   R.D.Mackay op cit p.102
37   10 Cl.& Fin.200 p.210
38   *R v Codère* [1916] 12 Cr.App.R.21
39   J.Fitzjames Stephen op cit p.166
40   Since *R v Quick and Paddison* [1973] 3 All.E.R.347
41   Since *R v Sullivan* [1983] 2 All E.R.673
42   *R v Hennessy* [1989] 2 All E.R.9
43   Supra f.n.19
44   [1956] 3 All E.R.249
45   ibid p.253
46   [1955] 1 All E.R.859
47   [1963] A.C.386
48   ibid p.412
49   [1991] 2 All E.R.769 p.774
50   Supra f.n.40
51   Glanville Williams *Textbook of the Criminal Law* (2nd ed.) (London, 1983) pp.674 & 675
52   ibid p.675
53   By Glanville Williams ibid p.665
54   *R v Tolson* [1889] 23 Q.B.D.168
55   ibid p.187
56   [1963] A.C.386 p.409
57   ibid p.415
58   Described by N.Walker op cit p.170
59   ibid p.170
60   ibid pp.170 & 171
61   *The Times* and *The Guardian* 18 Feb.1961
62   (1978) *The Times* 3 May 1978
63   I.Mackay "The Sleepwalker is Not Insane" [1992] 55 M.L.R.714 p.719
64   [1990] 56 C.C.C.3d.449
65   ibid p.452
66   75 C.C.C.3d.287
67   [1983] 2 All E.R.673
68   [1955] 1 All E.R.859 p.861
69   [1963] A.C.386 p.409
70   Clause 33(1)
71   A.Norrie *Crime Reason and History A Critical Introduction to Criminal Law* (London, 1993) p.179
72   [1973] Q.B.910 p.922
73   There is some anecdotal evidence that sleep-walking may be caused by eating cheese before sleep.
74   G.Virgo "Sanitising Insanity - Sleep-walking and Statutory Reform" [1991] C.L.J.286 p.287
75   A.Norrie op cit p.179
76   R.D.Mackay op cit p.105
77   The *obiter dictum* of Lord Lane in *R v Smith* [1979] 1 W.L.R.1445 suggests that

sleep-walking will qualify for the defence of diminished responsibility

78   Described in these terms by Celia Wells "Whither Insanity?" [1983] Crim.L.R.787 p.788

79   See R.D.Mackay "Non-Organic Automatism - Some Recent Developments" [1980] Crim.L.R.350 pp.353-355 for a summary of these decisions.

80   54 C.C.C.3d.1

81   Glanville Williams op cit p.675; R.D.Mackay "Non-Organic Automatism - Some Recent Developments" op cit p.359

82   *R v Hennessy* [1989] 89 Cr.App.R.10

83   [1990] Crim.L.R.256

84   ibid p.258

85   *R v Sullivan* [1983] 2 All.E.R.673; *R v Burgess* [1991] 2 All.E.R.769

86   P.J.Sutherland and C.A.Gearty "Insanity and the European Court of Human Rights" [1992] Crim.L.R. 418 p.421

87   R.D.Mackay "Mental Condition Defences in the Criminal Law" op cit p.67

88   See P.J. Sutherland and C.A.Gearty op cit pp.422-424

89   Supra f.n.19

90   Supra f.n.67

91   *Winterwerp v The Netherlands* [1979] 2 E.H.R.R.387 para.39

92   E.Baker "Human Rights, M'Naghten and the 1991 Act" [1994] Crim.L.R.84 p.86

93   S.Glueck *Law and Psychiatry* (London, 1963) p.45

94   Report of the Royal Commission on Capital Punishment (1949-53) Cmd 8932 op cit para.232

95   R.D.Mackay *Mental Condition Defences* op cit p.102

96   ibid p.104

97   R.R.Mowat *Morbid Jealousy and Murder* (London, 1966) p.7

98   W.C.Sullivan *Crime and Insanity* (London, 1924) p.243

99   Report of the Royal Commission on Capital Punishment (1949-53) Cmd 8932 op cit para.261

100   R.James Simon *The Jury and the Defense of Insanity* (Boston, 1967) p.177

101   ibid p.178

102   Cf: ibid pp.199 &200

103   ibid para.290

104   S.Glueck, *Mental Disorder and the Criminal Law* op cit pp.173,180,184,423 & 425.

105   *Holloway v U.S.* [1945] 148 F.2d. 665 [1945] p.667

106   S.Glueck *Mental Disorder and the Criminal Law* op cit p.170

107   G.W.Keeton *Guilty but Insane* (London, 1961) p.193

108   ibid

109   S.Glueck, *Mental Disorder and the Criminal Law* op cit pp. 124,125, 424, & 426.

110   C.Mercier, *Criminal Responsibility* (London, 1905) pp.174 & 176.

111   W.C.Sullivan, op cit p.130; C.Mercier op cit p.125; S.Glueck *Mental Disorder and the Criminal Law* op cit p.177

112   A.Norrie op cit p.179

113   J.Fitzjames Stephen op cit p.162

114   Perkins and Boyce *Criminal Law* (3rd edition) (New York, 1982) p.967.

115   W.C.Sullivan op cit p.130

116 P.J.Sutherland and C.A.Gearty op cit
117 F.McAuley *Insanity, Psychiatry and Criminal Responsibility* (Dublin, 1993) p.62
118 S.Glueck *Mental Disorder and the Criminal Law* op cit p.429
119 W.C.Sullivan op cit p.242.
120 A.Goldstein *The Insanity Defense* (New Haven and London, 1967) pp.53 & 54
121 ibid p.212
122 Report and Minutes of Evidence before the Select Committee on the Homicide Law Amendment Bill B.P.P.,1874, Vol.ix p.475 p.27
123 Lady Wooton "Mental Disorder and the Problem of Moral and Criminal Responsibility" in *Social Science and Social Pathology* (London, 1959) p.229
124 ibid p.230
125 Lord Devlin "Mental Abnormality and the Criminal Law" in R.St.J.Macdonald *Changing Legal Objectives* (Toronto, 1963) p.83
126 ibid p.85
127 S.Glueck *Mental Disorder and the Criminal Law* op cit pp.173 & 180
128 ibid p.173
129 [1991] 2 All E R 769 p.772

2 The Defence of Irresistible Impulse

The defence of irresistible impulse will mean little or nothing to today's jurist. However, for over a century it was urged by members of the medical and legal professions, both in England and Ireland, either as a replacement for or a supplement to the right-wrong test embodied in the McNaghten Rules. By examining this defence and its application, I will illustrate a facet of the dissatisfaction with the McNaghten Rules which pervaded medico-legal thinking in England until the late 1950's when the defence of diminished responsibility was introduced into English law.

Medical witnesses felt that there were many cases of insanity which McNaghten excluded but which would be covered by a defence of irresistible impulse. In England, for reasons which I deal with below, McNaghten finally emerged triumphant. In Ireland the defence of irresistible impulse, albeit in modified form, was eventually appended to the McNaghten Rules. The defence of irresistible impulse was also accepted by the Judiciary in the United States. In this chapter I intend to trace the development of the irresistible impulse defence and the consequent reform of the McNaghten Rules in Ireland and the United States. Furthermore, with the help of those committees and debates which rejected irresistible impulse as a test of insanity for Great Britain, I will illustrate that it is not the solution to the defects contained in the McNaghten Rules.

The conflicting interests of law and medicine were represented in the debate over irresistible impulse as a criminal law defence. The medical profession at the time was seeking to enhance its professional status and to obtain an increased role in criminal trials. Judicial opposition to the medical theories of the day often represented an opposition to the medical profession's ambitions. This medico-legal acrimony was resolved in more ways than one by the introduction of the diminished responsibility defence in 1957. The operation of this defence will be examined in Chapter Six but for now I will address the full extent of the medico-legal controversy which raged over irresistible impulse as a species of insanity.

The idea of irresistible impulses, arising from volitional or moral insanity, has its roots in the faculty psychology of Aristotle's time, which held that the mind was composed of localised independent faculties such as will, imagination and understanding,[1] any one of which was liable to disease. In the course of the eighteenth century faculty psychology regained lost popularity as a result of the spread of the doctrine of phrenology,[2] whose origin has been described in Chapter One.

The French psychiatrist Pinel's teachings that the reasoning faculties could remain intact during insanity, were taken up by James Cowles Prichard (1786-1848), the Bristol asylum superintendent, who by combining Pinel's *manie sans delire*[3] and Esquirol's monomania, was responsible for "identifying" the eclectic category of moral insanity in 1833.[4] In this form of insanity, due to disease of the "moral" faculties, "the passions were under no restraint" and the will was surrendered impetuously to the emotions.[5] In his article on *Soundness of Mind (1835)* Prichard argued that

> There is a form of insanity existing independent of any lesion of the intellectual powers, in which connected in some instances with evident constitutional disorder and with affections of the nervous system excited according to the well known laws of the animal economy, a sudden and often irresistible impulse is experienced to commit acts, which under a sane condition of mind would be accounted atrocious crime.[6]

Five years later Prichard was less convinced that irresistible impulse was a form of moral insanity.[7] In *The Different Forms of Insanity in Relation to Jurisprudence*, published in 1842, he said "Instinctive madness seems to be rather an affection of the will or voluntary powers than of affections", describing it in the following terms:

> In this disorder the will is occasionally under the influence of an impulse, which suddenly drives the person affected to the perpetration of acts of the most revolting kind, to the commission of which he has no motive. The impulse is accompanied by consciousness but it is in some instances irresistible.[8]

Although the identification of moral insanity may be attributed to Prichard, it appears that Etienne Georget (1795-1828), a disciple of the French psychiatrist Esquirol, was responsible for the "discovery" of volitional insanity.[9] In a series of pamphlets he identified the condition of *monomania instinctive.*[10] Georget proclaimed that murderers were insane even though they showed no signs of intellectual disturbance.[11] He acknowledged that they reasoned perfectly well and were even morally repelled by their deeds, but maintained that the murderers had been propelled by an irresistible urge, committing crimes with full knowledge of their horror.[12] This he attributed to a "lesion of the will" which left the rational faculties intact and moral discernment unimpaired.[13] In this respect volitional insanity differed from moral insanity where the moral faculties were impaired. However as Smith notes[14] "[i]mpulsive insanity and moral insanity were rarely thought to exist in a pure form; rather, they were two overlapping classes. In the former, the dominant feature was uncontrollable, motiveless, sharp and spasmodic violence; in the latter, it was disordered emotion leading to general violence and aggressiveness".

With a climate favourable to the reception of psychological theories reconcilable with phrenology, Prichard's moral and instinctive insanity were readily accepted in English medical circles,[15] as is evidenced by the plethora of cases *below*, where these conditions were offered as evidence of insanity. However the concept of moral insanity did not gain widespread lay and legal notice until the trial of Edward *Oxford* in 1840 for treason, for the attempted murder of Queen Victoria.[16] There Lord Denman C.J. directed the jury that

> If some controlling disease was, in truth, the acting power within [the defendant] which he could not resist, then he will not be responsible.[17]

When *McNaghten* was tried for the murder of Drummond, defence counsel Cockburn argued that the accused was the "creature of delusion, and the victim of ungovernable impulses, which wholly [took] away from him the character of a reasonable and responsible being".[18] Drawing on the medical theories of the day Cockburn continued:

> The mistake existing in ancient times, which the light of modern science has dispelled, lay in supposing that in order that a man should be mad..it was necessary that he should exhibit those symptoms which would amount to total prostration of the intellect; whereas modern science has incontrovertibly established that any one of these intellectual and moral functions of the mind may be subject to separate diseases, and thereby man may be rendered the victim of the most fearful delusions, the slave of uncontrollable impulses impelling or rather compelling him to the

commission of acts such as that which has given rise to the case now under your consideration.[19]

After an array of medical experts had testified in these terms Tindal C.J. stopped the trial. Although Tindal C.J. instructed the jury that the relevant question for their consideration was whether at the time of the crime McNaghten knew right from wrong in relation to the act, he left no doubt in their minds that he was entirely convinced by the uncontradicted medical evidence.

A moral panic ensued as a result of McNaghten's acquittal which was interpreted as "a precedent for every lunatic to take the law into his or her own hands".[20] As a result, the judges of England were asked to clarify the law's position on insanity. In their reply, no mention was made of the test used in *Oxford*, but this is undoubtedly attributable to the fact that their answers were confined to the questions put to them regarding persons who suffered from delusion. The Rules were no more than a set of answers to specific questions and were not intended as a general statement of the law.[21] This is evident from statement of Tindal C.J. to the effect that

> They deemed it at once impracticable, and at the same time dangerous to the administration of justice, if it were practicable, to attempt to make minute application of the principles involved in the Answers.[22]

and his caution that the Rules "should be accompanied by such observations and explanations as the circumstances of each particular case may require".[23] It was not long, however, before they had evolved into an inflexible yardstick of legal insanity and as a result, in 1848 a plea of irresistible impulse was swiftly dismissed in *Reg v Stokes*,[24] Baron Rolfe stating that

> It is true that learned speculators, in their writings, have laid it down that men with a consciousness that they were doing wrong were irresistibly impelled to commit some unlawful act. Who enabled them to dive into the human heart and see the real motive that prompted the commission of such deeds.

In *R v Barton*[25] Baron Parke approved Baron Rolfe's view and noted that

> The excuse of an irresistible impulse co-existing with the full possession

of reasoning powers, might be urged in justification of every crime known to the law - for every man might be said, and truly, not to commit any crime except under the influence of some irresistible impulse. Something more than this was necessary to justify an acquittal on the ground of insanity and it would be therefore for the jury to say whether..the impulse under which the prisoner had committed the deed was one which altogether deprived him of the knowledge that he was doing wrong. Could he distinguish between right and wrong?.[26]

Smith has uncovered some unreported cases in the medical literature of the day, where medical evidence of an irresistible impulse led to a successful defence of insanity. When *Mary Ann Brough* was tried for the murder of her six children in June 1854, medical opinion at her trial argued that there was a general syndrome in which brain disease led to an inability to control movements and Mrs Brough was classified as belonging to this group. Mrs Brough was acquitted by reason of insanity.[27] At the trial of *Martha Prior* in 1848 for the murder of her baby, although Lord Denman attacked the notion of irresistible impulse, he nevertheless conceded the jury would act on the medical testimony in order to acquit her[28] and in 1862 Dr Hood from Bethlem successfully argued that disease had led to uncontrollable conduct at the trial of *Mrs Vyse* for the murder of her two children.[29] Smith opines[30] that in Mrs Brough's case it was the extreme and exceptional nature of the crime coupled with awe and humanitarian sentiment towards a mother who had killed her children which led to the acquittal, rather than deference to the medical viewpoint. It is worth noting at this point that women at this time were viewed as mentally weaker than men, especially in matters connected with reproduction,[31] and therefore more prone to insanity - a view which no doubt influenced the introduction of the partial defence of infanticide in 1922. Hence the success of *Martha Brixey* in an insanity plea in 1845, where the defence argued that obstructed menstruation led to an irresistible impulse to murder (there was no evidence of delusion or intellectual aberration).[32] Disordered menstruation ("amenorrhoea") was the reason for *Shepherd's* acquittal for stealing a fur boa and for the acquittal of *Amelia Snoswell* for killing her baby niece,[33] but whether evidence of uncontrollable impulses was tendered here is unclear.

At the trial of *James Hill* in 1856 for cutting off his nephew's head Willes J. asserted that

> Such a thing as a person not being able to control himself in the doing of an act which he knows to be wrong, is a phrase that is not known to the law of this country.

but he finally compromised by inferring that as the question was the consciousness of right and wrong at the moment of the deed, consciousness might have been swept aside by the actual impulse.[34]

However each successful plea was matched by more cases where irresistible impulse was rejected. *John Smith* was hanged in 1849 following Lord Denman's direction to the jury to ignore the defence.[35] In *Alnutt* the plea was unsuccessful at the trial of a twelve-year-old boy who poisoned his grandfather.[36] At the trial of *Robert Pate* in July 1850 for hitting Queen Victoria on the head with his walking stick, Baron Alderson asserted that if a man claimed that he picked a pocket from some uncontrollable impulse, the law would have an uncontrollable impulse to punish him for it.[37] The failure of the defence in *Buranelli's* and *Dove's* cases are further illustrations of the law's antagonism to the medical theories of the day.

There were a number of reasons for the Judiciary's opposition to an insanity defence which considered irresistible impulse. A utilitarian theory of punishment prevailed which favoured deterrence and retribution[38] and the above-named medical entities proposed to excuse not only the mad but the bad in pursuit of reformation. As Prichard himself noted of moral insanity "there is scarcely an act in the catalogue of human crimes which has not been imitated..by this disease".[39] Further, there was no evidence that medicine could in fact cure these "illnesses".[40] The difficulty of identifying accurately who would be affected by the threat of sanction led to a preference for McNaghten's cognitive test over the irresistible impulse test.[41] With judges and prosecuting counsel seeing themselves as delegates of public morality and "society's guardians"[42] it was felt that errors should be made in the direction of more sanction rather than less.[43]

There were also competing professional and status claims involved in the conflict.[44] The medical profession was attempting to advance itself within the realm of the criminal law but encountered great difficulty. Judiciary and counsel had unquestionable professional autonomy compared with the alienists' questionable social authority.[45]

One of the frequent criticisms of the medical argument for re-phrasing the Rules to include irresistible impulse was that logical consistency meant that alienists were invoking the determinism of all human actions.[46] Deterministic theories threatened to undermine the law's traditional *modus operandi*, based on the theory of free will.[47] The law's normative approach and its concern to pass judgment on human conduct was directly opposed to medicine's concern to understand conduct.[48] Because the law's approach to criminals was entrenched it appeared natural and self evident.[49]

Finally, the notion of defective will power was unlikely to gain credence in Victorian Society where will power and restraint were values which were cherished.[50] Hence in *R v Haynes,*[51] Baron Bramwell gave the notion short shrift telling the jury:

> If the influence itself be held a legal excuse rendering the crime dispunishable you at once withdraw a most powerful restraint - [law] forbidding and punishing its perpetration.[52]

This observation reveals Baron Bramwell's distrust of the genuineness of truly irresistible impulses. In similar vein, Wightman J. observed that moral insanity was

> A most dangerous doctrine and fatal to the interests of society and security of life.[53]

He went on to hold that the notion was inconsistent with the rule laid down by the judges, namely that a man was responsible for his actions if he knew the difference between right and wrong.

By now the notion of irresistible impulse had gained widespread approval in medical circles. The discovery of reflex action of the cerebrum and spinal cord and increasing knowledge of the effects of epilepsy, whilst exposing the crudity of phrenology,[54] nevertheless bolstered the medical argument that there were uncontrollable movements which the law should recognise. In July 1864 the Association of Medical Officers of Hospitals and Asylums for the Insane passed a resolution to the effect

> That so much of the legal test of the medical condition of an alleged criminal lunatic as renders him a responsible agent, because he knows the difference between right and wrong, is inconsistent with the fact well known to every member of this meeting, that the power of distinguishing between right and wrong exists very frequently among those who are undoubtedly insane, and is often associated with dangerous and

uncontrollable delusions.[55]

The wording of the motion seems to suggest that some insane persons should be excused because their delusions led to uncontrollable impulses.[56]

This resolution was moved by Dr. Harrington Tuke who also gave evidence to the Royal Commission on Capital Punishment in 1865.[57] However, he stipulated in his evidence before the Commission that irresistible impulse should not be a defence in the case of a sane man and that he would require evidence of his insanity, except where the killing was without possible motive. This approach shows a willingness to deduce insanity from an ostensibly insane act without reference to *mens rea*, an approach which was utterly at odds with the law's emphasis on states of mind. If medical experts habitually took this approach then it is no wonder that the legal profession was opposed to a defence of irresistible impulse which could be only too easily inferred from the perpetration of a criminal act. In any event, the Royal Commission in its report declined to make any recommendation on the law of insanity on the ground that this issue was not confined to capital cases but affected the entire administration of criminal law. It did, however, recommend further investigation of this area of law.[58]

The most relentless judicial advocate of irresistible impulse was to be Sir James Fitzjames Stephen (1829-94). In a paper to the Juridical Society in 1855 he appeared wary of the notion of irresistible impulse.[59] The same attitude pervaded his *General View of the Criminal Law of England*.[60] Stephen was of the opinion that the commonest and strongest cases of irresistible impulse were those of women who, without motive or concealment, killed their children after recovery from childbirth.[61] With regard to moral insanity, his view was that if proved, it would be a ground for acquitting the accused on the ground of lack of malice.[62] However, he stated

> The evidence given in support of the assertion that a man is "morally insane" is, generally speaking, at least as consistent with the theory that he was a great fool and a great rogue, as with the theory that he was the subject of a special disease, the existence of which is doubtful.[63]

By the 1870's Stephen had altered his stance. In 1872 Stephen prepared a draft of a Homicide Law Amendment Bill to codify the law relating to homicide.[64] When this was referred to a Select Committee in

1874 the provision on insanity had been amended slightly to provide

> 24. Homicide is not criminal, if the person by whom it is committed is, at the time when he commits it, prevented by any disease affecting his mind
> (a) from knowing the nature of the act done by him;
> (b) from knowing that it is forbidden by law;
> (c) from knowing that it is morally wrong; or,
> (d) from controlling his own conduct.
> But homicide is criminal, although the mind of the person committing it is affected by disease, if such disease does not in fact produce some one of the effects aforesaid in reference to the act by which death is caused, or if the inability to control his conduct is not produced exclusively by such disease.
> If a person is proved to have been labouring under any insane delusion at the time when he committed homicide it shall be presumed, unless the contrary appears or is proved, that he did not possess the degree of knowledge or self-control hereinbefore specified.[65]

What is noteworthy is the emphasis on mental disease rather than on lack of will which marked his earlier discussions on the subject.[66] Lord Chief Justice Cockburn was opposed to the provision on delusion but expressed his approval of Stephen's main proposal. However the other witnesses were opposed to the provision on irresistible impulse, Mr. Justice Blackburn on the ground that it would exclude cases which ought to be included[67] and Baron Bramwell on the ground that it would weaken the deterrent value of the criminal law. His view on the subject was summed up in the following statement

> It is obvious that what is called an uncontrollable impulse is one as to which the deterring or controlling motives are not strong enough; and this is a proposition in all cases to take away from a man in a state of mind in which he is more likely to do mischief than anything else, a deterring motive.[68]

However his approach to mothers who killed their children under an irresistible impulse was in marked contrast to the above. Of these he stated

> Surely such a case as this is a case of misfortune and not of crime..The act is a spasmodic one, like a cough or winking of the eye. It gives a man no practical pleasure to cough or wink, but if you threatened to flay him alive

for it he would not be able to abstain for any length of time.[69]

Baron Bramwell was also opposed to the presumption proposed in cases of delusion. In any event, the Select Committee decided not to proceed with partial codification.[70]

In 1878 Stephen included a provision on similar lines in the Draft Criminal Code Bill. However, in a deliberate attempt to placate the Bramwellian opposition[71] he provided

> No act shall be an offence if the person who does it is at the time when it is done prevented, either by defective mental power or by any disease affecting his mind,
> (a) from knowing the nature of his act; or
> (b) from knowing either that the act is forbidden by law or that it is morally wrong; or
> (c) if such person was at the time when the act was done, by reason of any such cause as aforesaid, in such a state that he would not have been prevented from doing that act by knowing that if he did do it the greatest punishment permitted by law for such an offence would be instantly inflicted upon him, provided that this provision shall not apply to any person in whom such a state has been produced by his own default.[72]

Nonetheless the Commission remained sceptical of irresistible impulse as a test of insanity, being of the view that there would be difficulty distinguishing such a state of mind from a criminal motive.[73]

By 1879 the revised form of the Code showed that the orthodox view had prevailed over Stephen's.[74] By the time he wrote *A History of the Criminal Law of England*[75] Stephen was casting doubt on the authority of the McNaghten Rules.[76] He also felt that something more than an implied assertion was necessary to reject disease effecting the emotions and will, due to the monstrous consequences which would follow.[77] Stephen even opined that in cases of insanity judges might rightly feel themselves at liberty to direct the jury in such terms as they felt appropriate,[78] in other words, to ignore the Rules. Although he continued to require that an impulse be irresistible[79] he was of the view that a man who by reason of mental disease was prevented from controlling his conduct was in any event covered by the McNaghten Rules.[80] This is because of the broad interpretation which he ascribed to knowledge within the Rules, saying

> Knowledge has its degrees like everything else and implies something

more real and more closely connected with conduct than the half knowledge retained in dreams.[81]

A requirement of a deeper level of knowledge would cover cases of irresistible impulse. According to Stephen knowledge and self-control were inter-dependent:

> It is as true that a man who cannot control himself does not know the nature of his acts as that a man who does not know the nature of his acts is incapable of self-control.[82]

In *R v Davis (1881)*[83] Stephen took the initiative himself. Two medical men gave evidence that the accused, who was charged with feloniously wounding his sister-in-law with intent to murder her, was suffering from *delirium tremens,* as a result of which his actions would not be under his control and he would not be able to distinguish between moral right and wrong at the time he committed the act. Stephen's summing-up had all the appearance of orthodoxy, for he told the jury that they must follow "the great test laid down in McNaughten's case" but then he did his best to show the dependence of knowledge of right and wrong on possession of self control:

> As I understand the law, any disease which so disturbs the mind that you cannot think calmly and rationally of all the different reasons to which we refer in considering the rightness or wrongness of an action - any disease which so disturbs the mind that you cannot perform that duty with some moderate degree of calmness and reason may be fairly said to prevent a man from knowing that what he did was wrong... both the doctors agree that the prisoner was unable to control his conduct, and that nothing short of actual physical restraint would have deterred him from the commission of the act. If you think there was a distinct disease caused by drinking, but differing from drunkenness, and that by reason thereof he did not know that the act was wrong, you will find a verdict of not guilty on the ground of insanity.[84]

The jury returned a verdict of not guilty on the ground of insanity. Stephen J. again used irresistible impulse as evidence of lack of knowledge of right and wrong in *R v Burt (1885)* and *R v Davies (1888)*[85]

Soon other judges were going a step further than Stephen J. In *R v Duncan (1890)* Lawrence J. added, as an alternative to the usual charge, the question:

> Was the prisoner unable to control his actions in consequence of a disordered mind?.[86]

In *Jordan (1872)* Baron Martin had said "When such impulses come upon men, according to the medical view they were unable to resist them. It would be safe in such a case to acquit the accused on the ground of insanity".[87] The defence was again admitted in *Gill (1883)*.[88]

Irresistible Impulse in the Court of Appeal

In 1910 the recently formed Court of Criminal Appeal had its first opportunity to settle whether irresistible impulses could lead to a successful defence of insanity. *Victor Jones*[89] was convicted of the murder of a schoolteacher friend before Grantham J., at the Monmouth Assizes. He appealed *inter alia* on the ground of misdirection as to the law relating to insanity as a defence. Counsel for the appellant contended that his crime showed all the characteristics which Taylor and other writers on medical jurisprudence recognised as notes of homicidal mania or impulsive insanity, namely no motive, the victim an object of sincere love, no concealment, no attempt to escape, confession of the act and an outward appearance of utter coolness and indifference.

Defence counsel contended that even if these facts were not of themselves sufficient to show insanity, taken together with the appellant's mental history, they were of great moment. Arguing that knowledge and self control are interdependent he drew support from *Stephen's History of the Criminal Law of England* [90] and from Baron Rolfe's dictum in *Layton,*[91] to justify of his argument that, "knowing" that an act is right or wrong requires something more than mere consciousness. That the Court of Appeal was not satisfied that either McNaghten madness or irresistible impulse had properly been made out is evident from the words of Alverstone L.C.J.:

> There is no need here to enter upon a disquisition as to the terms in which the question ought to be left, where a person is prevented by defective mental power or mental disease from knowing the nature of his acts or from controlling his conduct. It is not made out in this case that the

appellant was not in a condition to be aware of the nature of his acts or that he was prevented from exercising self control.[92]

The Court of Appeal decided to postpone determination of the issue for an occasion when the facts established uncontrollable impulse. Alverstone L.C.J. asserted that

> When that day comes the Court will not shrink from the duty of deciding those matters of controversy and declaring the law. But in this case they do not arise.[93]

The plea of irresistible impulse enjoyed success for some time after the trial of *Victor Jones*. In *R v Hay*[94] Darling J. directed a jury that they would be justified in finding the accused insane, if through disease of the mind he was unable to control a homicidal impulse, although he knew the nature and quality of his act and knew that it was wrong. That same year the Court of Criminal Appeal was required to consider an uncontrollable impulse in *R v Thomas*.[95] Thomas was convicted of murder and appealed on the ground that the trial judge erred in not allowing irresistible impulse to go to the jury. Darling J., now sitting in the Court of Criminal Appeal, found that the trial judge's direction was perfectly adequate in light of the evidence and that "Impulsive insanity is the last refuge of a hopeless defence".[96]

It is submitted that this ruling cannot be taken as a rejection of irresistible impulse by the Court of Criminal Appeal. The Court was merely urging for caution where uncontrollable impulse was pleaded. In the face of the Court of Appeal's indecision, trial judges continued to give approval to the doctrine of irresistible impulse. In *R v Fryer*,[97] where medical witnesses offered conflicting evidence regarding the accused's insanity, Bray J. (referring to the McNaghten rules) directed the jury in the following terms

> That is the recognised law on the subject but I am bound to say it does not seem to me to completely state the law as it now is and for the purposes of to-day I am going to direct you in the way indicated by a very learned judge, Fitzjames Stephen and follow his direction, that, if it is shown that he is in such a state of mental disease or natural mental infirmity as to deprive him of the capacity to control his actions I think you ought to find him what the law calls him - 'insane'.[98]

Not long after, Bray J. directed a jury in similar terms, where a plea of guilty but insane was based on evidence that the prisoner was an epileptic and had acted under the influence of an uncontrollable impulse.[99]

In *R v Coelho*[100] the Court of Appeal refused to set aside a conviction for murder on the ground that the trial judge should have allowed a defence of irresistible impulse to go to the jury. Again the decision seems to have been based on lack of evidence of the condition as nothing in the judgment suggests a rejection of irresistible impulse per se.

However, resistance to recognition of irresistible impulse as a defence reasserted itself and in *R v Holt*[101] the Court of Appeal put an end to the notion. The question of whether the accused was suddenly overcome by an uncontrollable impulse was left to the jury by the trial judge (Greer J.) but they decided against the appellant. On appeal, the Court of Appeal (Reading L.J. speaking on behalf of Avory J. and surprisingly Bray J., who had presided over *R v Fryer* and *R v Jolly*) held that

> The tests in McNaughten's case must be observed, and it is not enough for a medical expert to come to the Court and say generally that in his opinion the criminal is insane.[102]

Soon afterwards Darling J., hearing an appeal against a conviction for murder, held

> The contention..that the prisoner was insane was based upon grounds never yet admitted in any English Court of Justice.[103]

This is a surprising observation considering that he himself had accepted these grounds as evidence of insanity in *R v Hay*.

Despite the Court of Appeal's recent pronouncements, in *True 1922*[104] the trial judge, McCardie J., allowed a defence of irresistible impulse to go to the jury but they rejected it. On appeal, the Court of Appeal reasserted the supremacy of the McNaghten Rules, saying:

> There is no foundation for the suggestion that the rule derived from McNaghten's case has been in any sense relaxed.[105]

Furthermore Greer J. denied that in *Holt* he had directed the jury that irresistible impulse was a defence. The medical view of insanity prevailed when *True* was reprieved by the Home Secretary on the grounds of his mental condition. (To secure a reprieve a medical report by two doctors was necessary, which in this instance the Home Secretary treated as conclusive evidence of *True's* insanity). As a result of this, the Home Secretary came under an onslaught of criticism.[106] However, the controversy generated by this reprieve did have the effect of bringing into the open the tension between the law's definition of insanity (the McNaghten Rules) and the medical theories of the day.[107] The outcome of all this was the appointment by the Government of a Committee on Insanity and Crime "to consider what changes, if any, are desirable in the existing law and practice relating to criminal trials in which the plea of insanity as a defence is raised, and whether any and, if so, what changes should be made in the existing law and practice in respect of cases falling within the provisions of section 2(4) of the Criminal Lunatics Act, 1884"[108] (the section dealing with psychiatric inquiries instituted after sentence by the Home Secretary).

The Committee was chaired by Lord Justice Atkin and its members were appointed by the Lord Chancellor, the Earl of Birkenhead. By subsequent correspondence it was made clear that the Lord Chancellor intended the inquiry to have a wide scope and to include consideration of the Rules in McNaghten's case.[109] The Committee on Insanity and Crime (Atkin Committee) received memoranda from both the British Medical Association and the Medico Psychological Association.

In composition the Committee was overwhelmingly legal and official to an extent that could be considered quite improper.[110] It is clear that by appointing such a legally representative body of members the Lord Chancellor was doing his best to ensure that their report would preserve the *status quo*.[111] Surprisingly however, the Atkin Committee favoured the British Medical Association's proposal to add the defence of irresistible impulse to the McNaghten Rules by an express statutory provision.[112] The Atkin Committee was most convinced of the genuineness of irresistible impulses in the case of "mothers who have been seized with the impulse to cut the throats or otherwise destroy their children to whom they were normally devoted" and who in practice were found insane.[113] This was the only example which they gave in support of their argument for an insanity defence accommodating irresistible impulse.

On 6/3/1924 the Home Secretary made it clear that the Government did not contemplate proposing any legislation on this subject,[114] possibly because of the introduction of infanticide as a partial defence in 1922. To some, no doubt, this rendered the Atkin Committee's recommendation otiose. As a result of the Government's inertia Lord Darling introduced a private members bill in 1924, the Criminal Responsibility (Trials) Bill, designed to give effect to these recommendations.[115]

Clause One of this bill enacted in statutory form the existing McNaghten Rules, with the addition of a defence of uncontrollable impulse. The House of Lords refused to give the bill a second reading after a debate in which it was opposed by Lord Sumner, the Lord Chancellor (Lord Haldane), Lord Dunedin, Lord Cave and the Lord Chief Justice (Lord Hewart) who said that he had consulted 12 of the 15 judges of the King's Bench Division and 10, like himself, emphatically opposed the bill.[116]

The arguments on which the opposition to the bill was founded have been summarised by the Royal Commission on Capital Punishment (1949-53) as follows[117]:-

> 1) Even if it were accepted that there was such a thing as an irresistible impulse, cases were uncommon and could be satisfactorily dealt with under the existing law. The McNaghten Rules were sufficiently flexible to allow a verdict of guilty but insane to be founded in those cases of irresistible impulse where it was justified.
>
> 2) There was no clear criterion by which to decide whether an impulse was irresistible or only unresisted, and the proposed addition to the McNaghten Rules would place juries in an impossible position, besides making it much more difficult for the judge to give an adequate direction to the jury.
>
> 3) In practice this defence would be most often raised when no other defence had any chance of success. Juries were apt to take a merciful view and would be reluctant to reject medical evidence that an impulse was irresistible. Thus, responsibility would, in effect, be transferred from the jury to the doctors, with the result that many offenders would escape just punishment.
>
> 4) The proposed change would apply to other crimes as well as murder and might lead to a serious increase in crimes of violence, especially in offences against women and children. Sane and insane persons alike were subject to such impulses as anger and sexual passion and there would be a great danger that sane persons who committed crimes under such impulses would successfully plead that the impulse was irresistible.
>
> 5) There was no justification for suggesting that everyone who was insane was wholly irresponsible for his actions. The penalties of the law were, in fact, a restraining influence on many persons of unsound mind and if this

restraint were removed, many would yield to impulses which they would otherwise have resisted.

In the writer's opinion much of the opposition to irresistible impulse was based on the law's fear that the medical profession would usurp insanity trials. Lord Haldane L.C's. distrust of the medical profession is evident from the debate on the Criminal Responsibility (Trials) Bill when he commented that psychology was "a most dangerous science to apply to practical affairs" and scientists "excellent servants but not always reliable masters".[118]   A lecture delivered by Lord Hewart before the Medical Society of London shortly afterwards revealed his fear of medical dominance in cases where insanity was pleaded when he said of the defence of irresistible impulse

> If the law were relaxed in the way which has been suggested..the result might be to transfer to a section of the medical profession the question whether a great number of ordinary criminals should be held responsible to the law.[119]

It will be seen in Chapter Six that this medico-legal tension dissipated with the introduction of the partial defence of diminished responsibility which recognises lesser degrees of mental abnormality and is not restricted to cognitive defects.

Any doubt as to the status of the defence of irresistible impulse was resolved by *Kopsch (1925)*.[120] Kopsch had strangled his uncle's wife with his tie at her request. There Hewart L.C.J. categorically rejected irresistible impulse as a defence, saying:

> It is the fantastic theory of uncontrollable impulse which if it were to become part of our criminal law would be merely subversive. It is not yet part of the criminal law and it is to be hoped that the time is far distant when it will be made so.[121]

Flavell[122] was the last case in the series to reject the defence of irresistible impulse and *Sodeman*[123] marked the end of its life in the dominions. Nonetheless the controversy over the McNaghten Rules continued unabated and in 1930 the report of the Select Committee on Capital Punishment[124] stated:

We are satisfied that there is a strong case for bringing the McNaghten

Rules up to date, so as to give the fullest scope to general medical considerations and to extend in some way the area of criminal irresponsibility.[125]

Once again no action was taken on their recommendation and when the Royal Commission on Capital Punishment of 1953 reported,[126] the Rules were unaltered from their form in 1843. The British Medical Association was still urging extension of the McNaghten Rules to cover irresistible impulse. Although the Association received express and implied support from a substantial number of witnesses,[127] the majority of witnesses felt that the Rules were by now being interpreted so loosely that cases of irresistible impulse caused by disease of the mind were now embraced by them.

Rejecting all the traditional arguments against adopting irresistible impulse as a defence, the Royal Commission felt that if anything, the addition of irresistible impulse would be too narrow a test of responsibility,[128] saying:

> If therefore, the McNaghten Rules are to be extended by the addition of a third limb to meet the case of insanity affecting not the reason but the will, it is important that this should be formulated not merely in terms of inability to resist an impulse, but in wider terms which will allow the court to take account of those cases where an insane person commits a crime after a long period of brooding and reflection or is gradually carried towards it without any real attempt to resist this tendency.[129]

Although the Commission preferred that the jury be left free to determine whether, at the time of the act, the accused was suffering from disease of the mind or mental deficiency to such a degree that he ought not to be held responsible, it felt that the British Medical Association's proposal was preferable to leaving the McNaghten Rules intact.[130] The Commission recommended that a formula on the following lines should be adopted in the alternative to their main recommendation:-

> The jury must be satisfied that, at the time of committing the act the accused, as a result of disease of the mind or (mental deficiency) (a) did not know the nature and quality of the act or (b) did not know that it was wrong or (c) was incapable of preventing himself from committing it.[131]

However every one of the Commission's major recommendations

were rejected by the conservative Government of 1953 whose primary concern was the preservation of the *status quo ante*.[132] One of the reasons given for rejecting the Commission's proposals on the law of insanity, was that they extended beyond the law on murder.[133]

This was the last word in England on irresistible impulse as a criminal law defence but it was later admitted, in modified form, into Irish Law as part of the insanity defence. It appears that the English medical profession eventually lost interest in it as the categories of volitional and moral insanity became outmoded but this did not deter the Irish Courts from recognising an outdated psychiatric theory when re-writing the insanity defence.

Irresistible Impulse in Irish Law

Although independence was obtained from Great Britain in 1922 it was not until 1933 that irresistible impulse first arose for consideration in the Irish courts.[134] Between this time and 1974 irresistible impulse was frequently urged by medical witnesses as a replacement of the McNaghten Rules.[135] In *A.G. v O'Brien*[136] Kennedy C.J. in the Court of Appeal stated that the enactment of a new insanity defence was the Legislature's role and not the Judiciary's. In most of the cases which were to follow, the Judiciary evaded answering the question of whether irresistible impulse was part of Irish law by deploying the strategy of finding that there was no evidence of the condition in the case at hand.[137]

It was not until the end of the 1960's that a reformulation of the Irish insanity defence was adopted by an Irish judge, when Henchy J. accepted a control test as part of Irish law in *The People (A.G.) v Hayes*.[138] Hayes, who was charged with the murder of his wife, was not professionally represented. Submissions were made to the trial judge by counsel on behalf of the Attorney General, as to the form in which the issue of insanity should be left to the jury. Henchy J. acknowledged the shortcomings of the McNaghten Rules, saying

> In the normal case, tried in accordance with the McNaghten rules, the test is solely one of knowledge; did he know the nature and quality of his act or did he know that the act was wrong? The rules do not take into account the capacity of a man on the basis of his knowledge to act or to refrain from acting and I believe it to be correct psychiatric science to accept that

certain serious mental diseases such as paranoia or schizophrenia, in certain cases enable a man to understand the morality or immorality of his act or the legality or illegality of it, or the nature and quality of it, but nevertheless prevent him from exercising a free volition as to whether he should or should not do that act.[139]

He went on to hold that

If it is open to the jury to say, as say they must, on the evidence that this man understood the nature and quality of his act, and understood its wrongfulness, morally and legally, but that nevertheless he was debarred from refraining from assaulting his wife fatally because of a defect of reason due to his mental illness, it seems to me that it would be unjust, in the circumstances of this case, not to allow the jury to consider the case on those grounds.[140]

This however, was a decision of the High Court and Supreme Court confirmation was required before irresistible impulse could be considered to be part of Irish Law.[141]

The following year in the case of *James Coughlan*[142] Kennedy J. in the Central Criminal Court gave as his view that the issue for the jury in any case where the plea of insanity was relied on was the following - *"Was the act caused by disease of the mind?"*. He proposed to leave that broader issue to the jury, while stating by way of example of acts caused by disease of the mind which exempted from criminal responsibility, the three cases cited by Sir James Stephen - where the accused did not know the nature and quality of his act, its wrongness or was prevented by defective mental power or by any disease affecting his mind from controlling his own conduct, unless the absence of the power of control was produced by his own default.[143] Here Kenny J. went a step further in his decision than Henchy J. had in *Hayes*, as this criterion does not necessarily confine the defence of insanity within the bounds of the three tests laid down by Sir James Stephen, but recognises the possibility of a valid defence of insanity being raised, even in a case which doesn't appear to fall strictly within Stephen's formula.[144] Not surprisingly, the jury returned a verdict of guilty but insane after an absence of only ten minutes.

There does not appear to be any recorded case in which *Coughlan* has been approved[145] and in *A.G. v McDonagh*[146] Gannon J. told the jury that

> If it be established by evidence to your satisfaction that at the time of committing the act the will of the accused was so defective that he was unable to control his actions and that such defect of will was due to mental illness the proper verdict would be guilty but insane.[147]

The accused, a butcher, had an argument with a neighbour outside his house. He went into his own house, went up to his bedroom and took a butcher's knife from the top of his wardrobe, came out again and stabbed his neighbour, killing him instantly. A psychiatrist gave evidence for the defence that at the time of the killing the accused was responding to auditory delusions in a psychotic state. So powerful and so intense was the pressure on his mind that he did not have control over his volition. Gannon J., having dealt with the McNaghten Rules, charged the jury in the above terms. After retiring to consider their verdict, the jury returned to court and asked to be furnished with a copy of the McNaghten Rules. This was given to them and they retired again. The jury returned a second time to ask a question about the law applicable where the will is defective through mental illness, and Gannon J. repeated the passage quoted above. The jury retired and came back with a verdict of guilty but insane.

It was Henchy J.'s *dictum* in *Hayes* which the Supreme Court opted to approve in *Doyle v Wicklow County Council*.[148] The applicant applied to the respondents for compensation under the criminal injury code, after a seventeen year old set fire to his abattoir. At the hearing of the application in the Circuit Court it was established that the youth had caused the damage deliberately with the intention of damaging or destroying the applicant's abattoir. The issue was whether the boy had been capable of forming the requisite "malicious intention" because of his alleged insanity.

The medical evidence given was to the effect that the boy O., was suffering from a mental disorder which led him to believe that he shouldn't be charged or punished for setting the fire, although he knew his act was one forbidden by society or contrary to law. His reason for this belief was his love of animals, the killing of which he was very much opposed to. Dr.Noel Browne, the defendant's medical witness, was of the opinion that O. believed his act was right and that the doing of that act showed that O's. judgement was distorted and he was emotionally disturbed, and to that extent he could not be called sane, and he needed psychiatric treatment and detention.

The Circuit Court stated a case to the Supreme Court asking, *inter alia*:- Where on the trial of an application for compensation for criminal injury, there is evidence of the insanity of the person who caused the damage at the time he did so, should the judge determine the issue of insanity as an issue of fact solely on the evidence offered, or should he in addition apply the principles laid down in *McNaghten's case*.

The Supreme Court ruled that the judge, in determining such issue of insanity, should apply the standards or rules appropriate to a criminal trial and that

> The McNaghten Rules do not provide the sole or exclusive test for determining the sanity or insanity of an accused. The questions put to the judges were limited to the effect of insane delusions and I would agree with the opinion expressed by the Court of Criminal Appeal in AG v O'Brien that the opinions given by the judges must be read with the like specific limitation.[149]

This appears to have been a *sub silentio* rejection of *R v Windle*,[150] which held that the McNaghten Rules govern the entire law of insanity, not just instances of insane delusion.[151] Griffin J., speaking on behalf of the Supreme Court, then approved *Hayes* as the correct test to be applied by the Circuit Court judges in determining whether the act was malicious or not. He noted that a civil case was not the most appropriate circumstance in which to consider the application of rules which have been widely applied in criminal trials for upwards of 130 years but that the enactment of the Criminal Justice Act, 1964 (abolishing the death penalty with certain exceptions) made it less likely that the Supreme Court would be required to consider the McNaghten Rules in a criminal appeal.

It is noteworthy that nowhere in the Supreme Court judgment is there any mention of the requirement of an impulse, so that strictly speaking the Supreme Court was recognising a control test and not a defence of irresistible impulse. This is in keeping with the recommendation of the Royal Commission (1949-53) that

> If..the M'Naghten Rules are to be extended by the addition of a third limb to meet the case of insanity affecting not the reason but the will, it is important that this should be formulated not merely in terms of inability to resist an impulse, but in wider terms, which will allow the court to take account of those cases where an insane person commits a crime after a long period of brooding and reflection or is gradually carried towards it without any real attempt to resist this tendency.[152]

The Court approved Henchy J's. test *verbatim* that certain

> Serious mental diseases such as paranoia or schizophrenia, in certain cases enable a man to understand the morality or immorality of his act or the legality or illegality of it, or the nature and quality of it, but nevertheless prevent him from exercising a free volition as to whether he should or should not do that act.[153]

and that insanity should be made out where a defendant

> Understood the nature and quality of his act and understood its wrongfulness, morally and legally, but..nevertheless..was debarred from refraining from [committing the act] because of a defect of reason, due to his mental illness.[154]

It is not entirely clear whether the control test is to be interpreted literally or liberally. McAuley asserts that a literal stance may have been taken by the Supreme Court, as evidenced by Griffin J's. opinion, although *obiter*, that a satisfactory defence of insanity had not been made out in *Doyle*.[155] His opinion is that the judge's misgivings appear to have stemmed from the fact that the claim that the boy was unable to control his behaviour was not easy to reconcile with the uncontested evidence that he was determined to burn down the abattoir.[156] McAuley points out that the fact that a defendant was determined to do something does not entail and may exclude the conclusion that he was unable to refrain from doing the act, under a literal interpretation of the control test.[157] This approach may result in depressives, drug addicts and even schizophrenics (the very offenders envisaged by Henchy J. as deserving of an insanity defence) being held responsible if there is any evidence of planning or purposive action involved.[158]

The writer's view however, is that the fact that a defendant was determined to do something does not preclude the conclusion that his act was uncontrollable[159] although it may show that his act was not impulsive.[160] This should not lessen the success prospects of an insanity plea which uses the control test, as nowhere in the Supreme Court judgment does it mention the requirement of an uncontrollable "impulse".[161] My view is that the Irish defence of volitional insanity may indeed be very wide. This view is given weight by the *obiter* of Finlay C.J. in the Supreme Court decision of *D.P.P. v Mahony*[162] where he observed that the appellant in the English Court of Appeal decision *R v Byrne,*[163] a sexual psychopath who suffered from violent perverted sexual desires which he found difficult or impossible to control, if tried in accordance with the law of Ireland on the same facts, would have been properly found to be not guilty by reason of insanity. This statement suggests that substantial difficulty in controlling one's acts, as opposed to an inability, will lead to a successful plea of volitional insanity.

On the assumption that *McNaghten* is limited to cases of delusion since *Doyle*, its harshness is greatly alleviated by its narrower application than in England and there is no danger that "disease of the mind" will be interpreted, as in England, to include epileptics, diabetics in a state of hyperglycaemia and sleep-walkers. However it remains a very narrow test of insanity in terms of its foundation on a test of knowledge which excludes true understanding, of wrongness which excludes the *accused's* appreciation of wrongness and of nature and quality which means no more than the physical nature of the act. Similarly, McNaghten requires the Irish courts to excuse some delusions but not those which would not excuse a sane man (which the accused is not).

Nor can it be said that psychiatrists have any special competence in answering the philosophical conundrum which is posed by the Irish insanity defence: Was the accused debarred from refraining from committing the act because of a defect of reason due to mental illness?. The very existence of the control test places defence psychiatrists under considerable pressure to tailor their evidence to it,[164] an objection which has been repeatedly levelled at the McNaghten Rules.

A liberal interpretation of the Irish control test, requiring merely substantial difficulty in the control of acts, may make the application of the Irish insanity defence very wide. That the Irish courts might follow the English approach and interpret "mental illness" to cover epilepsy, hyperglycaemia and sleepwalking remains a constant threat. Add to this the effect of the Court of Appeal's ruling in *People (A.G.) v Messitt,*[165] which held that where evidence of insanity is available to the prosecution and the defence does not choose to raise the issue, the prosecution are under an obligation to do so themselves, and the true scope of Irish insanity defence becomes evident. As there has been no amending legislation to the insanity verdict akin to the English Criminal Procedure (Insanity) Act, 1964, it is likely that there is still no right of appeal from an acquittal on the ground of insanity, in the Irish courts.[166]

The regime of compulsory hospitalisation following a finding of insanity in Ireland is exacerbated by the unsatisfactory procedure for release of those found "guilty but insane" from detention, once cured of their mental affliction. In *People (D.P.P.) v Patrick Ellis*[167] O'Hanlon J. in the Central Criminal Court placed the burden of deciding their release on the Government, on the grounds that this was not a decision which came under the umbrella of "law and justice". Soon after in *People (D.P.P.) v Neilan*[168] Keane J. in the same court replaced this function on the Judiciary. Then the Supreme Court in *D.P.P. v John Gallagher*[169] ruled that release following a finding of insanity is an Executive function. What is of interest in this case is the submission to the contrary by the Attorney General, which suggests that neither the courts nor the Government wished to have this function vested in them.

The Government is not obliged to carry out a review of detention in cases where the detainee has not sought one.[170] As a result, in *Ellis* it was two years before a review was carried out despite abundant evidence of his sanity.[171] The controversy over John Gallagher's detention in the State Mental Hospital has been documented by the writer elsewhere.[172]

During the course of the English controversy over recognition of irresistible impulse as a species of insanity, its limitations were exposed by opponents of the defence. No doubt aware of these limitations with the benefit of experience, reform of the insanity defence was proposed in 1978 by the Interdepartmental Committee on Mentally Ill and Maladjusted Persons which reported under the chairmanship of the now Supreme Court Judge, Mr Justice Henchy. Its Third Interim Report entitled *Treatment and Care of Persons Suffering from Mental Disorder who Appear before the Courts on Criminal Charges*, stated that because of the law on insanity as stated in *Doyle* "many persons are dealt with by the courts as "normal" offenders who are either not responsible (or not fully responsible) for the conduct charged against them".[173] This statement, which echoes that of the Butler Committee (whose proposals will be discussed in Chapter Four), is a surprising allegation given the broadness of the Irish control test.

After considering the various formulae in different jurisdictions, the Committee opted for the following tripartite test of insanity, which asks:

1) Did the accused commit the act or omission charged?
2) If so, was he suffering at the time from mental disorder (as defined)? and

3) If so, was it such that he should not be found guilty of the offence?[174]

"Mental Disorder" was defined[175] as mental illness or mental handicap but as not including violent personality disorder. From this, it is tempting to infer dissatisfaction on the part of the author of the Irish control test, with the applicability of his test to the psychopath and almost certain from his recommendation of an alternative insanity defence that he was not satisfied with his own handwork, the Irish defence of irresistible impulse.

D.P.P. v Penny Ann Dorricott[176], decided in the Central Criminal Court on 3/2/1982, shows that the control test is firmly entrenched in Irish law. There Finlay J. asked the jury to consider as the third proposition (the first two comprising the McNaghten Rules) whether the accused, at the time of the act, was suffering from a disease of the mind which prevented her from exercising a free volition. The defendant was suffering from insane delusions.

More recently, *Sean Courtney* was found guilty of murder after his plea of insanity, based on evidence of post-traumatic stress disorder, occasioned while serving as a soldier in the Lebanon,[177] was rejected by the jury. Mr Justice Lynch asked the jury "At the time when the accused..killed the deceased..was he acting under the influence of an irresistible impulse caused by a defect of reason due to mental illness which debarred him from refraining from killing her?".[178] Given that the irresistible impulse test is more stringent than the control test and that irresistible impulse has no place in Irish law, the propriety of the judge's direction is open to question.

Rather than constituting an appendix to the Rules, the control test has emerged in Irish law as McNaghten's successor in all cases except delusion. In recent years the Supreme Court's decision in *Doyle* has come under attack, most notably by Irish judges. Speaking of the detention and release of those found guilty but insane in Irish law, O'Hanlon J. in *Ellis* commented

> The problem has been compounded by developments in the law as to insanity as a defence to a criminal charge, which have taken place in this jurisdiction in the last quarter-century or so.[179]

It is therefore surprising to see the recently elected Irish Government's proposal to maintain McNaghten and irresistible impulse in the Criminal Justice (Mental Disorder) Bill 1996. Section 4(1) requires a finding of not guilty by reason of mental disorder where the jury/court finds that the defendant

(a) committed the act alleged
(b) was suffering at the time from mental disorder and
(c) the mental disorder was such that he should not be held responsible for the act by reason of the fact that-
(i) he did not know the nature and quality of his act,
(ii) he did not know that what he was doing was wrong, or
(iii) he was unable to refrain from committing the act.

The Irish Government's proposed alternative pays lip service to the Henchy Committee's test and is in reality a reformulation of the McNaghten and irresistible impulse tests.[180] The defects inherent in the Irish control test and in the Henchy Committee's proposed alternative, which will be examined further in Chapter Three, underscore the futility of attempting to palliate the controversy over the McNaghten Rules by reformulating the insanity defence.[181] The writer has argued elsewhere that the Irish insanity defence is in breach of the European Convention on Human Rights and breaches Irish Constitutional Rights[182] but further discussion of these issues is outside the scope of this work.

Irresistible Impulse in the United States

The Judiciary of some States were less hesitant in embracing the medical theories of the day via the medium of the insanity defence. This was demonstrated by the early recognition of irresistible impulse as a test of legal insanity. The most influential of the early cases recognising irresistible impulse[183] was *Parsons v State of Alabama*.[184] Here Judge Somerville said that legal responsibility had two constituent elements - "capacity of intellectual discrimination" and "freedom of will" and that a just and reasonable test of responsibility must take account of both elements, and that it was a question of fact, not of law, whether insanity can so affect the mind "as to subvert the freedom of the will, and thereby destroy the power of the victim to choose between the right and wrong, although he perceive it".

The Royal Commission on Capital Punishment (1949-53) noted that the doctrine of irresistible impulse was or had at some time been recognised in 17 States and in the District of Columbia and the Federal Jurisdiction.[185] As in Ireland the test in the United States was often formulated in the broader terms of "inability to control acts"[186] and like in Ireland this revision of the McNaghten Rules was equally unsatisfactory. Many of the critics drew on the English commentators' criticisms of irresistible impulse, outlined above.[187] Others criticised its foundation on an out of date psychology.[188] This was no doubt, due in some measure to the fact that moral and volitional insanity had by now been abandoned by the psychiatric profession. In particular, the accepted psychiatric view of personality as integrated seemed irreconcilable with irresistible impulse as a defence[189] where either volitional or moral faculties were impaired but reason remained intact. This, and the fact that the irresistible impulse test also restricted psychiatric testimony on the defendant's insanity, eventually led to its abandonment in D.C. in favour of a new test designed to facilitate psychiatric testimony on all aspects of a defendant's mental state. The new test arose out of the decision in *Durham v U.S.*[190] and was based on New Hampshire's test of insanity.

However rather than resolve the polemic over the insanity defence *Durham* was to be the beginning of a new controversy.

Notes

1   A.R.Hayward "Murder and Madness: *A Social History of the Insanity Defence in Mid-Victorian England*" M.Litt., (Oxford, 1983) p.32

2   ibid

3   translated by N.Walker *Crime and Insanity* Vol.2 (Edinburgh, 1973) p.207 as "mania without confusion"

4   A.R.Hayward op cit p.73

5   ibid p.77

6   Quoted ibid p.89

7   ibid

8   Quoted by R.Smith *Trial by Medicine* (Edinburgh, 1981) p.39

9   R.Harris *Murders and Madness: Medicine Law and Society in the Fin de Siecle* (Oxford, 1989) pp.8 & 9

10   ibid

11   ibid p.9

12   ibid

13   ibid

14   R.Smith op cit p.97

15   A.R.Hayward op cit p.95

16   ibid p.106
17   *R v Oxford* 9 C.& P.525 p.546
18   *R v McNaghten* 4 St.Tr.N.S.847 p.875
19   ibid p.887
20   A.R.Hayward op cit p.108
21   ibid p.109
22   10 CL.& F.200 p.208
23   ibid p.211
24   A.R.Hayward op cit p.113
25   (1848) 3 Cox C.C.275
26   ibid p.276
27   R.Smith "The Boundary Between Insanity and Criminal Responsibility in Nineteenth Century England" in A.Scull (ed) *Madhouses, Maddoctors and Madmen* (Philadelphia, 1981) pp.372 & 373
28   R.Smith *Trial by Medicine* op cit p.109
29   ibid p.112
30   R.Smith "The Boundary Between Insanity and Criminal Responsibility in Nineteenth Century England" op cit p.373
31   R.Smith *Trial by Medicine* op cit pp.143 and 144
     (For further insight on medical views of women and sexuality during this era see E.Showalter "Victorian Women and Insanity" (1980) 23 Victorian Studies 157 pp.169-171 and V.Bullough and M.Voigt "Women, Menstruation, and Nineteenth-Century Medicine" (1973) 47 Bull.Hist.Med.pp.66-82)
32   Described by R.Smith ibid pp.155 & 156
33   Both of these cases are described by R.Smith ibid p.156
34   ibid p.111
35   ibid p.109
36   ibid
37   ibid p.126
38   ibid pp.73 & 74
39   Quoted by R.Smith ibid p.39
40   A.Goldstein *The Insanity Defense* (New Haven, 1967) p.21
41   ibid p.211
42   R.Smith *Trial by Medicine* op cit p.75
43   A.Goldstein op cit p.21
44   See A.R. Hayward op cit, generally.
45   R.Smith *Trial by Medicine* op cit p.67
46   R.Smith "The Boundary Between Insanity and Criminal Responsibility in Nineteenth Century England" op cit p.375
47   F.McAuley "The Civilian Experience of the Insanity Defence" (1989) 24 Ir.Jur.227 p.235
48   J.Hall "Psychiatry and Criminal Responsibility" (1956) 65 Yale L.J.761 p.764
49   R.Smith *Trial by Medicine* op cit p.67
50   ibid p.72
51   (1859) 1 F.& F.666
52   ibid p.667

53   *R v Burton* (1863) 3 F.& F.772 p.780
54   A.R.Hayward op cit p.49
55   N.Walker *Crime and Insanity in England* Vol.1 (Edinburgh, 1968) pp.105 and 106
56   ibid p.106
57   Report of the Royal Commission on Capital Punishment (1949-53) Cmd.8932 (London, 1953) appendix 8 (d) p.398
58   ibid p.li
59   On the policy of maintaining the limits at present imposed by law on the criminal responsibility of madmen - Papers read before the Juridical Society, 1855-8 (London, 1855) p.81
60   *A General View of the Criminal Law of England* (London, 1863) p.95
61   ibid
62   ibid
63   ibid pp.95 & 96
64   B.P.P.,1872, Vol.2 p.241
65   B.P.P.,1874, Vol.2 p.370
66   Supra f.n.59
67   B.P.P.,1874, Vol.ix p.527
68   ibid p.513
69   ibid p.514
70   ibid pp.iii and iv
71   S.Davies "Irresistible Impulse in English Law" (1930) 17 Can.B.R.147 p.159
72   B.P.P.,1878, Vol.2 p.31
73   B.P.P.,1878-9, Vol.20 p.186
74   S.Davis op cit p.159
75   *A History of the Criminal Law of England* Vol.ii (London, 1883)
76   ibid pp.153 & 154
77   ibid p.159
78   ibid pp.154 & 155
79   ibid p.172
80   ibid p.167
81   ibid p.166
82   ibid p.171
83   (1881) 14 Cox.C.C.563
84   ibid p.564
85   These cases were cited by the Royal Commission on Capital Punishment (1949-53) Cmd 8932 op cit appendix 8(d) p.400
86   The Law Times (1960) Vol.229 p.192
87   H.Barnes "A Century of the McNaghten Rules" (1944) 8 C.L.J.300 p.316
88   ibid
89   (1910) 4 Cr.App.R.207
90   Stephen *A History of the Criminal Law of England* Vol.ii op cit
91   (1849) 4 Cox.C.C 155
92   (1910) 4 Cr.App.R.207 p.217
93   ibid p.218
94   22 Cox.C.C.268

95   (1911) 7 Cr.App.R.36
96   ibid p.37
97   (1915) 24 Cox.C.C.403
98   ibid p.405
99   *R v Jolly* 83 J.P.296
100 (1914) 10 Cr.App.R.210
101 (1921) 15 Cr.App.R.10
102 ibid p.12
103 *R v Quarmby* (1921) 15 Cr.App.R.163 p.164
104 *R v True* (1922) 16 Cr.App.R.164
105 ibid p.170
106 H.C.Deb.1922, Vol.155 p.201
107 Cf: ibid p.2421
108 Report of the Committee on Insanity and Crime Cmd 2005 (London, 1924) p.787
109 Report of the Committee on Insanity and Crime Cmd 2005 op cit.p.3
110 N.Walker *Crime and Insanity in England* Vol.1 op cit p.108
111 ibid p.109
112 ibid
113 ibid p.8
114 H.C.Deb.1924, Vol.170 p.1576
115 See the debate on the Criminal Responsibility (Trials) Bill H.L.Deb.1924, Vol.57 p.443
116 Report of the Royal Commission on Capital Punishment (1949-53) Cmd 8932 op cit appendix 8 (d) p.405
117 ibid pp.405 & 406
118 Seaborne Davies op cit p.165
119 Excerpts of the lecture have been published by the Law Times (1927) Vol.164 p.384
120 (1925) 19 Cr.App.R.50
121 ibid pp.51 & 52
122 (1926) 19 Cr.App.R.10
123 (1936) 2 All.E.R.1138
124 Report of the Select Committee on Capital Punishment (London, 1930)
125 ibid p.xi, para.161
126 Report of the Royal Commission on Capital Punishment (1949-53) Cmd 8932 op cit
127 ibid para.266
128 ibid para.314
129 ibid para.315
130 Report of the Royal Commission on Capital Punishment (1949-53) Cmd 8932 op cit para.333
131 ibid para.317
132 N.Walker *Crime and Insanity in England* Vol.1 op cit p.111
133 ibid
134 *A.G.v O'Connor* (1933) L.J.Ir.130
135 Cf: F.Boland "Insanity, the Irish Constitution and the European Convention on Human Rights" (1996) 47 N.I.L.Q.260
136 (1936) I.R.263 p.271

137   eg. *A.G.v Patrick Boylan* (1937) I.R.449; *The People (A.G.) v Michael Manning* (1955) 89 I.L.T.R.155; *The People (A.G.) v Vincent McGrath* 1 Frewen 192

138   *Irish Times* 12 Oct.1974

139   Quoted in *Doyle v Wicklow County Council* (1974) I.R.55 p.71

140   ibid

141   F.Boland op cit p.266

142   *Irish Times* 28 Jun.1968

143   Professor R.O'Hanlon "Not Guilty Because of Insanity" (1968) 3 Ir.Jur.61 p.76

144   ibid pp.76 & 77

145   F.McAuley *Insanity, Psychiatry and Criminal Responsibility* (Dublin, 1993) p.14

146   (1973) 107 I.L.T.R.169

147   ibid

148   (1974) I.R.55

149   ibid p.70

150   N.Osborough "McNaghten Revisited" (1974) 9 Ir.Jur.76 p.78

151   (1952) 2 All E.R.1

152   Report of the Royal Commission on Capital Punishment (1949-53) op cit para.315

153   (1974) I.R.55 p.71

154   ibid

155   F.McAuley op cit p.45

156   ibid

157   ibid

158   ibid pp.46-49

159   F.Boland "Diminished Responsibility as a Defence in Irish Law" (1995) 5 I.C.L.J.173 p.175

160   ibid p.176

161   ibid

162   (1986) I.L.R.M.244 pp.248 & 249

163   (1960) 3 All E.R.1

164   F.McAuley op cit p.59

165   (1972) I.R.204

166   In 1978 the *Henchy* Committee recommended a right of appeal from an acquittal by reason of insanity but its proposals have never been implemented.

167   (1990) 2 I.R.291

168   (1990) 2 I.R.267

169   (1991) 1 I.R.31

170   F.McAuley op cit p.121

171   ibid

172   F.Boland "Insanity, the Irish Constitution and the European Convention on Human Rights" op cit

173   Third Interim Report of the Inter-departmental Committee on Mentally Ill and Maladjusted Persons *Treatment and Care of Persons Suffering from Mental Disorder who Appear before the Courts on Criminal Charges* Prl (8275) (Dublin, 1978) p.3 para.4

174   ibid p.4 para.7

175   ibid p.15

176 P.Carney "Anachronism of our Criminal Insanity Laws" *Irish Times* 13 Jan 1990
177 *Irish Times* 22 Jan 1993 and *Irish Times* 21 Jan 1993
178 *Irish Times* 23 Jan 1993
179 (1990) 2 I.R.291 p.294
180 F.Boland "The Criminal Justice (Mental Disorder) Bill, 1996" (1997) 4 Web J.C.L.I.
181 ibid
182 Cf: F.Boland "Insanity, the Irish Constitution and the European Convention on Human Rights" op cit
183 A.Goldstein *The Insanity Defense* op cit p.68
184 (1866) 81 Ala.588, 2 So.854
185 Appendix 8(d) p.409
186 See S.Glueck *Mental Disorder and the Criminal Law* op cit pp.267-273
187 Eg. R.H.Kuh "The Insanity Defense - An Effort to Combine Law and Reason" (1962) 110 U.Pa.L.Rev.771 p.787 criticised the requirement of an impulse saying that contemporary psychiatry knows of no such fleetingly serious mental disease
188 E.R.Keedy "Insanity and Criminal Responsibility" (1917) 30 Harvard L.Rev.535, 724 pp.555 & 736; H.Weihofen *The Urge to Punish* (London, 1957) p.100
189 J.Hall op cit p.775
190 214 F.2d 862 (1954)

3 United States Reform *Post* Irresistible Impulse

The Product Test of Insanity

I will begin by examining the "product test" of insanity which provides that an accused should be excused from criminal liability if his act was the product of insanity. Many variants on this theme have been proposed, all of which would have given the medical profession considerable authority in criminal trials by allowing the medical view of insanity to prevail. This test of insanity was first accepted in New Hampshire in 1845.[1] This chapter will examine the use of this defence and will highlight the magnitude of the polemic which followed in the wake of *Durham v U.S.*[2] where the product test of insanity was adopted in D.C.. Granting recognition to the medical view of insanity did not resolve the controversy over the McNaghten Rules and irresistible impulse, and if anything, exacerbated it. I will then discuss the reforms of the insanity defence which were proposed and enacted following *Durham* with the intention of abating the controversy over the insanity defence.

While irresistible impulse was being urged in English law, the McNaghten Rules were also receiving an onslaught of criticism from the psychiatric profession in the United States. Dr.Isaac Ray, one of the founders of the American Psychiatric Association, believed that mental illness, where the patient seems to be the victim of emotional or "moral" forces beyond his control, can exist in spite of seemingly intact intellectual ability and that the symptoms of mental disease are so diverse that no legal definition or test of universal application is possible.[3] These observations lead him to suggest in his *Treatise on the Medical Jurisprudence of Insanity* (1838) that

> If the mental unsoundness, necessary to exempt from punishment, were required by law to have embraced the criminal act within its sphere of influence, as much perhaps would then be accomplished as is practicable within a specific enactment.[4]

His personal influence on Judge Charles Doe[5] led the latter to introduce this principle in a trilogy of New Hampshire cases, starting with *Boardman v Woodman*.[6] This was a probate case in which Judge Doe offered as a dissenting opinion that delusions were not the test of insanity and that insanity is a question of fact for the jury to decide and not a question of law for the judge to direct the jury on. Judge Doe was aware that a new rule would be less likely to win acceptance than a return to basic principles of common law[7] which he felt had been corrupted by the failure of the "great lawyers" to distinguish issues of fact from issues of law. According to Reid, although Doe was concerned by the fact that the law advanced an outdated theory of mental disease, his primary concern was to restore the distinction between law and fact.[8] Hence his dissenting judgment in *Boardman*:

> The question whether Miss Blydenburgh had a mental disease was a question of fact for the jury, and not a question of law for the court. Whether a delusion is a symptom, or a test, of any mental disease, was also a question of fact, and the instructions given to the jury, were erroneous in assuming it to be a question of law. The jury should have been instructed that if the writing propounded in the probate court was the offspring of mental disease, the verdict should be that Miss Blydenburgh was not of sound mind.[9]

His eagerness to have his doctrine accepted by the legal profession was the reason for his failure to accredit Dr.Isaac Ray with it. Antagonism towards the medical profession from the legal profession also meant that insanity had to be put forward as an issue of fact for the jury to decide, without seeming to accommodate recent medical theories.[10]

In *State v Pike*[11] Judge Doe, serving as junior to Chief Justice Ira Perley, persuaded the latter to instruct the jury that

> Whether there is such a mental disease as dipsomania, and whether the defendant had that disease, and whether the killing of Brown was the product of such disease, were questions of fact for the jury.[12]

Under the law as it then stood, the justices of the Supreme Judicial Court who presided as *nisi prius* judges at trial term, also reviewed their own decisions as appellate judges during law term. Thus when Pike appealed his conviction, Doe was able to develop in a concurring opinion, the theoretical basis for Perley's charge.[13]   After this decision, Doe sought to minimise his role in it and maximise Perley's, hoping that the latter's prestige would lend it respectability in the eyes of the legal profession.[14]

Six months after the *Pike* decision was handed down, Doe presided at another murder trial in which the plea of insanity was entered. Hiram Jones of Newmarket was an uxoricide who had slit his wife's throat from ear to ear with a razor because, he said, she was unfaithful to her marriage vows. The defence specifically asked the court to charge the jury that delusion, knowledge of right and wrong, and irresistible impulse were all tests of criminal responsibility. Doe refused and instead gave substantially the same charge Perley C.J. had given in *Pike*. Jones appealed but the New Hampshire Appellate Court unanimously approved Judge Doe's charge that if "the killing was the offspring or product of mental disease, the defendant should be acquitted", Ladd J. saying:

> Whether the defendant had a mental disease..seems to be as much a question of fact as whether he had a bodily disease; and whether the killing of his wife was the product of that disease, was also as clearly a matter of fact as whether thirst and a quickened pulse are the product of a fever. That it is a difficult question does not change the matter at all. The difficulty is intrinsic, and..symptoms, phases, or manifestations of the disease as legal tests of capacity to entertain a criminal intent..are clearly matters of evidence, to be weighed by the jury upon the question whether the act was the offspring of insanity: if it was, a criminal intent did not produce it; if it was not a criminal intent did produce it, and it was a crime.[15]

Among commentators there is disagreement about whether New Hampshire requires that the jury find that the defendant's mental illness *caused* the criminal act before he can be exculpated.[16] However in view of the evolution of the New Hampshire doctrine from the law of evidence and the fact that at no time did the New Hampshire judges attempt to define "product" and the fact that they expressly held that all definitions of "insanity" (or "responsibility" or "mental disease" etc.) are questions of fact for the jury, the better position is that the New Hampshire doctrine does not require that a causal connection between the mental disease and the act be shown, to exempt from legal responsibility.[17] With this in mind it would seem that, despite some contradictory words,[18] Judge Doe expressed the New Hampshire position on causation when he said:

Whether an act may be produced by partial insanity when no connection can be discovered between the act and the disease, is a question of fact.[19]

This has led Reid to conclude[20] that Doe intended not only the word "product" to be a question of fact, but also whether or not a finding of causation is necessary, to be a matter of fact for the jury.

Judge Doe confirmed his faith in jury competence and in the science of psychiatry in a letter to Dr. Ray dated 14/4/1868 which said[21]

Giving this matter to the jury leaves the way open for the reception of all progress in your science. One jury is not bound by the verdict of another jury on a general question of fact or science, as courts sometimes feel themselves bound by decisions on general questions of law. My result takes off the shackles of precedent and authority, - opens the subject to be decided in each case as an entirely new subject. Juries may make mistakes, but they cannot do worse than courts have done in this business.

Although the New Hampshire solution was praised by some, it was criticised by others on the ground that its inherent ambiguity left juries with insufficient guidance on the critical issue of responsibility.[22] The practical effect of the New Hampshire rule has been to transfer the decision on insanity to the psychiatrists, as prosecution and defence alike almost unquestioningly accept the psychiatric evidence tendered by the State Mental Hospital.[23] Reid reveals that the medical experts tend to limit insanity to psychosis[24] and to require a causal connection between the act and the illness,[25] some experts even requiring McNaghten madness before they will return a finding of insanity.[26] The obvious inference is that the medical profession decides the issue of insanity based on a misunderstanding of the prevailing test, whilst the true New Hampshire rule is, in effect, ignored. On the other hand, it may be argued that the doctors had to take upon themselves the task which Judge Doe and his successors on the New Hampshire bench should have undertaken; namely to give a separate legal definition of mental illness as a legally excusing condition.[27] That the New Hampshire rule did not acquire success, is evident from the fact that for the next eighty three years, no other American jurisdiction adopted the New Hampshire rule or even gave it serious consideration.[28]

However, this approach to insanity had some supporters in England, as is evident from the testimony of Blackburn J. before the Select

Committee on the Homicide Law Amendment Bill in 1874:

> On the question what amounts to insanity, that would prevent a person being punishable or not I have read every definition which I ever could meet with, and never was satisfied with one of them, and have endeavoured in vain to make one satisfactory to myself; I verily believe that it is not in human power to do it. You must take it that in every individual case you must look at the circumstances and do the best you can to say whether it was the disease of the mind which was the cause of the crime, or the party's criminal will.[29]

The proposal formulated by the Medico Psychological Association before the Atkin Committee in 1922 was also clearly influenced by the New Hampshire test. That proposal was that

> (1) The McNaghten rules be abrogated and the responsibility of a person should be left as a question of fact to be determined by the jury on the merits of the particular case.
> (2) In every trial in which the prisoner's mental condition is in issue the judge should direct the jury to answer the following questions
> (a) Did the prisoner commit the act alleged?
> (b) If he did was he at the time insane?
> (c) If he was insane, has it nevertheless been proved to the satisfaction of the jury that his crime was unrelated to his mental disorder?.[30]

The Atkin Committee's main reason for rejecting this recommendation was their belief that it treated insanity as co-extensive with irresponsibility. The Atkin Committee feared the far-reaching effect of granting immunity to everyone of unsound mind, especially since unsoundness of mind was no longer regarded as a disorder of the intellectual or cognitive faculties but as a morbid change in the emotional and instinctive activities with or without intellectual derangement.[31] All the witnesses agreed that the requirement that the prosecution satisfy the jury that the act was unrelated to the mental disorder would cast a burden which could not be discharged,[32] and when the vagueness of "unrelated" was pointed out, the phrase was altered to "the mental disorder was not calculated to influence the commission of the act".[33] However, the Atkin Committee felt that this failed to alter the difficulty of burden of proof.[34]

The Committee's reasons for rejecting the recommendation of the Medico Psychological Association were firstly, their view that during the early stages of insanity the defendant would be affected by every motive for committing or abstaining from committing a criminal act that would be likely to affect a person of sound mind and in substantially the same degree. Secondly, they felt that the difficulty of diagnosis and when some unsoundness of mind was indicated, of establishing the non-relation of the act to the unsound state of mind would introduce so much uncertainty into the administration of the criminal law as to create a public danger.[35] Thirdly, they felt that much of the criticism directed from the medical side at the McNaughten Rules was based upon the misapprehension that the Rules contain a definition of insanity, so that the legal definition was contrasted with the medical conception of insanity. In the Committee's view the judges who framed the Rules were not professing to define "disease of the mind" but only to define what degree of disease of the mind negatived criminality; Once it was appreciated that the question is a legal question, and that under the present law a person of unsound mind may be criminally responsible, the criticism based upon a supposed clash between legal and medical conceptions of insanity disappears.[36]

Although in 1953, in evidence given before the Royal Commission on Capital Punishment, the Medico Psychological Association (which had now added Royal to its name) were content to rely on the "increasing elasticity" with which the Rules were being interpreted and were no longer in favour of their abrogation, the Royal Commission felt (with one dissentient) that the test of responsibility encompassed by the McNaghten Rules was so defective that the law on the subject ought to be changed.[37] The Commission's main recommendation (with three dissentients) was that the McNaghten Rules be abrogated and the jury be left free to determine whether, at the time of the act, the accused was suffering from "disease of the mind or mental deficiency to such a degree that he ought not to be held responsible".[38]

Although at first glance this does not appear to resemble Isaac Ray's formulation, the Commission was certainly influenced by it. The Commission categorically denied that mental disease or mental defect of any type is co-extensive with irresponsibility[39] but stated that

> If it appears that the crime was wholly or very largely caused by insanity then [the accused] ought to be treated as irresponsible; for to punish a person for a crime caused by insanity would in effect be to punish him for his insanity.[40]

This echoes the words of the Supreme Court of New Hampshire in *State v Jones* that

> No argument is needed to show that to hold that a man may be punished for what is the offspring of disease would be to hold that he may be punished for disease. Any rule which makes that possible cannot be law.[41]

In assessing causation the Commission stated that

> Where a person suffering from a mental abnormality commits a crime, there must always be some likelihood that the abnormality has played some part in the causation of the crime; and generally speaking, the graver the abnormality and the more serious the crime, the more probable it must be that there is a causal connection between them. But the closeness of this connection will be shown by the facts brought in evidence in individual cases and cannot be decided on the basis of any general medical principle.[42]

The Commission justified its proposal to allow the jury wide general discretion by saying

> Whatever the rule of law may say, and however broadly it may be interpreted, it can never be all-embracing and it must be expected that members of the jury will sometimes find that their common sense drives them to look behind the rule and to address their minds directly to the essential question of responsibility.[43]

The Commission denied that their proposal would lay a difficult or impossible task on the jury and asserted the advantages of the judges' new freedom to direct the juries' attention to all the evidence for and against a finding of insanity.[44] However the dissentients, Mr Radzinowiz, Dame Florence Hancock and Mr McDonald objected that a standard of responsibility was necessary to limit arbitrariness on the part of the jury, to promote uniformity of decision, and to aid the jury in deciding between the conflicting testimony of the experts.[45] It is interesting to note that the majority of witnesses who gave evidence to the Commission felt that a standard of responsibility was necessary for similar reasons.[46]

The Commission's proposals were never enacted and the law on insanity remained precisely the same as it was in 1843. The Commission's recommendation on the wording of the insanity defence has been adopted by a 1978 Interdepartmental Committee on Mentally Ill and Maladjusted Persons (the Henchy Committee) which recommended that a variant of it replace the McNaghten-irresistible impulse test of insanity which prevails in Irish law.[47] This test appears to have been revived by the recently defeated Irish government when it threatened to pay particular attention to the Henchy Committee's proposals in the course of reforming the law on insanity[48] but the present Government's draft bill[49] only pays lip service to the Royal Commission's justly responsible test.[50]

The Durham Rule

The Royal Commission's report also influenced developments in the U.S., and one year later Judge David Bazelon, in *Durham v U.S.*,[51] ruled that if the defendant's act was the product of mental disease or defect he was not criminally responsible. In doing so he overruled the right-wrong test supplemented by the irresistible impulse test which had prevailed until then in D.C.. The Court in *Durham* stated that the "rule we now hold..is not unlike that followed by the New Hampshire court since 1870",[52] a statement which has led to the two decisions being twinned together and jointly criticised although they are not in fact the same, as causation is not a legal requirement under the New Hampshire "rule".

Although not well articulated, the court in *Durham* wished to remedy the well known criticism directed at the insanity tests, that experts were required to testify on issues beyond their competence.[53] Whilst the medical experts would advance evidence of disease or defect, the jury would determine the ultimate question of whether the act was the product of mental disease or defect. What *was* clear from the *Durham* decision was its foundation on the premise that factfinders should be able to weigh any and all expert information about the accused's behaviour.[54] The advantage of Durham (as with the New Hampshire test) was that unlike irresistible impulse it did not attempt to crystallise one set of medical theories in place of another and that it was sufficiently broad to embrace future developments in psychiatry.[55] Thus the new test would remedy the defects of McNaghten and irresistible impulse which limited psychiatric testimony to cognitive and volitional defects.

Durham heralded the arrival of a new reformative era of

punishment instead of the previous utilitarian one and hinted that increasing numbers would be removed from the criminal justice system to the mental health system because they suffered from mental disease[56] . The new rule promised an increased role for psychiatry in criminal trials where insanity was pleaded, and in the disposal of insane offenders.

The shortcomings of *Durham* soon became obvious. The only explanation given of "mental disease" and "mental defect" was that disease is "a condition which is considered capable of either improving or deteriorating" whereas defect is a nonchanging condition "which may be either congenital, or the result of injury, or the residual effect of a physical or mental disease".[57]   The vagueness of these phrases was pointed out in *Wright v U.S.*[58] where the court said "the terms "disease" and "defect" are not so self-explanatory and our definition of them in Durham is not so definitive as to make elucidation always superfluous".[59]   One of the earliest critics of the *Durham* rule observed that

> The decision left unresolved the question whether the controlling criterion, "mental disease or defect", was intended to be *psychiatric* (in the sense that psychiatric conceptions of "mental disease" would legally be equated to "insanity") or *jural* (in the sense that the jury's view of "mental disease" would control). Upon this "pending" decision hangs the critical issue of whether psychiatrist or jury will have the final say of criminal responsibility.[60]

That the issue of mental disease was to be turned over to the medical witnesses was confirmed in *Wright*, where the D.C. Court of Appeals defined mental disease as synonymous with mental illness. Then in *Carter v U.S.*[61] the court stated that

> Mental "disease" means mental illness. Mental illnesses are of many sorts and have many characteristics. They, like physical illnesses, are the subject matter of medical science..The problems of the law in these cases are whether a person who has committed a specific criminal act..was suffering from a mental disease, that is, from a medically recognized illness of the mind.[62]

As the psychiatric view of insanity was to prevail the psychiatric profession had at last won its hard fought battle. Now "mental disease" would exculpate anyone whom psychiatrists chose to label as "mentally diseased." This was to become controversial, the problem being dramatically highlighted by the "weekend flip flop case", *In Re Rosenfield* 63 where the petitioner was described as a sociopath. A psychiatrist from St.Elizabeth's hospital testified that a person with a sociopathic personality was not suffering from a mental disease. That was on a Friday afternoon. On the following Monday morning, through a policy change at the hospital, it was determined, as an administrative matter, that the state of a psychopathic or sociopathic personality did, afterall, constitute a mental disease. The immediate consequence of this policy change was a ten-fold increase in acquittals by reason of insanity in D.C.64 Antagonism to the psychiatric profession became increasingly obvious and it was said that whatever the psychiatrist testified amounted to "mental disease", he was making a judgment about criminal responsibility, a judgment that he was not authorised to make and with respect to which he is not expert.65 (In this respect *Durham* differed from the New Hampshire doctrine and the recommendation of the Royal Commission on Capital Punishment (1953) where the issue of insanity is clearly a jural question). The effect of the reduction of insanity to a scientific question was to minimise the relevance of moral judgment, although *pace* Fletcher, I do not feel that this was the implicit ambition of *Durham*.66 The end result was that in *McDonald v U.S.*67 the D.C. Court of Appeals stated that "a "mental disease or defect" for clinical purposes..may or may not be the same as mental disease or defect for the jury's purpose in determining criminal responsibility",68 thus replacing the issue of "mental disease or defect" on the jury.

Where there was agreement on the existence of mental disease the controversy shifted to "product".69 The jury was left entirely dependent on the expert's classification of conduct as the "product" of mental disease.70 Furthermore, it was said that the "product" requirement assumed a compartmentalised mind, like McNaghten had done, because it implied that mental disease "caused" some unlawful acts and not others.71 Although the New Hampshire test also requires that the act be a product of mental disease, their requirement of causation is less objectionable as it does not amount to a substantive legal rule. On a philosophical level, the problem with the requirement of causation in *Durham* was the failure to see the possibility of there being differing sets of equally sufficient conditions existing to cause the same event. To say that a bodily movement is the product of an abnormal condition of the brain does not preclude one from describing that movement as an action performed by an agent for reasons.72 The practical effect of *Durham* was that it shifted the court-room controversy from the words of the insanity defence to the nature of the particular disease and to whether the criminal act was the product of such disease.[73] *Wright* and *Carter* attempted to clarify the "product test" by the adoption of a "but for" test (i.e. the crime would not have occurred "but for" the mental disease or defect). Because it is not possible to say that a crime would have been committed if mental disease or defect had not been present, the result of the "but for test" was a direct move from a finding of mental disease to a finding of lack of responsibility.[74] This was especially true in the case of the psychopath,[75] who it is commonly asserted, exhibits an abnormality only in the repetitious performance of antisocial or criminal acts.[76] The jury's role had been usurped by the psychiatric profession. For this reason in *Washington v U.S.,*[77] psychiatric testimony on the issue of productivity was prohibited.

While thirty four acquittals on the basis of Not Guilty by Reason of Insanity had been given during the four years previous to the application of the *Durham* rule, in the four years after *Durham* was decided the number of acquittals from insanity pleas rose to one hundred and fifty.[78] The public perception must have been that *Durham* was responsible for this rise, although there is reason to believe that the increase was the result of a redirection into the insanity defence of individuals who had previously been held incompetent to stand trial.[79] *Durham* left lawyers feeling that the liberty of the individual was seriously threatened: One concern was that the mental hospitals where indeterminate confinement took place were really prisons in disguise with only a pretence of treatment and with gross disregard of civil liberties and due process.[80] The individual was no longer regarded as a person with rights but as an object of control according to scientific techniques.[81]

While *Durham* centred on the effect of mental disease or defect on the conduct of the actor, it provided no measure of the necessary effect which was present in the McNaghten Rules and even in the irresistible impulse test. In these formulations at least the jury was presented with the task of determining whether the mental disease had the effect of impairing cognitive or volitional capacities.[82] With no standard by which to judge the evidence the jury was left with the burden of deciding between conflicting expert testimony as to whether the defendant was suffering from "mental disease" and whether his act was the "product" of disease.

The erosion of Durham began in 1962 with *McDonald v U.S.* where the court said

Neither the court nor the jury is bound by *ad hoc* definitions or conclusions as to what experts state is a disease or defect..The jury should be told that a mental disease or defect includes any abnormal condition of the mind or emotional process that substantially impairs behaviour controls. The jury would consider testimony concerning the development, adaptation and functioning of these processes and controls.[83]

It was said that *Durham* had travelled a remarkably circuitous path towards the conclusion that the jury needed some guidance, that words like mental disease and product were inadequate and that the standard would have to incorporate somehow, a description of the sorts of effects of disease that were relevant to compliance with the criminal law.[84] That the jury is left with no standard with which to judge the evidence, is an objection that applies equally to the New Hampshire rule, to the recommendation of the Royal Commission on Capital Punishment (1949-53) and to that of the Henchy Committee (1978). A variation of the Royal Commission's test had been approved by a minority of the American Law Institute, a body of noted attorneys, judges and scholars which had undertaken to revise the criminal law and to write a model penal code that could be adopted by the states,[85] as an alternative to the test adopted in the code. This variation of the Royal Commission's test was urged as a replacement of the *Durham* test by Bazelon J. in *Brawner*. Bazelon's new test proposed that

A defendant is not responsible if at the time of his unlawful conduct his mental or emotional processes or behavior controls were impaired to such an extent that he cannot justly be held responsible for his act.[86]

However the court in *Brawner*[87] was impressed by Goldstein's warning in *The Insanity Defense*[88] that the

Overly general standard [*whether the accused may justly be held responsible*] may place too great a burden upon the jury. If the law provides no standard, members of the jury are placed in the difficult position of having to find a man responsible for no other reason than their personal feeling about him. Whether the psyches of individual jurors are strong enough to make that decision, or whether the "law" should put that obligation on them, is open to serious question. It is far easier for them to perform the role assigned to them by legislature and courts if they know - or are able to rationalize - that their verdicts are "required" by law.

This refers to the concern, also advanced by Weihofen,[89] that in a serious case it is distressing enough having to find a man guilty even when the jury is shielded from guilty feelings by the knowledge that the law is clear and permits no other verdict. If the law is unclear and leaves the decision of life and death, or of a life sentence or hospitalisation to the conscience of the jury with no definite rule to bind them, the burden can be more than we have a right to impose. Some weight may be lent to this argument by Simon's research on jury deliberations in insanity trials which has shown that juries who were uninstructed on insanity deliberated longer than their counterparts who were given the McNaghten Rules.[90]   They were also more likely to acquit the defendant on the grounds of insanity than under the McNaghten Rules.[91]

Rejecting the Royal Commission's proposal as an alternative to the *Durham* rule, the court in *Brawner* expressed the view[92]

> That an instruction overtly cast in terms of "justice" cannot feasibly be restricted to the ambit of what may properly be taken into account but will splash with unconfinable and malign consequences.

Whilst admitting that

> There may be a tug of appeal in the suggestion that law is a means to justice and the jury is an appropriate tribunal to ascertain justice

it claimed[93]

> This is a simplistic syllogism that harbors the logical fallacy of equivocation, and fails to take account of the different facets and dimensions of the concept of justice..The thrust of a rule that in essence invites the jury to ponder the evidence on impairment of the defendant's capacity and appreciation, and then do what to them seems just, is to focus on what seems "just" as to the particular individual. Under the centuries-long pull of the Judeo-Christian ethic, this is likely to suggest a call for understanding and forgiveness of those who have committed crimes against society but plead the influence of passionate and perhaps justified grievances against that society, perhaps grievances not wholly lacking in merit..The judgment of a court of law must further justice to the community, and safeguard it, against undercutting and evasion from overconcern for the individual. What this reflects is not the rigidity of retributive justice..but awareness how justice in the broad may be

undermined by an excess of compassion as well as passion. Justice to the community includes penalties needed to cope with disobedience by those capable of control, undergirding a social environment that broadly inhibits behavior destructive of the common good. An open society requires mutual respect and regard and mutually reinforcing relationships among its citizens, and its ideals of justice must safeguard the vast majority who responsibly shoulder the burdens implicit in its ordered liberty. Still another aspect of justice is the requirement for rules of conduct that establish reasonably generality, neutrality and constancy. This concept is neither static nor absolute, but it would be sapped by a rule that invites an ad hoc redefinition of the "just" with each new case.

As a result of the *Durham* experience, when the American Law Institute (A.L.I.) made its recommendations on insanity for its Model Penal Code, a year after the decision in *Durham*, it rejected the advice of its psychiatric advisory committee, which endorsed *Durham*.[94] Instead the A.L.I. adopted the following test:-

(1) A person is not responsible for criminal conduct if at the time of such conduct as a result of mental disease or defect he lacks substantial capacity either to appreciate the criminality of his conduct or to conform his conduct to the requirements of law.

(2) As used in this Article, the terms "mental disease" do not include an abnormality manifested only by repeated criminal or otherwise antisocial conduct.

Although signalling a return to the McNaghten and irresistible impulse tests, the A.L.I.'s formula contained two important changes. It used "appreciate" instead of "know" in the McNaghten Rules, which suggested that responsibility required a deeper level of understanding than mere knowledge or perception. The wording of section 2 was designed to ensure that psychopaths would not be encompassed by the insanity defence.[95] Although the formulation did not use the words "irresistible impulse", the terminology "to conform his conduct" made it clear that impairment of volition as well as impairment of cognition should be considered in determining criminal responsibility. The substitution of language avoided the criticism directed at the "irresistible impulse" test by the Royal Commission in 1953, that volitional control may be impaired not only by a sudden occurrence but may be impaired after brooding.[96] Furthermore, the word "substantial" eliminated the need to show total impairment of cognitive or control capacities.[97]   Because no more than three essential facts were required under the A.L.I. test, if psychiatry decided in the future to classify other abnormal behaviour as symptomatic of a mental illness that impaired a person's ability to obey the law, the individual afflicted could raise insanity as a defence to criminal charges arising from such behaviour.[98]

Court after court refused to adopt *Durham*, using the occasion to reaffirm its faith in free will and deterrence, its hostility to psychiatry and the deterministic view of human behaviour, its scepticism about psychiatry's status as a science and its fear that the concept of mental disease was so broad that it might encompass all or most serious crime and especially the psychopath.[99]   The Durham rule was attacked in the same court that enunciated it and rejected by every other court that considered it.[100]   The author of the *Durham* formula, Judge Bazelon, has described his own reasons for abandoning it in the following terms:

> In the end, after eighteen years, I favoured the abandonment of the Durham rule, because, in practice it had failed to take the issue of criminal responsibility away from the experts. Psychiatrists continued to testify to the naked conclusion instead of providing information about the accused so that the jury could render the ultimate moral judgment about blameworthiness. Durham had secured little improvement over McNaghten.[101]

Professor Goldstein is of the view that *"Durham's* principal contribution has been less as a "solution" to the insanity problem than as a dramatic demonstration that there are no solutions".[102]   The truth of this statement will be questioned at length in Chapter 4. *Durham* was finally overruled in *U.S. v Brawner* in favour of a variant of the Model Penal Code rule, a rule which has been urged (albeit unsuccessfully) in court, as the appropriate test of insanity in Irish Law.[103]

The A.L.I. rule was far more successful,[104] possibly a reaction of the legal profession against the degree to which *Durham* had been championed by psychiatrists and in part, as a result of the widespread acceptance of the stereotyped view of McNaghten and irresistible impulse - a view which *Durham* did a great deal to intensify.[105]   In 1961 only one state had a standard similar to the A.L.I. test. By 1985 approximately half of the states used the A.L.I. test, either *verbatim* or with slight modifications.[106]

However this flight to the A.L.I. formula did not continue. The Model Penal Code was open to the same objection as *Durham* in its reference to "mental disease or defect" but its second limb raised other problems. In particular, the test of capacity to conform had to face a well-known philosophical criticism. How can one tell the difference between an impulse which is irresistible and one which is merely not resisted?.[107] Judge David Bazelon, author of the *Durham* rule, stated squarely in *U.S. v Brawner* that

> Instead of asking a jury whether the act was caused by the impairment, our new test asks the jury to wrestle with such unfamiliar if not incomprehensible concepts as the capacity to appreciate the wrongfulness of one's action, and the capacity to conform one's conduct to the requirements of law. The best hope for our new test is that jurors will regularly conclude that no-one - including the experts - can provide a meaningful answer to the question posed by the ALI test.[108]

It was said that, despite the intention of section 2, the psychopath would not be excluded from A.L.I. insanity because it was unlikely that any psychiatrist would base his diagnosis of psychopathy solely on criminal or antisocial conduct.[109] Furthermore, it would be impossible for the defence of insanity, supported largely by evidence of prior crimes, to be denied as a matter of law and because the prosecutor's attempt to prove a history of similar prior crimes would be met with the objection that the evidence was inadmissible because of its prejudicial effect.[110] It is not necessary to criticise the A.L.I. formula in much depth as it is no more than a reformulation of the McNaghten and irresistible impulse tests[111] and the main defects in those two tests (which have been well rehearsed in Chapters One and Two) are present in the A.L.I. formulation. The phrase "as a result of" prolongs the requirement of a causal connection which was the cause of so much controversy while *Durham* reigned and use of the words "substantial capacity" and "appreciate" has been questioned on the ground that they are bound to encourage differences among expert witnesses and also among jurors over whether the defendant's degree of impairment or depth of awareness was sufficient.[112] No doubt these objections influenced the rejection of the A.L.I. test by a majority of the Canadian Royal Commission on the Law of Insanity, the Massachusetts Special Commission on Insanity and by the New Jersey Supreme Court.[113] There is weak but provocative support for the conclusion that switching from the McNaghten test which prevailed in most states, to the A.L.I. test, also resulted in more successful insanity pleas. Between 1966 and 1972, Oregon had only 44 successful insanity pleas using the McNaghten test; between 1972 and 1982, a total of 734 insanity acquittals occurred using the A.L.I. standard. Maryland experienced an increase of 143% in the proportion of defendants found not guilty by reason of insanity in the years after that state changed from McNaghten to the A.L.I. test.[114]

Major controversy followed the *Hinckley* verdict, when President Reagan's would-be assassin was acquitted by reason of insanity, using the A.L.I. test. As a result of "unprecedented criticism surrounding the Hinckley verdict"[115] several states restricted the test of legal insanity. Four jurisdictions changed from the A.L.I. or McNaghten plus irresistible impulse tests[116] to the simple McNaghten test.[117] Idaho and Utah abolished the insanity defence. As well as a plethora of procedural reforms, the much criticised[118] verdict of guilty but mentally ill was introduced in several jurisdictions to accompany restrictions of the insanity defence. Being no more than a dressed up verdict of guilty it will not be examined in the context of insanity defence reform. At this time, reports of the American Psychiatric Association and the American Bar Association were advocating a cognitive test of insanity.[119] Thus, despite the attempts to accommodate the psychiatric profession by widening the scope of the insanity defence, the psychiatric profession had now done a u-turn.[120] The American Psychiatric Association was now of the view that

> Psychiatric information relevant to determining whether a defendant understood the nature of his act, and whether he appreciated its wrongfulness, is more reliable and has a stronger scientific basis, than for example, does psychiatric information relevant to whether a defendant was able to control his behavior.[121]

The American Bar Association rejected the "control" test in favour of an exclusively cognitive test because it concluded that "there are occasional mistakes, and..these mistakes are most likely to be associated with the volitional criterion".[122] It added that "any volitional inquiry involves a significant risk of 'moral mistakes' in the adjudication of responsibility".[123]

Early in the twentieth century, statutes had been passed in Washington State, Mississippi and Louisiana preventing defendants from pleading insanity under any conditions.[124] Although these statutes had been declared unconstitutional,[125] after the *Hinckley* verdict public pressure to abolish the insanity defence began to accumulate. In what has been viewed as an attempt to save the insanity defence from complete extinction,[126] the United States Congress in 1984 enacted the Insanity Defense Reform Act. This piece of legislation took the power to decide which version of the insanity defence to adopt away from the federal circuit courts of appeal, and mandated that a uniform insanity test be used in all federal prosecutions.[127] Several of the bills introduced in Congress in the aftermath of the *Hinckley* verdict would have eliminated the insanity defence altogether and limited evidence of mental illness solely to the issue of the defendant's *mens rea*.[128]   As a result, Congress responded by passing legislation which restricted the scope of the insanity defence even further than McNaghten had done and would excuse a criminal defendant only

> If at the time of the offense, the defendant, as a result of *severe* mental illness or defect, was *unable* to appreciate the nature and quality or the wrongfulness of his acts.[129]

Abolition of the Insanity Defence

Any discussion of the insanity defence must involve consideration of why we excuse the insane. If a defence for the insane cannot be justified then we would be better off abolishing it, a view which has been adopted in recent years by many American academics and has even appealed to Judge Bazelon,[130] the author of the Durham Rule. This view will be discussed *below*.

Bracton's 13th century treatise *On the Laws and Customs of England* excused the insane on the basis of the principle *furiosus solo furore punitur* - a madman is punished by his madness alone. This justification of the insanity defence was borrowed from Roman law[131] but it is difficult to accept it as a justification for the insanity defence today. In practice it has been subsumed by a more rational justification. This is that a madman cannot be blamed as he is *amens (id est) sine mente*, without his mind or discretion and *actus non facit reum nisi mens sit rea*. This approach is similar to the law's treatment of children under ten years of age, who are treated as being incapable of having *mens rea* and who cannot be found guilty of a criminal offence. This rationale for the insanity defence goes back at least as far as 1280 when a Nottingham jury, who tried a man who had hanged his daughter in a frenzied state, certified that "he did as aforesaid, and not feloniously or through malice afore-thought".132   However, unless the state of *mens rea* presupposes a guilty *healthy* mind it is not easy to see that the insane offender does in fact lack *mens rea*, particularly if the state of mind required for the offence is objective recklessness or strict liability. Fingarette feels that the equating of insanity with lack of *mens rea* has been responsible for the assumption that the specific conditions that normally show absence of *mens rea* are also the ones that must be shown to be present where there is insanity.133   As a result, the insanity defence has been limited to cognitive and volitional impairment. Furthermore, the use of this justification may render the insanity defence otiose134 since any person who lacks *mens rea* will in any event be acquitted.

A third justification which is commonly urged on behalf of the insanity defence is Bentham's view that the deterrent effect of the law cannot have its usual impact on insane offenders and hence, punishing an insane offender will not deter those who can identify with him. As Fletcher notes, the problem with this justification is that there is no way to say *a priori* that some people should be excluded from the category of potential deterrables and without empirical evidence the argument of pointless punishment hardly generates a rationale for the existing excusing conditions in the law.135

Another justification which is commonly urged on behalf of the special verdict is that an insane offender lacks blame for what he has done. Although closely allied to the *mens rea* principle it seems to be based on compassionate rather than academic grounds, what Fingarette speaks of "as a matter of deep intuition, evident through several centuries of Anglo-American law".136   The York plea rolls for the year 1212 record a case in which

> The King must be consulted about an idiot who is in the prison because in his witlessness he confessed that he is a thief, although in fact he is not to blame.137

This was the justification underlying *Durham v U.S.*, which held "[o]ur collective conscience does not allow punishment where it cannot impose blame".138   No one would doubt that the grossly psychotic lacks blame, that a "residual category of persons [exists] whose mental disorientation is so severe that they are incapable of culpability".[139] This must be because of their failure to reason or rationalise[140] like a normal individual who is deserving of the law's sanction. The difficulty lies in discerning *when* an insane person lacks blame, in other words how ill must one be before blameworthiness is absent. The debate over the insanity defence discussed *above* shows that the medical profession often wished to treat all or most insane persons as irresponsible whereas the law wished to treat some insane persons as responsible, both to deter others and to punish the wrongdoer. Reduced blameworthiness is a justification for the defence of diminished responsibility, examined further in Chapters Five and Six, which reduces the legal responsibility of those who are less blameworthy for their criminal acts.

A final rationale for excusing the insane is that the process of prosecution, conviction and imposition of sanctions which serves to educate the public by making known what conduct is prohibited by the criminal law, cannot serve this function by punishing the insane. Because this group is regarded as not blameworthy their punishment could only blur the distinction between good and bad conduct and thus work against the education theory.[141] Presumably this argument refers to the moral repugnance that the community would feel towards punishing the insane. Closely allied to this idea is the notion that the citizen needs the insanity defence to symbolise and reinforce his/her belief in personal responsibility:[142] by identifying the individuals who are not responsible for their actions we induce in the remainder of the population the belief that they are responsible.[143] However, although belief in personal responsibility is an important determinant of the citizen's law abiding behaviour[144] it is impossible to say how the insanity defence affects this perception.[145]

Thus, it seems that an insanity defence can be justified for the insane as a means of preserving respect for the law and reflecting their absence of blameworthiness. However as a result of the American experience, many academics have abandoned attempts to reformulate the insanity defence and prefer instead to advocate its abolition.[146] They have questioned the purpose of the insanity defence, stating that this "either has been assumed to be so obvious as not to require articulation[147] or has been expressed in such vague generalizations as to afford no basis for evaluating the multitude of formulae".[148] Examination of the *mens rea* rationale has led the abolitionists to the conclusion that "[w]ithout the essential element of *mens rea* there is no crime from which to relieve the Defendant of liability and consequently, since no crime has been committed, there is no need for formulating an insanity defense".[149] Some abolitionists favour the invocation of insanity, as evidence bearing on the presence or absence of *mens rea* (the *mens rea* model). According to Morris[150] this was the *status quo* until the 19th century

> But by the time of McNaghten (1843) this clear position was frustrated by the increasing tendency of lawyers, psychiatrists, public opinion and legislators to turn questions of evidence into matters of substance and to transmute medical evidence about legal issues into substantive legal rules. McNaghten was just such a substantive rule confusing evidence for a proposition with the proposition itself.

By far the most radical proposal has been the removal of the concept of responsibility from the law and with it the insanity defence (the behavioural model). These abolitionists would have insanity considered at the sentencing stage, in deciding how to dispose of the offender.

A variety of arguments have been put forward in favour of abolition. Firstly, the abolitionists claim that the administration of the insanity tests has been a failure[151] because at the end of the day the jury's decision depends on either over-identification with or alienation from the defendant.[152] The jury's decision will often be largely governed by the credentials and presentation of the psychiatric experts[153] who are encouraged to parade their opinions, guesses and speculations under the banner of scientific expertise.[154] Thus insanity is a "rich man's defense" in that it favours the wealthy who can afford the array of experts needed to mount a convincing defence whilst discriminating against the poor who cannot afford the time of influential experts - experts who are in short supply and whose time would be better spent treating those who have been committed to hospital or imprisoned.[155] Because of the above, and the fact that there is no workable distinction between responsibility and irresponsibility, psychiatry should not frame the dividing line between the two.[156] La Fave and Scott have advanced three further arguments in favour of abolition.[157] Firstly, the crucial decision to be made concerns the proper disposition of mentally abnormal persons who commit criminal acts, and this is a matter which is better dealt with in a direct way following conviction than indirectly during trial. Secondly, a number of informed observers believe that it is therapeutically desirable to treat behavioural deviants as responsible for their conduct rather than as involuntary victims playing a sick role. Thirdly, persons channelled out of the criminal process following a finding of insanity are not protected against administrative abuse of their rights to the same degree as they would be if they remained within the criminal justice system.

Those in favour of abolition also stress that the defence of legal insanity is of little practical importance. With increasing frequency, issues concerning the mental abnormality of the offender are being taken into account after conviction rather than before.[158] The insanity defence's inquiry into the defendant's mental state *at the time of offence* seems misplaced.[159] Another abolitionist argument is that the retention of the distinction between those to be punished and those only to be treated is unfortunate and invidious because it is in all cases, not only in some, that persons who do harms should be treated and held in the interest of the public's protection. In most crimes psychical and social determinants inhibit the capacity of the actors to control their behaviour.[160] The abolitionists assert that the present situation is bad and that abolition could only make it better.[161]

The abolitionist argument has not fallen on deaf ears. Rising crime rates and the coincident widening of the insanity defence convinced many Americans that the two were related.[162] Strict commitment criteria applied following a finding of insanity, with the result that insane offenders, if not considered mentally ill *and* dangerous, could be released within hours of acquittal. When the American public learned that John Hinckley could be released from Saint Elizabeth's Hospital at virtually any time, public awareness of the insanity defence changed dramatically.[163] An Associated Press-NBC newspoll in 1981 following the *Hinckley* verdict, showed that 70% of the American public favoured total elimination of the insanity defence. Montana had abolished the insanity defence in 1979 and now the state Legislatures of Idaho and Utah followed suit.[164] The Supreme Courts of Montana and Idaho upheld the constitutionality of abolishing the insanity defence and the U.S. Supreme Court indicated that it too, would not strike down as unconstitutional, legislation that abolished the insanity defence.

However, this is not to say that the abolitionist argument has received unanimous support. Kadish has answered many of the abolitionists arguments. He concedes that the administration of the insanity defence is very bad indeed but scarcely the only feature of our criminal justice system which is badly administered in practice.[165]   Inefficiency and inequity are endemic to a system committed to an adversary process but not committed to supplying the resources of legal contest to the typically penurious who make up the bulk of criminal defendants.[166]   The lesson of all this would not be to abandon the adversary method on that score, but to improve its operation. Likewise with the insanity defence, improvement of its operation rather than its abolition would seem to be the more appropriate response.[167]

To the extent that the case for abolition rests on the inequitableness and irrationality of its administration, the very infrequency with which the insanity defence is invoked reduces the import of the criticism.[168]   The defences of necessity or duress are invoked in a minute fraction of criminal cases, yet few would regard this as a reason for abandoning them.[169]   The function of a legal defence is not measured by it use but by its usefulness in the total framework of the criminal justice system.[170]

If a crime requires mere negligence then absence of an insanity defence would leave the defendant with no defence at all, since all that is required is that the defendant has fallen substantially below the standard of the reasonable man and this, by definition, a McNaghten defendant has done[171] (except, of course, to the extent that the subjective feature of the concept of negligence were enlarged, to embrace his special cognitive disabilities).[172]

The proposal for abolition opens to the condemnation of a criminal conviction a class of persons who, on any common sense notion of justice are beyond blaming and ought not to be punished.[173]   It is true that a person adjudicated Not Guilty by Reason of Insanity suffers a substantial social stigma but this results from the misinterpretation placed upon the person's conduct by people in the community.[174]   It is not, like the conviction of the irresponsible, the paradigmatic affront to the sense of justice in the law of convicting a morally innocent person of a crime, of imposing blame when there is no occasion for it.[175]   Here Kadish uses the justifications of the insanity defence outlined by the writer *above*, as reasons for retaining it.

Further arguments for retaining the insanity defence include the requirement that the decision be made by a jury, representative of the public, rather than by experts.[176]   The much criticised expert dominance of insanity trials would be exacerbated by abolition of the insanity defence. Where a *mens rea* model prevailed psychiatrists would doubtless give conclusive evidence that *mens rea* was absent[177] thus rekindling the controversies which prevailed under *Durham*. Given the constant expansion of the concept of mental illness there is every reason to doubt Morris' view that cases involving the effect of mental abnormality on *mens rea* would be rare.[178] The American experience of abolition has shown that efforts to keep the insanity question out of the criminal trial have been largely unsuccessful[179] with the result that psychiatric evidence has to be heard twice, firstly, as bearing on the issue of *mens rea* and secondly, in deciding the appropriate disposition. The result is that the defendant is given "two shots at the same thing". In addition to the extra cost to the state, a defendant may be handicapped by financial incapacity to procure psychiatric testimony for two hearings.[180] Expert dominance would be even more obvious under the behavioural model where all defendants who committed an *actus reus* would be held responsible but expert testimony in relation to mental illness and all aspects of their social upbringing including poverty and abuse, would govern their disposal. Nonetheless, not all psychiatrists favour abolition and the American Psychiatric Association has expressed the view that retention of the insanity defence is necessary to the moral integrity of the law.[181] It is clear that the receipt of psychiatric input in a trial which is subject to traditional adversary procedures, filters out the genuine from the fraudulent.[182] Furthermore, under the behavioural model conviction would not be as aversive as at present, possibly resulting in a diminishing of the law's ability to deter potential criminals.[183]

The Butler Committee on Mentally Abnormal Offenders has more recently rejected proposals made by the British Psychological Society and others to abolish the special verdict.[184] Two kinds of two-stage trial were proposed. According to the first, the jury (in a trial on indictment) would find the external facts and it would then be for the sentencer (the judge) to find what was the defendant's mental state at the time of the act, as one of the matters bearing upon sentence. Under this system the trial would not be concerned with the notions of guilt and responsibility except insofar as such matters had a bearing on the appropriate measures to be taken to prevent a recurrence of the forbidden act. The Committee felt that it would not be acceptable to remove these questions altogether from the jury and that in theory, the proposal would render a person involved in a fatal accident through no fault of his own, liable to detention for life, in the same way as if he had committed murder. Such protection as he would have would rest only on a wise use of discretion by the sentencing tribunal. The

Committee felt that sentencers would apparently be left with no guidance on the relative importance that the community attaches to different prohibitions and some parts of the present law which rest particularly upon proof of intention, such as the law of conspiracy and attempt, would become unworkable.[185]

The second form of the proposal the Committee felt to be less extreme: it would allow the jury to decide the question of guilt in the first stage and hear and pronounce on psychiatric evidence in the second stage. However, they felt[186] that this makes the mistake of supposing that the question of guilt can be decided merely by establishing the external facts. The defendant's state of mind, with possible psychiatric evidence bearing upon it, necessarily arises in the first stage and cannot be removed from it. In consequence, this form of two-stage trial would sometimes lead to the jury having to consider the same psychiatric evidence twice: in the first stage, on the issue of guilt in relation to the definition of the offence, and in the second stage, on the issue of exemption from responsibility on account of mental disorder. In these circumstances there is no advantage, and some disadvantage in separating the trial into two stages, as was found in California when this form of trial was introduced there.

The Committee felt that the decline in the use of the special verdict to the point where it is scarcely used at all, did not indicate that the law need no longer provide for total exemption from criminal responsibility for the mentally disordered offender[187] and it then went on to reformulate the insanity defence.

Notes

1   *Boardman v Woodman* 47 N.H.120 (1845)
2   214 F.2d 862 (1954)
3   L.E.Reik "The Doe-Ray Correspondence: A Pioneer Collaboration in the Jurisprudence of Mental Disease" [1953] 63 Yale L.J.183 pp.184 & 185
4   Quoted by N.Walker *Crime and Insanity in England* Vol.1 (Edinburgh, 1968) p.90
5   See L.E.Reik op cit *generally*
6   47 N.H.120 [1845]
7   L.E.Reik op cit p.185
8   J.Reid "Understanding the New Hampshire Doctrine of Criminal Insanity" [1960] 69 Yale L.J.367 p.372
9   47 N.H.120 [1845] pp.147 & 148
10 J.Reid op cit p.376

11   49 N.H.399 [1870]

12   ibid p.402

13   J.Reid op cit p.377

14   ibid pp.376 & 377

15   *State v Jones* 50 N.H.369 [1871] pp.398 & 399

16   J.Reid "The Companion of the New Hampshire Doctrine of Criminal Insanity" [1962] 15 Vand.L.Rev.721 p.740

17   ibid p.741

18   "An act produced by mental disease is not a crime..Insanity is not innocence unless it produced the killing of his wife". *State v Jones*, 50 N.H.369 [1871] p.370

19   ibid

20   J.Reid "The Companion of the New Hampshire Doctrine of Criminal Insanity" op cit p.741

21   See J.Reik op cit p.188

22   La Fave and Scott Jr *Substantive Criminal Law*, Vol.1 (St.Paul, 1986) p.455

23   J.Reid "The Working of the New Hampshire Doctrine of Criminal Insanity" [1960] 15 U.Miami L.Rev.14 p.16

24   ibid p.18

25   ibid p.27

26   ibid p.28

27   M.S. Moore *Law and Psychiatry: Rethinking the Relationship* (London, 1984) p.228

28   La Fave and Scott Jr. *Substantive Criminal Law* Vol.1 (Minnesota, 1986) p.455

29   Report and Minutes of Evidence before the Select Committee on the Homicide Law Amendment Bill B.P.P., 1874, Vol.ix p.525

30   Report of the Committee on Insanity and Crime Cmd 2005 (London, 1924) p.4

31   ibid p.5

32   ibid p.4

33   ibid p.5

34   ibid

35   ibid p.6

36   ibid

37   Report of the Royal Commission on Capital Punishment [1949-53] Cmd 8932 (London, 1953) para.333

38   ibid

39   ibid para.280

40   ibid para.285

41   50 N.H.369 [1871] p.394

42   Report of the Royal Commission on Capital Punishment op cit para.280

43   ibid para.323

44   ibid para.332

45   A.Goldstein *The Insanity Defense* (New Haven and London, 1967) p.81

46   Report of the Royal Commission on Capital Punishment op cit para.274 &275

47   Third Interim Report of the InterDepartmental Committee on Mentally Ill and Maladjusted Persons *Treatment and Care of Persons Suffering from Mental Disorder who Appear Before the Courts on Criminal Charges* (Dublin, 1978) p.4 para.7

48   *Irish Times* Apr.25 1996

49   *Criminal Justice (Mental Disorder) Bill, 1996*

50   F.Boland "The Criminal Justice (Mental Disorder) Bill, 1996" [1997] 4 Web J.C.L.I.

51   214 F.2d 862 [1954]

52   ibid p.874

53   See the dissenting judgment of Bazelon J. in *U.S.v Brawner* 471 F.2d.969 [1972] p.1014

54   D.Bazelon "Justice Stumbles on Science" [1966] 1 Ir.Jur.273 p.277

55   S.E.Sobeloff "Insanity and the Criminal Law: From M'Naghten to Durham and Beyond" [1955] 41 A.B.A.J.793 p.795

56   A.Goldstein op cit p.82

57   214 F.2d 862 [1954] p.875

58   250 F.2d 4 [1957] p.11

59   ibid

60   E.De Grazia, "The Distinction of Being Mad" [1955] 22 U.Chi.L.Rev. 339 p.347

61   252 F.2d 608 [1957]

62   ibid p.617

63   157 F.Supp 18 [1957]

64   B.L.Diamond "From M'Naghten To Currens and Beyond" [1962] 50 Calif.L.Rev.189 p.192

65   H.Fingarette *The Meaning of Criminal Insanity* (Los Angeles, 1972) pp.31 & 32

66   G.P.Fletcher *Rethinking Criminal Law* (Boston, 1978) p.840

67   312 F.2d 847 [1962]

68   ibid p.851

69   A.Goldstein op cit p.85

70   ibid p.84

71   ibid

72   M.S.Moore op cit p.226

73   A.Goldstein op cit p.85

74   S.Glueck *Law and Psychiatry* (London, 1963) p.103

75   H.Weihofen *The Urge to Punish* (London, 1957) p.87

76   La Fave and Scott Jr. op cit p.439

77   390 F.2d 444 [1967]

78   Winslade and Ross *The Insanity Plea* (New York, 1983) p.211

79   A.Goldstein op cit p.84

80   B.L.Diamond op cit p.202

81   A.Norrie *Crime Reason and History A Critical Introduction to Criminal Law* (London, 1993) p.184

82   D.H.J.Hermann *The Insanity Defense: Philosophical Historical and Legal Perspectives* (Illinois, 1983) p.46

83   312 F.2d 847 [1963] p.851

84   A.Goldstein op cit p.86

85   La Fond and Durham *Back to the Asylum: The Future of Mental Health Law and Policy in the United States* (New York, 1992) p.36

86   471 F.2d.969 [1974] p.1032

87   ibid p.988

88   A.Goldstein op cit pp.81 & 82

89   H.Weihofen op cit p.33
90   R.James Simon *The Jury and the Defense of Insanity* (Boston, 1967) p.75
91   ibid p.73
92   471 F.2d.969 [1972] p.987
93   ibid p.988
94   A.Goldstein op cit p.87
95   S.Glueck *Law & Psychiatry* (London, 1963) p.68
96   D.H.J.Hermann op cit pp.50 & 51
97   ibid p.50
98   La Fond and Durham op cit p.42
99   A.Goldstein op cit p.92
100 R.H.Kuh "The Insanity Defense - An Effort to Combine Law and Reason" [1962] 110 U.Pa.L.Rev.771 p.789
101 Quoted by the Butler Committee on Mentally Abnormal Offenders Cmnd 6244 para.18.15 from Bazelon, "Psychiatrists and the Adversary Process", [1974] Sci.Am.230
102 A. Goldstein op cit p.213
103 *People A.G.v Michael McGlynn* [1967] I.R.232
104 Perkins & Boyce *Criminal Law* (New York, 1982) p.978
105 A.Goldstein op cit pp.92 & 93
106 R.F.Schopp "Returning to McNaghten to Avoid Moral Mistakes" [1988] 30 Ariz.L.Rev.135 p.137
107 Report of the (Butler) Committee on Mentally Abnormal Offenders op cit para.18.16
108 471 F.2d.969 p.1031
109 R.H.Kuh "The Insanity Defense - An Effort to Combine Law and Reason" op cit p.799
110 ibid pp.799 & 800
111 S.Glueck op cit pp.68 & 69
112 La Fave and Scott Jr.op cit p.466
113 S.Glueck op cit p.69
114 La Fond and Durham op cit p.136
115 R.D.Mackay *Mental Condition Defences in the Criminal Law* (Oxford, 1995) p.112
116 Callahan, Mayer and Steadman "Insanity Defense Reforms in the U.S. - post-Hinckley" 2 Mental and Physical Disabilities Law Reporter (1987) 54 p.55
117 In California a conjunctive McNaghten Test was passed by a referendum, requiring inability to know the nature and quality of the act *and* to distinguish right from wrong at the time of the offence but the California Supreme Court held in *People v Skinner* 39 Cal 3d 765, 217 Cal Rptr 685, 704 P 2d 752 [1985] that the new test must be read disjunctively.
118 R.D.Mackay op cit p.119
119 D.B.Wexler "Redefining the Insanity Problem" [1985] 53 Geo.Wash.L.Rev.528 p.532
120 P.E.Johnson "Review of N.Morris *Madness and the Criminal Law*" [1983] 50 Uni.Chi.L.Rev.1534 p.1546
121 American Psychiatric Association Insanity Defense Working Group "American Psychiatric Association Statement on the Insanity Defense" [1983] 130 Am.J.Psychiat.681 p.685

122   D.B.Wexler op cit p.532
123   ibid
124   R.D.Mackay op cit p.l24
125   ibid
126   LaFond and Durham p.64
127   ibid p.63
128   ibid p.64
129   ibid p.63
130   A.L.Halpern "Reconsideration of the Insanity Defense and Related Issues in the Aftermath of the Hinckley Trial" [1982] 54 Psychiat.Quart. p.260 at p.261
131   N.Walker op cit p.24
132   ibid p.19
133   H.Fingarette op cit p.136
134   C.Wells "Whither Insanity" [1983] Crim.L.R.787 p.794
135   G.P.Fletcher op cit p.817
136   H.Fingarette op cit p.5
137   N.Walker op cit p.19
138   214 F.2d 862 [1954] p.876
139   P.E.Johnson op cit p.1541
140   H.Fingarette op cit p.128
141   La Fave and Scott Jr.op cit p.432
142   J.Monahan "Abolish the Insanity Defense? - Not Yet" [1973] 26 Rutgers Law Rev.719 p.720
143   ibid p.721
144   ibid p.720
145   ibid p.725
146   N.Morris op cit; Goldstein and Katz "Abolish the "Insanity Defense"-Why Not?" [1963] 72 Yale L.J. 853; Winslade and Ross op cit; C.Wells op cit; H.Wechsler "The Criteria of Criminal Responsibility" [1955] 22 Uni.Chi.L.Rev 367
147   The [1949-1953] Royal Commission on Capital Punishment's justification has been specifically targeted as an object of this criticism.
148   Goldstein and Katz op cit p.859
149   ibid p.863
150   N.Morris op cit p.55
151   S.H.Kadish "The Decline of Innocence" [1968] 26 C.L.J.273 p.277
152   Winslade and Ross op cit p.198
153   S.H Kadish op cit p.277
154   Winslade and Ross op cit p.198
155   La Fave and Scott Jr. op cit p.433
156   N.Morris op cit pp.55 and 56
157   See La Fave and Scott Jr. op cit pp.433 and 434
158   S.H.Kadish op cit p.277
159   J.B.Brady "Abolish the Insanity Defense? - No!" [1971] 8 Houston Law Rev.629 p.630
160   N.Morris op cit p.59
161   S.H.Kadish op cit p.278

162 La Fond and Durham op cit p.151
163 ibid p.76
164 ibid p.65
165 S.H.Kadish op cit p.278
166 ibid
167 ibid
168 ibid p.279
169 ibid
170 ibid
171 ibid p.280
172 ibid
173 ibid pp.282 & 283
174 ibid p.283
175 ibid
176 LaFave and Scott Jr. op cit p.435
177 H.W.Wales "An Analysis of the Proposal to "Abolish" the Insanity Defense in S.1: Squeezing a Lemon" [1976] 124 U.Pa.L.Rev. 687 pp. 694 & 695
178 J.Monahan op cit p.728
179 See Louisell and Hazard ""Insanity Defense" The Bifurcated Trial" [1961] 49 Calif.L.Rev.805 for an insight into the operation of the bifurcated trial in California, Colorado Texas and Louisiana
180 ibid p.823
181 American Psychiatric Association Insanity Defence Work Group op cit p.683
182 ibid
183 J.Monahan op cit p.736
184 Report of the (Butler) Committee on Mentally Abnormal Offenders op cit paras.18.10-18.13
185 ibid para.18.12
186 ibid para.18.13
187 Report of the (Butler) Committee on Mentally Abnormal Offenders op cit para.18.10

4 Butler and Beyond

Report of the (Butler) Committee on Mentally Abnormal Offenders (1975)

In 1972 the Butler Committee embarked upon the formulation of an insanity defence suitable for the Law Commission's Draft Criminal Code. The history of the insanity defence had taught them that certain requirements must be met by any reformulated insanity defence,[1] namely that it should
(a) avoid the use of medical terms about which there may be disputed interpretations or whose meaning may change with the years; and
(b) be such as to allow psychiatrists to state the facts of the defendant's mental condition without being required to pronounce on the extent of his responsibility for his offence. Degrees of responsibility are legal, not medical concepts.

Moreover, to the extent that the question of "insanity" is to remain one for the jury to decide the defence must
(c) avoid the use of words and expressions which may confuse the jury and
(d) be capable of being the subject of a clear direction by the judge.
The extent to which these concerns have been met by the Butler Committee's reformulation of the insanity defence will now be discussed.

The Committee reported in 1975 and recommended[2] that the jury be directed to return a verdict of "not guilty on evidence of mental disorder" where satisfied

> (1) That the defendant is not proved to have had the state of mind necessary for the offence and where they are satisfied on the balance of probability that at the time of the act or omission he was mentally disordered or
> (2) Where they are satisfied on the balance of probability that at the time he was suffering from severe mental illness or severe subnormality.

The judge would be required not to leave (2) to the jury unless the defence was supported by the evidence of two psychiatrists, who must be medical practitioners, approved by an area health authority as having special experience in the diagnosis or treatment of mental disorders (with

86

an exception for transient states of mental disorder).

For the purposes of section (1), "mental disorder" means the same as it does in section 4 of the Mental Health Act, 1959 - that is "mental illness, arrested or incomplete development of mind, psychopathic disorder and any other disorder or disability of mind".

The Committee stressed[3] that "mental disorder" would not embrace transitory states not related to other forms of mental disorder and arising solely as a consequence of (a) the administration, mal-administration or non-administration of alcohol, drugs or other substances, or (b) physical injury.

For the purposes of section (2), the Committee defined mental subnormality by drawing on its meaning under section 4(2) of the Mental Health Act, 1959 as "a state of arrested or incomplete development of mind which includes subnormality of intelligence and is of such a nature or degree that the patient is incapable of living an independent life or of guarding himself against serious exploitation, or will be so incapable when of an age to do so".

The Committee stated[4] that "A mental illness is severe when it has one or more of the following characteristics:-
(a) Lasting impairment of intellectual functions shown by failure of memory, orientation, comprehension and learning capacity.
(b) Lasting alteration of mood of such degree as to give rise to delusional appraisal of the patient's situation, his past or his future, or that of others, or to lack of any appraisal.
(c) Delusional beliefs, persecutory, jealous or grandiose.
(d) Abnormal perceptions associated with delusional misinterpretation of events.
(e) Thinking so disordered as to prevent reasonable appraisal of the patient's situation or reasonable communication with others".

Finally the Committee stressed[5] that severe mental illness or severe subnormality would not include psychopathic disorder, subnormality or the other abnormal states of mind mentioned in section 4 of the Mental Health Act, nor the transient states excluded under the Committee's proposals for section (1) of the special verdict.

To summarise, section (1) excludes from criminal liability one who did the prohibited act without *mens rea* and who is proved to have been suffering from "mental disorder" at the time of the act. Section (2) would save from conviction one who did the act with *mens rea* but who is proved to have been suffering from "severe mental illness" or "severe subnormality" at the time of his offence.

As with every other insanity test that I have discussed, the Butler Committee criteria are equally open to objection. Limb 1 has been criticised, firstly, on the grounds that McNaghten's ghost will still be with us insofar as the mental disorder must be sufficient to create a reasonable doubt that the defendant had the intention, foresight or knowledge required for the offence. Those varieties of mental disorder which affect not cognition but motivation and will power would strictly fall outside this ground for the special verdict.[6] Secondly, it has been pointed out that the inclusion of psychopathic disorder within section 1 of the Mental Health Act, 1959 will be of little avail to the psychopath who will only qualify for a mental disorder verdict in the unlikely event of his lacking *mens rea*.[7] However, for reasons advanced in Chapter Six, the writer does not endorse this particular criticism, being of the view that diminished responsibility is a preferable defence for the psychopath.

It is not clear that the Butler Committee's insanity defence will meet requirement (d)[8] that is, that it be capable of being the subject of a clear direction by the judge. In fact the Butler test may be far from clear to the doctors who are required to testify as to the accused's mental state. Although "severe subnormality" is already defined in section 4(2) of the Mental Health Act, 1959 the term "severe mental illness" is not a term of art in law or psychiatry.[9] The 1959 Mental Health Act does not provide a definition of mental illness and the criteria Butler list for "severity" increase the likelihood of disagreement among experts. If the practical effect of the Butler formula is that medical witnesses are to be entrusted with the decision as to what constitutes mental illness, then the Butler Committee defence will meet with the same response as the Durham rule was. Despite the Committee's own statement that psychiatrists should not be required to pronounce on the accused's responsibility, the defence has been criticised for handing over to the psychiatrists[10] "what is essentially an ethico-legal question".[11]   In fact the Medical Advisory Committee of Broadmoor Hospital has rejected the definition altogether, suggesting that "the psychiatric disorder in this context is something which the jury should decide".[12]

It is noteworthy that in the Butler formulation there is no requirement of causal connection, as the Committee thought that the disorders specified are of such severity that a causal connection can safely be presumed. Treating insanity as a status exempting from responsibility signals a return to the policy of the eighteenth century and earlier, when the mentally disordered were regarded as a category outside the bounds of responsibility like children under ten are today.[13] Kenny points out two bad effects of this approach to insanity.[14] On the one hand, it gives a certified mental patient a licence which is not given to others (he knows that there are certain things which he may do without being held criminally responsible, while all others not of the same status will be held responsible). On the other hand, it attaches a stigma to insanity by assuming, without any need of proof, that insanity, as such, predisposes to criminal action. The debate surrounding the Butler Committee's test involves a resurfacing of the age-old conflict between lawyers and psychiatrists. From the lawyers' perspective the accused might be suffering from a severe mental illness, but still retain a residue of responsibility for his actions; from the psychiatrists', the accused's medical condition explains all his/her actions.[15] Although the Butler approach avoids the criticism that was directed at Durham's "product test", the Law Commission felt that a requirement of causal connection is necessary and Clause 35(2) of the Draft Criminal Code provides that the mental disorder verdict does not apply if the court or jury is satisfied beyond reasonable doubt that the offence was not attributable to the severe mental disorder. Aside from the difficulties of proof facing the prosecution, Norrie points out that "[i]n this apparently innocuous clause, there lurks the germ of the old law/psychiatry conflict, unresolved..[and] the possibility..of an open power struggle in the courts between lawyers and psychiatrists remain[s]".[16]

The Butler Committee comment that, regarding mental subnormality, the phrase "arrested or incomplete development of mind" in section 4 of the Mental Health Act, 1959 should be wide enough to cover not only all dangerous mentally handicapped people but also persons of limited intelligence who might otherwise gain an outright acquittal. Yet the Committee do not specify whether the danger of a person repeating the offence is part of the definition of mental subnormality or whether limited intelligence by itself is sufficient to bring a person within this definition.[17] Similarly the Committee do not specify the relevance of the danger of recurrence when they recommend that expressly excluded from the special verdict should be any case in which the mental disorder is a transient state, not related to other forms of mental disorder, and caused by physical injury or by the abuse of alcohol, drugs or other substances but that "all other cases now regarded as non-insane automatism would be left to fall under the special verdict".[18]   Whilst expressing a wish to exclude from their mental disorder verdict a person who had failed to take insulin, who was concussed or who had unintentionally become intoxicated,[19] they fail to discuss the issues of somnambulism, fainting and strokes which, it appears, may still result in a mental disorder verdict. In this respect the Committee seems to have fallen short of its aim of clarifying the distinction between the special verdict and the existing law on non-insane automatism.[20]

The enactment of the Mental Health Act, 1983 has posed problems for the Butler Committee formulation. Severe subnormality has now given way to severe mental impairment. Now "arrested or incomplete development of mind" must also be "associated with abnormally aggressive or seriously irresponsible conduct".[21]   Two meanings of this phrase might cause confusion. The Butler Committee's reformulation of the insanity defence must be the most complex and confusing that has been devised yet. As one commentator has noted

> The Butler report was the innocent victim of that process of producing more complexities. Everyone was straining to do what they possibly could to make matters better, but each time that the subject was examined different conclusions were reached. That should not be surprising because the concepts involved were complex and it has been difficult to devise workable solutions.[22]

The Draft Criminal Code Bill contains some radical alterations. The Code requires a finding of "severe mental illness" or "severe mental handicap" under section 35(1). The Code has defined severe mental handicap as

> A state of arrested or incomplete development of mind which includes severe impairment of intelligence and social functioning.

The Law Commission excludes the 1983 Mental Health Act's requirement of abnormally aggressive or seriously irresponsible conduct. Mackay has stated that despite the Commission's belief that this will give effect to Butler's intention, it is likely to ensure that a narrower range of mentally impaired persons will qualify for the special verdict.[23]

In Clause 34 of the Code Bill "mental disorder" is defined as

Severe mental illness, arrested or incomplete development of mind, or a state of automatism (not resulting only from intoxication) which is a feature of disorder, whether organic or functional and whether continuing or recurring, that may cause a similar state on another occasion.

In light of the history of the insanity defence it should not be assumed that the Draft Criminal Code definition will fare any better than previous tests of insanity. It will be impossible for the prosecution to prove that the crime was unattributable to the mental disorder. Thus, the decision on responsibility will hinge on the expert's testimony of severe mental illness or severe mental handicap, a move which proved fatal to the Durham Rule. Underlying the Law Commission's reformulation is the concern that Butler's wide definition would subject too many insanity acquittees to "a possibly stigmatising or distressing verdict and to inappropriate control through the courts' disposal powers".[24] Hence their decision to exclude "mental illness" (not being severe) and "any other disorder or disability of mind" from the mental disorder verdict.[25] However, the Commission's inclusion of disorders that may cause a similar state on another occasion retains the stigma of insanity for diabetics and sleepwalkers. Although this approach takes account of social defence considerations it affronts common sense by leading to an insanity verdict for those who are palpably not insane.

The Criminal Procedure (Insanity and Unfitness to Plead) Act 1991

As noted by White, the Butler Committee's recommendations proved too controversial for speedy implementation[26] but their proposal that discretionary disposal consequences follow a finding of insanity was eventually introduced in the Criminal Procedure (Insanity and Unfitness to Plead) Act 1991. The 1991 Act allows the court to make such one of the following orders that it thinks most suitable in all the circumstances of the case, namely a guardianship order within the Mental Health Act 1983, a supervision and treatment order or an order for the defendant's absolute discharge. Alternatively, a hospital order may be made with or without restrictions. The bill had unanimous support in both Houses of Parliament,[27] one commentator observing that there was "no risk" that an unfit person who was a danger to the public would be allowed to go free in the community.[28] This confidence is not shared by the writer. Rather, this piece of legislation, which has been anticipated as the solution to the McNaghten dilemma, is likely to revive the United States polemic on English territory. The first case under the new act was reported under the provocative headline "'Drink Mad' Attacker Walks Free".[29] The defendant was a 36-year-old Petty Officer who suffered from serious brain damage such that small amounts of alcohol could motivate him without warning to dangerous acts of violence. The jury found him not guilty of attempted rape on the grounds of insanity and Auld J. discharged him.

Mackay and Kearns' research on the first cases dealt with under the 1991 Act has revealed the imposition of a supervision and treatment order in disposing of a defendant who pleaded somnambulism to a charge of attempted murder.[30] Protection of the public was doubtless the reason for the Court of Appeal's decision in *Burgess* that sleepwalking warrants a finding of insanity, rather than automatism which results in an outright acquittal. This very concern is likely to provoke public controversy at the release of such sleepwalkers who have been found insane. The absence of available legal sanctions to deal with an offender who does not comply with treatment or the conditions of a supervision and treatment order[31] creates a huge potential for public outrage.

On the other hand the failure of the Act to provide for discretionary disposal consequences in murder cases and insanity defences at Magistrates Court level[32] makes this piece of legislation a very half-hearted measure. As a result of the latter failure, unconditional liberation is the likely result of a successful insanity defence at Magistrates Court level.[33] This view is reinforced by the provision that in choosing between orders for guardianship, supervision and treatment and absolute discharge the court must select that which "in all the circumstances of the case is the most suitable means of dealing" with the defendant but no similar requirement governs the making of a hospital order. The implication is that a court may make an admission order even though it does not think such an order to be the most suitable disposition, for example, where a special verdict has been returned following an atrocious attempted murder by a defendant whose sanity is restored by the time of trial but whose outright release might provoke public outrage.[34] This half-heartedness is also evident in the absence of any provision allowing for appeal against a decision of the Crown Court to choose one disposition rather than another. In Chapter One I have discussed the failure to surrender any degree of sovereignty to the medical profession, by the requirement of medical evidence under section 1(1) which, although appearing to defer to the medical view of insanity, in reality is to have no binding force.[35] Thus the 1991 Act not only fails to bring the English insanity defence into line with Article 5(1)(e) of the European Convention on Human Rights but is also open to the criticism that it preserves the McNaghten Rules as the test of insanity.

Conclusions

The previous chapters have demonstrated that all reformulations of the insanity defence in the United States and Ireland have been surrounded by controversy. The aim of these reformulations was initially to give recognition to the psychiatric view of mental illness. It was felt that the McNaghten Rules restricted psychiatric testimony to one aspect of mental functioning, *cognition*. The test of irresistible impulse was intended to recognise impairment of *volition* but as this was based on the same outmoded psychology of phrenology and restricted expert evidence in the same way, the psychiatric profession was soon advocating reform. The Durham Rule contained no standard of impairment of mental functioning, merely requiring that the crime was a product of the defendant's mental illness. The psychiatric profession at last had the opportunity to testify on any and all aspects of the defendant's mental illness.

However the Durham experiment[36] was not successful. Granting the psychiatric profession autonomy in insanity trials led to a usurpation of the much revered jury system. Legal professionals became increasingly disillusioned with the medical profession's dominance of insanity trials. Not only could the psychiatrists not agree on whether the defendant's crime was a product of mental illness, as evidenced by the notorious battles of the experts, but their classification of mental illness was liable to change, as evidenced by "the weekend flip flop case", described in Chapter Three. As increased numbers were transferred from the criminal justice system to the mental health system scepticism began to accrue regarding the profession's ability to relieve these patients of their mental illness and of the use of the insanity defence by undeserving accused as a means of avoiding conviction. The end result was a reformulation of the insanity defence by the American Law Institute to take account of volitional and cognitive impairment. This test was drafted in wider terms than the McNaghten and irresistible impulse tests but was criticised by lawyers and medics alike. Then the trial of John Hinckley for the attempted assassination of President Ronald Reagan led to criticism on an unprecedented scale. Hinckley's success in using the A.L.I. test led to a public furore, resulting in calls to restrict and abolish the insanity defence.

The above discussion of insanity defence reform has shown the impossibility of formulating a test of insanity that will prove satisfactory to all. As early as 1896 the Criminal Responsibility Committee of the Medico Psychological Association reported that

> The framing and answering of new abstract questions [on the criminal responsibility of the insane], if it could be brought about, would be but the beginning of a new controversy and of new heart-burnings.[37]

Similarly, the Royal Commission on Capital Punishment concluded in 1953 "that it is not possible to define with any precision the state of mind which should exempt an insane person from responsibility". As the irresistible impulse rule and the product test were beleaguered by criticism the difficulty of reformulating the insanity defence became increasingly apparent. The Fourth Draft of the American Law Institute's Model Penal Code[38] commented that

> No problem in the drafting of a penal code presents larger intrinsic difficulty than that of determining when individuals whose conduct would otherwise be criminal ought to be exculpated on the ground that they were suffering from mental disease or defect when they acted as they did.

The fate of the A.L.I's reformulation reinforces their own statement on the difficulty of satisfactorily reformulating the insanity defence.

The controversy did not stem exclusively from the wording of the defence. Rather, it involved a wide range of social issues, for example, the decision who should be held responsible to the law and liable to punishment (or to the death penalty as the case may be) and who should be excused and receive treatment (or be released where this applies). Wexler suggests[39] that public distrust of the insanity defence today stems "almost exclusively" from its application in homicide cases.[40] Similarly Professor Norval Morris claims that "the insane killer" is "at the heart of the argument about the special defence".[41] Other observers feel that the polemic stems from the dispositional consequences attached to the insanity defence. This view is lent weight by the American controversy over the insanity defence, whose consequence was often immediate release unless mentally ill and dangerous. Hence the words of an American commentator

> The public's concern is less with ascertaining whether blame properly can be assigned to a particular defendant than with determining when he will get out. And the delusion of law professionals to the contrary notwithstanding, it is the public's concern that drives the debate on possible changes in the insanity defense.[42]

In the United States the focus of concern was whether insane defendants were released from custody before they had paid for their crime. In England and Ireland the controversy has been fuelled by the mandatory indefinite committal of insanity acquittees who are neither insane nor dangerous. With the advent of the Criminal Procedure (Insanity and Unfitness to Plead) Act 1991 the English concern is likely to be replaced by the American.

As is evident from the discussion of *Durham* and irresistible impulse *above*, the controversy also involved the issue of whether law or medicine should decide the dividing line between responsibility and irresponsibility. The Butler Committee and Law Commission reformulations of the insanity defence have once again illustrated the medico-legal tension underpinning the insanity defence when Butler's deference to the medical view of insanity was met with opposition by the Law Commission.

The psychiatric profession repeatedly claimed that the law's dividing line between sanity and insanity was too rigid and failed to take account of intermediate states of mental disorder, where the accused was of diminished responsibility. Thus, in England much of the controversy over the McNaghten Rules stemmed not from "any defect in themselves but the fact that..persons who [were] totally irresponsible [were] rarely at large, and if at large, [were] rarely put on trial: persons of diminished responsibility [were] frequently put on trial, and when they [were] convicted and sentenced to death, it [was] erroneously supposed that the McNaghten Rules [had] failed in their purpose".[43] This is a criticism whose import has been curtailed by the operation of diminished responsibility in English law, introduced by the Homicide Act, 1957. This defence reduces a charge of murder to manslaughter and is premised on the notion of partial or lesser responsibility when the accused was suffering from mental abnormality. Clearly enough time has been spent rewriting the boundaries between insanity and criminal responsibility. The remainder of this book will therefore be devoted to examining whether the time of legal commentators and legislators would be better spent examining if lesser degrees of mental abnormality should reduce the defendant's criminal liability without obliterating it altogether.

Notes

1   Report of the (Butler) Committee on Mentally Abnormal Offenders Cmnd 6244 (London, 1975) para.18.17
2   ibid para.18.37
3   ibid para.18.23
4   ibid para.18.35
5   ibid para.18.30
6   A.J.Ashworth "The Butler Committee and Criminal Responsibility" [1975] Crim.L.R.687 p.689
7   Ashworth and Shapland "Psychopaths in the Criminal Process" [1980] Crim.L.R.628 p.631
8   Report of the (Butler) Committee on Mentally Abnormal Offenders Cmnd 6244 op cit para.18.17
9   A.Ashworth op cit p.690
10   R.D.Mackay *Mental Condition Defences in the Criminal Law* (Oxford, 1995) p.88
11   ibid p.137
12   E.Griew "Let's Implement Butler on Mental Disorder and Crime!" [1984] C.L.P.47 p.56
13   A.Kenny "Anomalies of section 2 of the Homicide Act 1957" [1986] 12 J.Med.Ethics 24 p.25
14   ibid
15   A.Norrie *Crime Reason and History A Critical Introduction to Criminal Law* (London, 1993) pp.185 & 186
16   ibid p.186
17   A.J.Ashworth op cit p.689
18   Report of the (Butler) Committee on Mentally Abnormal Offenders op cit para.18.23
19   ibid
20   A.J.Ashworth op cit p.690
21   E.Griew op cit p.57
22   Mr.John Patten H.C.Deb.1991, Vol.186 p.1278
23   R.D.Mackay op cit p.133
24   Law Com. No.177 Vol.2 Criminal Law: A Criminal Code for England and Wales (London, 1992) para.11.27

25   Psychopathy is also excluded

26   "The Criminal Procedure (Insanity and Unfitness to Plead) Act" [1992] Crim.L.R.4 p.4

27   Cf: Mr.John Patten H.C.deb.1991, Vol.186, p.1277

28   Mr John Greenaway H.C.deb.1991, Vol.186, p.1274

29   *The Daily Telegraph*, 15 Jan.1992

30   R.D.Mackay and G.Kearns "The Continued Underuse of Unfitness to Plead and the Insanity Defence" [1994] Crim.L.R.576 p.578

31   M.C.Dolan and A.A.Campbell "The Criminal Procedure (Insanity and Unfitness to Plead) Act 1991" [1994] 34 Med, Sci & L.155 p.160

32   See P.Fennell "The Criminal Procedure (Insanity and Unfitness to Plead) Act 1991" [1992] 55 M.L.R.547 at pp.550 & 551

33   S.White "Insanity Defences and Magistrates' Courts" [1991] Crim.L.R.501 p.503

34   S.White "The Criminal Procedure (Insanity and Unfitness to Plead) Act" op cit p.10

35   E.Baker "Human Rights, M'Naghten and the 1991 Act" [1994] Crim.L.R.84 p.86

36   A.Krash "The Durham Rule and Judicial Administration of the Insanity Defense in the District of Columbia" [1961] 70 Yale L.J.905 p.951

37   C.Mercier *Crime and Insanity* (Oxford, 1905) p.220

38   Quoted by H.Fingarette *The Meaning of Criminal Insanity* (Los Angeles, 1972) p.1

39   D.B.Wexler "Redefining the Insanity Problem" [1985] 53 Geo.Wash.L.Rev.528 p.542

40   Later Wexler qualifies this by stressing the public's concern with "stranger killings"

41   N.Morris *Madness and the Criminal Law* (Chicago, 1982) op cit p.73

42   Ellis "The consequences of the insanity defense: Proposals to reform post-acquittal commitment laws" [1986] 35 Catholic Uni.L. Rev. 961 p.963 quoted by LaFond and Durham op cit p.77

43   P.Devlin "Responsibility and Punishment: Functions of Judge and Jury" [1954] Crim.L.R.661 p.685

5 The Homicide Act, 1957 and Its Origin

The Origin of Diminished Responsibility

Although a feature of ancient Irish and Germanic law, Roman law[1] and Dutch law of the middle ages,[2] diminished responsibility is relatively novel in English law. In this Chapter, I will trace its development in Scottish law, from which it was borrowed in 1957. (English Parliament had already gone half-way in 1922 by adopting a partial defence of infanticide, restricted to women who killed their children). By examining the Parliamentary debates which preceded the Homicide Act, 1957, I will show that it was hastily adopted to placate those M.Ps. who advocated the abolition of capital punishment. I will highlight a lack of discussion of the defence in Parliament, which would later lead to uncertainty as to its limits, with virtually the only guide-lines coming from Scottish law. As will be shown in Chapter Six, the end result was that the English Judiciary was placed in the difficult position of having to legislate which mental abnormalities would fall within the defence of diminished responsibility (and *vice versa*, which would not), a decision which ought to have been taken by the draughtsmen and Parliamentarians. The aim of this Chapter is therefore, to show the aspirations of those who created the English diminished responsibility defence with a view to examining in Chapter Six to what extent the defence has met those hopes.

As stated, the English defence of diminished responsibility has its roots in Scottish law where it was developed in order to avoid the consequences of the death penalty. In Scotland the defence made its first appearance in Sir George MacKenzie's *The Laws and Customs of Scotland in Matters Criminal* (1674) where he claimed that

> Since the law grants a total impunity to such as are absolutely furious therefore it should by the rule of proportions lessen and moderate the punishments of such, as though they are not absolutely mad yet are Hypochondrick and Melancholy to such a degree, that it clouds their reason.[3]

98

The earliest cases of diminished responsibility were non-capital charges where the court imposed a reduced sentence in view of the accused's mental condition.[4] (In capital cases mental weakness could be taken into account only by way of the Royal prerogative of mercy).[5] Mitigation of punishment because of partial insanity was in stark contrast to the English law at this time, of which Hale stated that "this partial insanity seems not to excuse them in the committing of any offence for its matter capital".[6]   As Diamond has pointed out,[7] the dichotomous dispositions of the death penalty for the sane and the equivalent of life imprisonment for the insane lent itself well to the development of an all-or-nothing, sane or insane, rule of criminal responsibility. There was no concept of responsibility that embraced diminished or intermediate grades of responsibility, because there were few, if any, possibilities for any intermediate form of punishment.

It was not until the decision in *Dingwall* [8] that the practice was established in Scotland of returning a verdict of culpable homicide rather than murder, in those cases in which responsibility was thought to be diminished. *Dingwall* was tried for the murder of his wife by stabbing her with a knife in the arm and side. "Habitually and irreclaimably addicted to drinking", he committed the fatal deed after his wife had hidden a pint bottle of whiskey and some money from him, to prevent him from getting more alcohol. Lord Deas pointed out to the jury that

> If [they] believed that the prisoner, when he committed the [murder of his wife], had sufficient mental capacity to know, and did know, that the act was contrary to the law, and punishable by the law, it would be their duty to convict him"[9] but he "could not say that it was beyond the province of the jury to find a verdict of culpable homicide if they thought that was the nature of the offence.[10]

In deciding whether to convict the accused of culpable homicide rather than murder, the relevant considerations were
1. The unpremeditated and sudden nature of the attack;
2. The prisoner's habitual kindness to his wife; of which there could be no doubt when drink did not interfere;
3. That there was only one stab or blow; this while not perhaps like what an insane man would have done, was favourable for the prisoner in other

respects;

4. That the prisoner appeared not only to have been peculiar in his mental constitution, but to have had his mind weakened by successive attacks of disease. It seemed highly probable that he had had a stroke of the sun in India, and that his subsequent fits were of an epileptic nature. There could be no doubt that he had had repeated attacks of *delirium tremens*, and if weakness of mind could be an element in any case in the question between murder and culpable homicide, it seemed difficult to exclude that element here.[11]

Dingwall was found guilty of culpable homicide and sentenced to ten years' penal servitude. It should be noted that Lord Deas did not regard the accused's mental weakness as the only basis for a verdict of diminished responsibility; Rather, it was one of a number of grounds which he thought might justify such a verdict[12] - a view which he continued to espouse until his retirement in 1887.[13] A culpable homicide verdict obviated any risk of a recommendation to mercy being rejected and also left the treatment of the accused in the hands of the judge who could impose what he considered to be a suitable sentence.[14]

Thus the doctrine of diminished responsibility took 193 years to come to fruition, a delay which Dr.Wright holds its creator, MacKenzie, partly responsible for.[15] The object of punishment in early days was primarily retribution and any interference with the revenge due to the lieges (higher Lords) was unlikely to be met with kindly. (The accused had to suffer the full penalty as a lesser penalty would not have appeased the wrath of the lieges at the heinousness of the crime).[16] MacKenzie was suggesting that punishment be moderated without explaining that the quality of the act was seriously to be questioned when the accused suffered from mental illness.[17] Part of the fault may also lie with the Scottish jurists Hume and Alison, neither of whom found MacKenzie's suggestion acceptable and who went to great lengths to ensure that there were only two classes of accused - the sane and the insane.[18] One must also bear in mind the absence of medical knowledge of the working of the brain and its disorders and the court, charged with the protection of society, was not willing to show too much compassion towards the accused lest it be accused of emotionalism.[19]

Dr.Wright has ventured to suggest that in *Somerville (1704)* and

Spence (1747) the court was very near to enunciating the doctrine and that had there been suitable cases following close upon their heels, it is doubtful whether Scotland would have had to wait until *Dingwall* before the unveiling of her humane doctrine.[20] The spirit of the doctrine had been living and there for any to take up and consider its possible application in practice.[21] Erskine admitted its existence when he said that the lesser degrees of fatuity saved from the *poena ordinaria* but he too, focused attention upon the moderation of punishment without linking it to a reduction in the quality of the crime.[22] Dr.Wright feels[23] that the doctrine was beginning to make itself felt as the nineteenth century approached but in *Kinloch (1795)* the Lord Advocate, Dundas, rejected this third category of accused - neither sane nor absolutely furious. Alison hesitantly acknowledged the lessening of responsibility but he was too closely allied to Hume to be able to unfetter his mind of the requirement of absolute alienation of reason.[24] At this point in time, a liberal exercise of the Royal prerogative of mercy enabled the court to adopt a strict interpretation of the kind of insanity which excused the prisoner and Dr.Wright considers that this also contributed to the delay in launching the doctrine.[25]

To some it was disappointing that such an important case as *Dingwall* had been heard on circuit and when *Tierney*[26] was tried for murder neither the prosecution nor the defence saw fit to refer Lord Ardmillan to *Dingwall*.[27] It was not to be long, however, before the opportunity arose again and this time the court ensured that the doctrine was accepted fully as part of the criminal law of Scotland. *John McLean's case*[28] was certified after the jury found him guilty, with a recommendation to mercy on account of his weak intellect. McLean's medical history showed a stay of two years in a lunatic asylum and for more than a year he had been in the refractory ward. It may be that the trial judge (Lord Moncrieff) had found himself unable to direct the jury on the lines of diminished responsibility as the charge was theft and the doctrine had been applied in a case of murder only. The court consisted of the Lord Justice-Clerk, Lord Deas, Lord Young and Lord Craighill. Lord Deas had no doubt that it was proper for the court to take into consideration, in awarding sentence, the mental weakness of the accused, saying

> I am of opinion that, without being insane in the legal sense, so as not to be amenable to punishment, a prisoner may yet labour under that degree

of weakness of intellect or mental infirmity which may make it both right and legal to take that state of mind into account, not only in awarding the punishment, but in some cases, even in considering within what category of offences the crime shall be held to fall.[29]

Lord Deas' example was followed by his fellow judges. In several of the cases in which this direction was given there was evidence of a weakness of the mind by alcoholism.[30] Lord McLaren also considered the doctrine of diminished responsibility to be relevant in a case of child murder.[31] The same judge in *H.M. Advocate v Robert Smith*[32] considered that the judge would be justified in giving effect to the defence if they found that the accused's mind had become so unhinged by a long course of verbal persecution that he had finally reacted to a trivial insult by shooting his tormentors. The Scottish defence of diminished responsibility was restricted to some debility amounting to brain disease in *Aitken*.[33]   By 1909, if not earlier, the phrase "diminished responsibility" was being used by judges and by the 1930's the stage had been reached at which the defence of insanity was rarely offered in a Scottish court to a charge of murder.[34]   Moreover, the Lord Advocate seems to have been willing to accept medical evidence of diminished responsibility to reduce the charge itself to culpable homicide.[35]   Thus, almost all the cases where the issue figured at trial were those in which the Lord Advocate's Crown Office had not been satisfied that responsibility had been diminished.[36]

Despite the finding of the Royal Commission on Capital Punishment (1949-53) that the Scottish defence of diminished responsibility worked well,[37] it was not introduced into English law until 1957. Given its creation in Scotland in 1867, the adoption of diminished responsibility into English law was a very lengthy process. By tracing this process it will be seen that, although hastily adopted in 1957 to placate the opponents of the death penalty, England had ample experience of the defence of diminished responsibility in the form of the Infanticide Acts of 1922 and 1938 and the evidence of its satisfactory operation in Scottish law. I will now trace the tentative steps towards creating the defence which were taken in the Infanticide Acts of 1922 and 1938, prior to the adoption of a full defence of diminished responsibility *via* the Homicide Act, 1957.

Infanticide

English law's first concession to the Scottish practice of reducing murder to manslaughter on evidence of mental unsoundness, was the introduction of the partial defence of infanticide in 1922. By tracing the history of this defence I will show its similarities with diminished responsibility in Scotland and how the adoption of a full defence of diminished responsibility in English law was just a short step away.

Throughout the nineteenth century determined efforts were made to circumvent the death penalty in cases of child-murder by women, with the last execution for this crime occurring in 1849.[38] The insanity defence played a significant role in the salvation of this class of female murderer from the damnation of the death penalty. As I have shown in Chapter Two, medical evidence of an irresistible impulse, which was so fervently resisted by the judiciary, was often taken seriously in the case of women who had killed their children. Medical theories of puerperal and lactational insanity were openly embraced by the courts in an endeavour to exculpate these women, as occurred in *Wilson (1864)*.[39] At the trial of *Eliza Dart*[40] for the attempted drowning of her daughter, Lord Justice Brett stated that "it was a mistake to suppose that, in order to satisfy a jury of insanity, scientific evidence must be adduced. If the evidence of facts were such as to indicate an unsound state of mind that was quite sufficient" and very often verdicts of insanity were returned where its only evidence was in the commission of the deed itself, particularly where the killing was accompanied by circumstances of poverty or other hardship.[41]

The Home Secretary's mercy was a final safeguard against the death penalty and it is at this point that parallels with the Scottish practice begin. According to Sir George Grey's evidence to the Royal Commission on Capital Punishment of 1866, Home Secretaries were aware that public opinion was against hanging for infanticide.[42] Reprieves were granted to women like *Maria Clarke (1851)* and *Mrs Maria Chitty*[43] where circumstances of poverty had prevailed at the time they had killed their children. Even in as notorious a case as that of *Celestina Somner*, "the Brighton murderess", the Home Secretary issued a reprieve after she had been found guilty of the murder of her ten-year-old stepdaughter.[44]

By the time the Royal Commission on Capital Punishment of 1866 reported, infanticide had emerged as an issue of national importance in England.[45]   This Behlmer attributes to four factors[46]: Firstly, that child-murder had reached such epidemic proportions by the 1860's as to demand attention from a public normally disposed to ignore unpleasant social realities. Secondly, that disturbing knowledge of the practice of child-murder as a custom in British India broke upon the popular consciousness just when medical journals were starting to decry domestic infanticide. The County Coroners Act of 1860 was followed by a 17% increase in the amount of money spent on inquests in England and Wales and this corresponded with a 31% increase in the number of verdicts of murder returned by coroners' juries. Fourthly, greater receptiveness to domestic subjects of a sensational nature during a time of peace ("peace must have offered dull reading") and increased circulation of the London dailies meant that news of infanticide could make a greater impact on the national consciousness.

Despite the perceived scale of infanticide, the evidence given before the Royal Commission on Capital Punishment of 1866 showed that the law had completely broken down in relation to child-murder.[47] Shee J. spoke of "the utter and hopeless failure of the existing theory of the law of murder as respects infanticide";[48] Lord Cranworth stated that infanticide was "practically never" treated as murder[49]; Bramwell B. had tried nine cases of infanticide and in eight of them the prisoner was either acquitted or found guilty of concealment of birth (a lesser alternative verdict) and in one exception the jury found the prisoner guilty of manslaughter.[50]   Lord Wensleydale had had a great number of cases of infanticide but never a conviction as "the woman always escaped"[51] (a plot, which evidence before the Royal Commission shows that the judges were conspirators to). Keating J. deposed "[i]t is in vain that Judges lay down the law and point out the strength of the evidence, as they are bound to do, juries wholly disregard them, and eagerly adopt the wildest suggestions which the ingenuity of counsel can furnish..Juries will not convict whilst infanticide is punished capitally"[52] and in similar vein, Byles J. thought that practically every case of concealment of birth was in fact a case of infanticide, a crime which had greatly increased and was of daily occurrence.[53]

Some explanations were offered for this reluctance to convict infanticidal mothers. According to Blackburn J. "the whole sympathies of everyone seem to me against the law which treats this crime as not different from other murders".[54]   Some witnesses were of the opinion that child murder was not as heinous as other forms of murder. A child could not be regarded in the same light as an adult; the loss to the child could not be estimated. The prevailing view was that the killing of a child by its mother did not create the same feeling of alarm in society as other forms of murder did and public opinion, consequently, did not insist upon the death sentence as a deterrent. The general opinion was that the common motive of hiding the shame of an illegitimate birth lessened the heinousness of the crime and that the execution of the law in its full severity would be barbarous. There was a widespread realisation that bad economic conditions frequently led to the commission of these crimes and that the malice was generally less in this class of murder because of the general state of health and mind of the perpetrators of them.

The judges' view was that the "solemn mockery" of the law, which compelled them to pass the death sentence where it would never be carried out, contributed to reduce the deterrent value of capital punishment and it was widely believed that the breakdown of the law was responsible for the perceived increase in the number of child murders. A minority of members recommended that infanticidal mothers be dealt with by giving jurors the power to bring in a verdict of "guilty of murder" with "extenuating circumstances". Keating J. would have allowed the jury to decide between capital and non-capital cases;[55] Sir Morduant Wells would have restricted this power to cases of infanticide[56] with the effect being to reduce murder to culpable homicide as in Scotland.[57]   However, the other proponents of this jury discretion were vague and unspecific and gave no indication that mental unsoundness should be a pre-requisite to this finding nor that the verdict of murder should be reduced to some lesser charge. The majority view was that this discretion would be better vested in the judges as juries would almost always find the accused guilty with extenuating circumstances rather than guilty of murder whose possible consequence was the death penalty.

As a result the Royal Commission recommended[58] that an act should be passed "making it an offence - unlawfully and maliciously to inflict grievous bodily harm or serious injury upon a child during its birth, or within seven days afterwards, in case such a child has subsequently died.

No proof that the child was completely born alive should be required". They objected to concealment of birth being an alternative verdict on an indictment of murder and felt that the accused should not be entitled to be acquitted on trial for the new offence, or for concealment if it should be proved that the offence amounted to murder or manslaughter. Finally, they recommended restoration of the judicial power to record the death sentence (which had been abolished by the Offences Against the Person Act, 1861). However no action was taken to implement these recommendations.

In 1872 the Homicide Law Amendment Bill provided that if a woman murdered her child "at or soon after birth, and whilst deprived of her ordinary power of self-control by the physical effects of its birth", the trial judge in his discretion could sentence her to penal servitude for any term of not less than five years.[59] The first attempt to have infanticide treated like manslaughter (and hence like the more recent Scottish defence of diminished responsibility) occurred when the above bill was reintroduced in 1874. Section 29(3) stated "[c]riminal homicide is manslaughter and not murder..[i]f the person whose death is caused is the child of the person who causes it, and if the act by which death is caused is done whilst such last-mentioned person, though not within the provisions of section 24 [which dealt with the exemptive effects of insanity] is deprived of the power of self-control by any disease or state of mind or body produced by bearing the child whose death is caused".[60]

Concurrently with the Homicide Law (Amendment) Bill another group of members was attempting to pass an Infanticide Law Amendment Bill introduced in 1873 and 1874, which in its amended form proposed that concealment of birth should be repealed as an alternative on an indictment of murder and that a new felony should be created to meet the case of a mother maliciously wounding or inflicting grievous bodily harm upon her child during or immediately after its birth, punishable with penal servitude for a term not exceeding ten years or with imprisonment for a term not exceeding two years.[61]

Both bills were referred to a Select Committee in 1874. Stephen J. justified according the mitigating effects of provocation to infanticide by reminding the witnesses of the practical impossibility of getting a jury to convict of infanticide when occurring at the time of the birth and by claiming that "a woman in that state is entitled to some kind of indulgence to human weakness".[62]   Although Baron Bramwell praised section 29(3) as "a very excellent one",[63] Cockburn L.C.J. demurred to the failure of the section to deal with child killing by omission.[64]   Blackburn J. appeared to favour the Infanticide Bill over Stephen's section 29(3).[65] He too, objected to the latter's failure to deal with child killing by omission, where it could not be proved that the mother had done violence to the child.[66]   He also protested at the treatment of this provision in a clause altering the law of murder, instead of making it a separate enactment.[67]   This approach appears to reveal a bias on the part of Blackburn J. in favour of according infanticide the status of a substantive offence as opposed to a defence to a charge of murder. Stephen countered by saying "I should look with great jealousy on any attempt to make a special offence, which is a kind of exception out of a major offence".[68] He did not like "a thing to be at once murder and something else for which you can try a person if you are so disposed"[69] and felt that the bill's approach was preferable: in these circumstances "the crime is extenuated".[70]

Following the objection to partial codification expressed by the Select Committee,[71] Stephen J. began preparing the Criminal Code (Indictable Offences) Bill, 1878.[72]   However, Blackburn J. had his way when Stephen J's. provision on infanticide, section 138, was deleted and replaced by sections 185 and 186.[73]   The first declared that every woman should be guilty of an indictable offence punishable with penal servitude for life, who, being with child and about to be delivered, with the intent that the child should not live, neglected to provide reasonable assistance in the delivery, if the child died immediately before, during, or shortly after birth, unless she proved that such death was not caused either by such neglect or by any wrongful act to which she was a party. The second created a similar, but minor offence punishable with seven years' penal servitude, in which the omission to obtain assistance was connected with an intent to conceal the fact of her having a child and which resulted either in the death of, or permanent injury to the child.[74]   One of the Commissioners' stated reasons for substituting sections 185 and 186 was their belief that these new provisions would often afford a means of punishing child-murder where there would be practical difficulty in obtaining a conviction of murder because of the necessity of proof of live-birth.[75]   The Criminal Code of 1878 was consigned to the Parliamentary shelves where it died a dusty death.

In 1880 another Criminal Code Bill was introduced by a group of private members which proposed that a woman who intentionally did an unlawful act from which the death of her child resulted, either in the act of birth or immediately thereafter, being at the time deprived of her self-control by reason of physical or mental suffering or distress, should be punished as for manslaughter and that proof of live-birth was not to be necessary for conviction, the proof of dead-birth being placed on the woman. Bodily harm inflicted on the child within fourteen days of birth by its mother in such circumstances was to be punishable, if it resulted in death, by a maximum term of twenty years' penal servitude.[76]

That amelioration of the legal position with regard to infanticidal women remained a pressing concern was demonstrated in 1908, when Mr George Greenwood introduced a Law of Murder Amendment Bill "to carry out the recommendations of the Royal Commission on Capital Punishment, 1866". It proposed to divide murder into two classes and specifically provided that no woman was to be indicted for killing her child at birth or within one month thereafter, but a woman who maliciously inflicted serious injury upon her child during that period, resulting in death, was to be guilty of an indictable offence punishable with penal servitude, imprisonment, or detention during H.M's. pleasure.[77]

At the committee stage of the Children Bill, 1908 the Lord Chancellor, Lord Loreburn, moved to insert a clause to the effect that "where a woman is convicted of the murder of her infant and that child was under the age of one year, the Court may, in lieu of passing a sentence of death, sentence her to penal servitude for life or any less punishment".[78] His main argument in support of it was that it would avoid the "solemn mockery" of pronouncing the death sentence in cases where it would not be carried out, a practice which was inhuman and contrary to public opinion.[79] He compared the Scottish position where a verdict of culpable homicide was returned in this kind of case, with the English position where juries took refuge in verdicts of concealment of birth,[80] presumably to illustrate that the position in Scotland was preferable, although adoption of diminished responsibility in its entirety does not seem to have occurred to him. In his opinion the English practice and the refusal of witnesses to give evidence in these cases, obstructed the administration of justice in

England.[81]   However, the Chief Justice, Lord Alverstone, doubted the propriety of dealing with infanticide within the Children Bill which related to the protection of children,[82] envisaging that the clause as it stood would lead to an increase in the worst kind of child murders.[83]   His main objection was that this discretion should be left to the Executive rather than be vested in the Judiciary.[84] The result would be "hanging judges and non-hanging judges".[85]   The clash between the two lawyers prompted the Bishop of Southwark to suggest that if the Lord Chief Justice did not like the Lord Chancellor's proposal he should take some other action himself.[86]

Thus Lord Alverstone was more or less trapped into introducing a bill of his own,[87] the Child Murder (Record of Sentence of Death) Bill, 1909. His bill would have restored the judges' discretion to record the death sentence in cases of child murder.[88]   Lord Loreburn objected on the ground that the bill would make no difference to the present state of the law.[89]   The death penalty would still hang over the prisoner unless the prerogative of mercy was exercised,[90]   the only difference being that the "sad pageant" of passing the death sentence in open court would be dispensed with.[91]   Consequently, the same influences would continue to operate on witnesses and juries, with the knowledge that capital punishment remained.[92]   In committee, Lord James who could find "no cause for enthusiastic support of the Bill",[93] moved an amendment to provide that if a mother who had not recovered from the effects of child-birth killed her infant, the judge *could* direct the jury that they might acquit of murder and convict of manslaughter.[94]   Lord Alverstone surrendered and accepted this amendment.[95]   Lord Ashbourne then moved an amendment which, in addition to the disturbances of childbirth, would take account of such circumstances as the desertion of the father, expulsion from her family, unemployment, sickness and destitution.[96]   In such cases the judges could direct a verdict of manslaughter if they considered that course proper, having regard to all the circumstances of the case. Lord Alverstone objected to vesting such a wide discretion in the judges,[97] but Lords Loreburn[98] and James[99] agreed with the substance of the amendment, the latter remarking that, in fact, the judges did exercise such discretion as they advised the Home Office on all questions of reprieve.[100] The amendment was withdrawn for reconsideration before the report stage and that was the last that was heard of it. The bill finally reached the

Commons in July, when they were already in difficulties with their timetable and it was probably a lack of Parliamentary time which prevented it from proceeding further.[101]

Thirteen years later Mr.Arthur Henderson, secretary of the Labour Party, introduced the Child Murder (Trial) Bill[102] which closely resembled its predecessor of 1909. However this bill left it open to the jury to bring in a verdict of manslaughter instead of murder (whenever evidence was given that at the time of the killing the woman "had not recovered from the effect of giving birth to the child") instead of leaving it to the judge's discretion whether or not to leave this decision to them. In the House of Lords Lord Phillimore expressed the view that the earlier proposals on infanticide had approached the problem in the wrong way.[103] He stated that the judges felt a strong aversion to the placement of this issue in their hands, being of the view that it was for the jury, under proper direction, to find the crime and for the judge to award the proper punishment.[104]

Although it was no wider than the principle on which the Home Secretary was using the prerogative of mercy[105] the Lord Chancellor, Lord Birkenhead, condemned it as "almost terrifying" in its lack of particularity.[106] He warned that the provision might appear to reflect on the jury's right to return a manslaughter verdict in any case and objected to the absence of a time limit on the operation of the defence; a woman might not recover from the physical consequences of giving birth to a child for as many as nine years.[107] Finally, there was nothing to connect the fact that the woman had not recovered from the effect of giving birth to the child with the commission of the offence,[108] with no requirement that her will power, judgment of right and wrong or capacity of judging right from wrong should be impaired.[109]

As a result he moved an amendment[110] which he had drafted and which had the approval of the D.P.P. and the law officers of the Crown, which restricted the scope of the bill to those cases "where a woman unlawfully by any direct means intentionally causes the death of her newly born child, but at the time..had not fully recovered from the effect of giving birth to such child, and by reason thereof the balance of her mind was disturbed". In such cases the jury were enabled to find her guilty of infanticide, for which the woman could be sentenced as if she were guilty of manslaughter. Following objections from Lords Parmoor[111] and

Phillimore[112] the bill was amended and the resulting Infanticide Act, 1922 ran

> Where a woman by any wilful act or omission causes the death of her newly-born child, but at the time of the act or omission she had not fully recovered from the effect of giving birth to such child, and by reason thereof the balance of her mind was then disturbed, she shall, notwithstanding that the circumstances were such that but for this Act the offence would have amounted to murder, be guilty of felony, to wit, of infanticide.

The limitations of the defence became obvious when in 1927, a woman named *O'Donoghue* who had killed her thirty-five-day-old infant, was not allowed to avail of the partial defence of infanticide since the child could not be said to be "newly-born".[113]

The Infanticide Bill of 1936 was a bold attempt to widen the scope of this legislation to correspond more closely both with public feeling and with the Home Secretary's use of the prerogative of mercy[114] Introduced by a number of Labour back-benchers, it would have exempted the killing of infants up to the age of eight years from the death penalty and would have widened the definition of an infanticidal mother's state of mind to cover "mothers who commit acts of this kind under extreme stress arising from other causes than the immediate effects of childbirth".[115] Following the abdication of the King the bill lapsed. The Home Secretary and Lord Chancellor, who saw "a number of difficulties" in amending the 1922 Act, would promise no Government legislation for this purpose.[116]

Finally Lord Dawson successfully introduced a bill which became the Infanticide Act of 1938. It made clear that the child could be of any age under twelve months and that the woman's mental imbalance was to be attributable either to the birth of the child or to the consequent lactation.[117] Although the bill received unanimous support in the House of Lords, the extension of the mitigatory effects of infanticide to cover the killing of children under the age of one year caused controversy, some commentators feeling that it was too broad and others feeling that it was too narrow. The bill received the Royal assent on 23/6/1938 and remains to this day the law on infanticide.

Although commentators speak of infanticide as a substantive

offence[118] it may also be viewed as a partial defence to murder. Walker, who describes infanticide as a crime,[119] goes on to describe it as "a crime which was expressly equated with manslaughter. It was an intermediate verdict of the same nature as that which was introduced thirty-five years later under the name of "diminished responsibility".[120] Parallels with the Scottish defence of diminished responsibility can be seen in the origin of the defence of infanticide in the use of the prerogative of mercy to secure release from the death penalty and both defences can be regarded as the handwork of the Judiciary. Edwards describes the Scottish defence of diminished responsibility as "a classic example of judge-made law"[121] while Seaborne Davies said of infanticide:

> If any legislation could be described as above all others the creation of the Judges, it is the Infanticide Act, 1922. Their evidence against "the solemn mockery" in 1866 really marks the starting point of this reform; it was they who frequently made proposals for the amendment of the law during the next two decades; it was they who revived the whole question in 1908 and 1909; it was they who mostly discussed in Parliament the proposals of the Bill of 1922 after it had been cast into more or less its final form by Lord Birkenhead and his collaborators.[122]

The above discussion is a vivid illustration of the law's preoccupation with women who killed their children. The tentative gropings for a satisfactory solution resulted in the Infanticide Acts of 1922 and 1938. In line with the Scottish defence of diminished responsibility, infanticide evolved into a partial defence, reducing murder to manslaughter and it also hinges on the requirement of a mental imbalance. The Infanticide Act 1922 was the first step taken to introduce diminished responsibility into English law and the adoption of a full defence of diminished responsibility in 1957 was, therefore, a natural progression.

Diminished Responsibility Imported

As stated above, the vesting of discretion in the jury to decide between capital and non-capital cases had been advocated by a minority of the 1866 Royal Commission on Capital Punishment. Only one proponent, however, linked it to a reduction of murder to culpable homicide. Stephen J. offered no evidence on the subject. By the time he wrote his *History of the Criminal Law of England* however, Stephen J., discussing cases in which self-control was weakened by insanity, was suggesting[123]

> the law ought..where madness is proved, to allow the jury to return any one of three verdicts: Guilty; Guilty, but his power of self-control was diminished by insanity; Not guilty on the ground of insanity.

No notice was taken of his suggestion however, and the Atkin Committee and the two medical associations that gave evidence to it in 1922 seem not to have considered it.[124]

By the time of the Royal Commission on Capital Punishment (1949-53) the British Medical Association was recommending not only the enlargement of the McNaghten Rules to cover irresistible impulse but also that the jury should be empowered to return a verdict of "guilty with diminished responsibility" if they found that the accused "at the time of the committing of the act was labouring, as a result of disease of the mind, under a defect of reason or a disorder of emotion to such an extent as not to be fully accountable for his actions".[125] The Association recommended detention in a special institution for an indeterminate period where such a verdict was returned, rather than a fixed term of imprisonment as in Scotland.[126] Their recommendation was based on a recognition of the gradation of intermediate states between full knowledge and complete lack of knowledge and that

> No revision of the McNaghten formula can completely solve the problem of determining responsibility for crime unless it is made possible for the defence in the English courts, as in the Scottish courts, to set up, as an alternative to the plea of insanity, a plea of diminished responsibility.[127]

The British Medical Association's proposal was also supported by the Scottish psychiatrists, the Institute of Psychoanalysis and Lord Denning.[128] The Scottish Crown Agent commented that

> This doctrine, which is now firmly established, has, in the view of the Criminal Authorities, worked satisfactorily and has the effect of

preventing convictions of murder in the technical sense and consequent sentences of death where the prisoners are abnormal from a mental aspect, and tends greatly to the side of mercy.[129]

However the majority of witnesses were against its introduction,[130] the psychiatrists on the grounds that it would place too much responsibility on medical witnesses and would give rise to conflicting testimony which could confuse the jury. Sir John Anderson thought that it would be hard to draft a statutory definition of diminished responsibility and that in any case the use made of it in Scotland between the wars had weakened the deterrent effect of capital punishment (an argument for which he did not offer any evidence).[131]

The Royal Commission noted that "mental abnormality varies widely in its intensity and in the extent to which it affects the behaviour of the patient and his capacity to conduct himself like a normal person. It follows that the extent to which a mentally abnormal person should be considered less responsible for his actions than a normal person varies equally widely; there is an almost infinite range of degrees of responsibility".[132] The Commission recognised that "no clear boundary can be drawn between responsibility and irresponsibility"[133] and saw no reason to apprehend that juries would find the issue too difficult or would take refuge in it unreasonably.[134] However they concluded that

> Although the Scottish doctrine of "diminished responsibility" works well in that country, we are unable to recommend its adoption in England.[135]

Their argument was that the conditions that gave rise to diminished responsibility were relevant to offences other than murder.[136] As their terms of reference were restricted to the law of murder they did not think "that so radical an amendment of the law of England would be justified for this limited purpose".[137] Some writers have interpreted this to mean that they advocated its introduction in relation to all offences.[138] This view may have arisen from the argument of Scottish witnesses that diminished responsibility was part of the general law of Scotland.[139] Instead, the Commission recommended that juries should be able to decide between life and death sentences, taking into account extenuating circumstances such as the mental state of the murderer.

It is important to know that the Government resorted to the appointment of the Royal Commission on Capital Punishment amidst growing agitation for abolition of the death penalty. However, the Commission was specifically forbidden by its terms of reference from considering the question of abolition and was therefore limited to considering how the law could be improved given that the death penalty persisted. The Gowers Commission's report was likely to be ignored since, as is well known, the appointment of a Royal Commission is a time-honoured device, used by all Governments, when they wish to fend off opposition and at the same time do nothing.[140] Not surprisingly, therefore, Mr.Lloyd George announced on 10/11/1955 that the Conservative Government rejected all the main recommendations of the Gowers Commission and would introduce no amending legislation to the law of murder.[141]

The Government's unwillingness to propose any legislation prompted a group of their supporters to take the initiative. The Inns of Court Conservative and Unionist Society appointed a committee of barristers and legally qualified M.P.s to take the initiative under the chairmanship of Sir Lionel Heald. The Heald Committee produced a short report[142] which recommended changes in the law regarding provocation, constructive malice, accomplices and the defence of insanity in trials for murder. Over the last of these they seem to have had great difficulty.[143] They sought advice from Dr Max Grünhut, the Oxford Criminologist, who was disposed in favour of the defence of diminished responsibility, and after listening to his advice the Heald Committee consulted the Scottish Lord Advocate, W.R.Milligan Q.C.[144] The Heald Committee rejected the Gowers Commission's recent proposal to allow the jury to decide whether or not the accused was suffering from disease of the mind (or mental deficiency) to such a degree that he ought not to be held responsible[145] and instead, recommended the adoption of the Scottish defence of diminished responsibility, pointing out that it was no innovation to provide a special defence which was confined to a specific crime.[146] They followed this with the recommendation that the result of a diminished responsibility verdict should be detention during Her Majesty's pleasure.[147]

The Government, fearing that if it remained obstinate it would be defeated by the abolitionists whose cause was attracting an increasing number of Conservatives, decided to throw its support behind the Heald Committee's recommendations.[148] The Government published its Homicide Bill later in the year, section 2(1) of which provided that

> Where a person kills or is a party to the killing of another he shall not be convicted of murder if he was suffering from such abnormality of mind (whether arising from a condition of arrested or retarded development of mind or any inherent causes or induced by disease or injury) as substantially impaired his mental responsibility for his acts or omissions in doing or being a party to the killing.

The words bracketed closely resemble the words of the definition of "mental defectiveness" in the Mental Deficiency Act 1927 - "arrested or incomplete development of mind existing before the age of 18 years". The 1927 Act however, seems to mean "however arising or caused" whilst the 1957 parenthesis is intended for the purpose of limitation rather than the avoidance of doubt.[149]

The following subsections of the Homicide Bill provided that it was for the defence to raise this issue, and if successful in doing so, the accused became liable to be convicted of manslaughter. The effect of this (which was not stated in the bill) would be to free the judge from the necessity of pronouncing the death sentence (or life imprisonment if the murder belonged to the newly created category of "non-capital murder") and to allow him a choice between life imprisonment, imprisonment for a specified term, a fine, a probation order, or an absolute or conditional discharge.[150] If the necessary medical evidence were forthcoming at the stage when he was considering sentence he could commit him to a mental hospital, but was not compelled to do so as he would have been by a verdict of "guilty but insane".[151]

The attempts to amend this clause during its passage through Parliament were not very determined, and the Attorney General and Lord Chancellor successfully resisted them.[152] At the committee stage in the House of Commons Mr.Silverman, who throughout took the leadership of the abolitionist members in the House of Commons,[153] proposed that the phrase should be amended so as to read "abnormality of mind (however arising)"[154] so that the law could keep abreast of advances in medical knowledge.[155] He himself gave no clear example of the sort of case which might otherwise be excluded, but his supporters instanced people who were partners in suicide pacts, or who were merely "simple" or irresponsible[156] without suffering from "arrested or retarded development of mind". Pointing out that Mr.Silverman's amendment would include murderers who were merely bad-tempered or who committed a murder as a result of an outburst of rage or jealousy,[157] the Attorney General stipulated that the chosen wording was intended "to bring English law into line with the Scottish doctrine, and not to go further than that"[158] and in the end the amendment was not accepted.

Another unsuccessful proposal of the abolitionists would have shifted the onus of proof from the defendant to the prosecution,[159] a move which has more recently been advocated by both the (Butler) Committee on Mentally Abnormal Offenders[160] and by the Criminal Law Revision Committee.[161] Its proponent Mr.Paget (M.P.for Northampton) stipulated that he wished to correct the anomaly of insanity, rather than add to it by putting diminished responsibility into the same category[162] and he pointed out that McNaghten's case was "rather a slim foundation on which the doctrine was built".[163] The reasons advanced in favour of this amendment were firstly, the convenience which would result if the onus was on the prosecution, as these are the people who have the evidence, the defendant being under constant observation in the prison hospital and secondly, the difficulty for defence counsel in obtaining instructions from a madman.[164] The Attorney General countered Mr.Paget's first argument by asserting that the prosecution make evidence of insanity available to the defence.[165] He claimed that the proposal would add considerably to the length of all trials, would amount to a radical change in our criminal administration and would be a change difficult to confine solely to murder charges.[166] He also pointed out that the defendant in a murder case may not wish to put forward a plea of insanity or diminished responsibility[167] and that such a change would prejudice the defence.[168] The amendment having failed, Sir Frank Soskice (M.P.for Newport) moved to leave out "prove" and insert "satisfy the jury"[169] to indicate that the burden of proof was on a balance of probability.[170] The Solicitor General made clear that this was what was intended by "prove"[171] and again this amendment failed.

Considerable discontent was expressed in the House of Commons at the Government's determination to rush this piece of legislation through,

in advance of a more far-reaching proposal on capital punishment.[172]
Mr.Anthony Greenwood (M.P.for Rossendale) expressed the view that

> It is becoming more and more obvious that the Government have not been
> motivated by a burning passion to amend the law, but rather with a
> determination to ditch [Mr.Silverman]. From some of the answers we
> have had to our queries, it seems obvious that the Government embarked
> upon the Bill with as little preparation and with as reckless a disregard of
> the results as in the case of a much graver enterprise that the Government
> have undertaken.[173]

Similarly, Mr.Paget claimed that

> The Clause is not nearly as good as it might be or as good as it would be
> if the Government were dealing with this matter with any measure of
> sincerity.[174]

Partly because of the haste with which the bill was rushed through
and the consequent lack of discussion of it, many M.Ps. were left in the
dark as to the working of the section.[175] Mr.Greenwood expressed the
view that "the Bill is just as far from clear to many of us who have been
considering it for that considerable length of time"[176] while Mr.Silverman
expressed disquiet that the proposed amendment on burden of proof

> Should ultimately be decided by votes cast one way or the other by
> hundreds of people who have not the slightest notion what question they
> are deciding, still less what are the arguments on either side.[177]

Mr.Silverman was also of the opinion that this was a matter that
should be decided by a free vote rather than according to the collective
political philosophy of each party.[178] No doubt the general ignorance of
this area of law and the fact that this was a party issue contributed to the
M.Ps'. failure to attend the debates.[179] Fewer than a half dozen members
on either side were present on 27/11/1956.[180]

In the House of Lords, similar discontent was expressed at the
Government's motives and actions.[181] Lord Chorley moved two
amendments, the first being to insert "environmental" after "inherent" and
the second to insert "or disorder of the mind" after "disease",[182] the object

being to include cases of diminished responsibility produced by external and environmental causes without disease.[183] However the Lord Chancellor, Lord Kilmuir, noted that the proposed amendments would go beyond the Scottish defence,[184] and Lord Chorley withdrew his amendment.[185] Lord Chorley also moved an amendment which would have made detention during H.M's. pleasure the automatic result of a successful defence under this clause.[186] His object was to eliminate the possibility of a fixed sentence, after two thirds of which, a man could claim his freedom although he might still be regarded by the authorities as dangerous. This was rejected by Lord Kilmuir on the grounds that there would also be cases in which the accused had virtually recovered by the time of trial[187] and in which it would be unduly severe to deprive the judge of discretion. After the Lord Chancellor asserted his faith in the judges to give appropriate sentences[188] Lord Chorley withdrew his amendment.[189]

The act received the Royal assent on 21/3/1957. The new Home Secretary, Mr.Butler, hailed the bill as a victory for the forces which represented majority opinion in the country.[190] There was not, in fact, the slightest support for such a contention.[191] All the evidence showed that public opinion was overwhelmingly either retentionist or abolitionist and that those who supported some middle position of grading murders were few in number, and expert opinion such as the Gowers Commission, had, whenever it had examined these proposals, decided that they were impracticable.[192] In fact there was nobody who favoured such a law on its own merits. The very Government which passed it had declared itself against it only two months before.[193] As Lord Templewood opined in the debate in the House of Lords, it was "nothing more than an expedient to extricate the Government out of a very difficult position".[194] However, as Hollis comments,[195] the right thing can be done for the wrong reasons;

> The motive for which the Act was passed is one thing. But, whatever its motive, we must examine objectively how it has worked. Parliament might have passed a wise act by a happy accident. Such things have happened before.[196]

Notes

1   M.Zeegers "Diminished Responsibility: A Logical, Workable and Essential Concept" [1981 4 Intl.J.Law and Psychiat.433 pp.435 & 436
2   N.Walker *Crime and Insanity in England* Vol.1 (Edinburgh, 1968) p.139 shows that the Scottish defence of diminished responsibility was borrowed from Dutch law.
3   ibid
4   G.H.Gordon *The Criminal Law of Scotland* (2nd ed) (Edinburgh, 1978) p.381
5   ibid
6   Hale *Historia Placitorum Coronae*, Vol.1 (London 1736), p.30
7   B.L.Diamond "From M'Naghten to Currens, and Beyond" [1962] 50 Calif.L.Rev.189 p.200
8   (1867) 5 Irv.466
9   ibid pp.475 & 476
10   ibid p.479
11   ibid
12   G.H.Gordon op cit p.382
13   F.McAuley *Insanity Psychiatry and Criminal Responsibility* (Dublin, 1993) p.155
14   G.H.Gordon op cit p.388
15   Dr.Wright *The Development of Legal Responsibility in the Criminal Law of Scotland* PhD 1954 Aberdeen University p.240
16   ibid
17   ibid
18   ibid p.241
19   ibid
20   ibid
21   ibid
22   ibid pp.241 & 242
23   ibid p.242
24   ibid
25   ibid
26   [1875] 3 Couper 152
27   Dr.Wright op cit p.245
28   [1876] 3 Couper 334
29   ibid p.337
30   *H.M. Advocate v Andrew Granger* [1878] 4 Couper 86; *H.M. Advocate v Thomas Ferguson* (1887) 4 Couper 552; *H.M. Advocate v John MacDonald* (1890) 2 White 517; *H.M. Advocate v David Kane* (1892) 2 White 386);*H.M. Advocate v John Graham* [1906] 5 Adam 212, all of which are discussed further in section 2.8 of this chapter.
31   *H.M. Advocate v Abercrombie* [1896] 2 Adam 163
32   [1893] 1 Adam 34
33   [1902] 4 Adam 88
34   N.Walker op cit p.144
35   ibid

36 ibid
37 Report of the Royal Commission on Capital Punishment [1949-53] Cmd 8932 (London, 1953) p.276
38 N.Walker op cit p.128
39 Described by R.Smith in *Trial by Medicine* (Edinburgh, 1981) pp.152 & 153
40 14 C.C.C.143 p.144
41 R.Smith op cit pp.148-160 describes a series of these cases.
42 Report of the Royal Commission on Capital Punishment 1866, B.P.P.1866, Vol.XXI p.193
43 R.Smith op cit pp.148 & 149
44 ibid p.154
45 G.K.Behlmer "Deadly Motherhood: Infanticide and Medical Opinion in mid-Victorian England" [1979] 34 Journal Hist.Med.403 p.406
46 ibid pp.406-409
47 D.Seaborne Davies "Child-Killing in English Law" [1937] 1 M.L.R.203 p.217. For the sake of convenience I treat the evidence before the 1866 Commission in substantially the same manner and order as Seaborne Davies does in this article.
48 Report of the Royal Commission on Capital Punishment 1866 op cit p.628
49 ibid p.4
50 D.Seaborne Davies op cit p.217
51 Report of the Royal Commission on Capital Punishment 1866 op cit p.49
52 ibid p.625
53 ibid p.627
54 ibid p.624
55 ibid p.625
56 ibid pp.468 & 469
57 ibid p.469
58 ibid p.1
59 B.P.P.1872, Vol.ii p.247
60 Homicide Law (Amendment) Bill 1874, B.P.P. 1874, Vol.ii p.372
61 B.P.P.1874, Vol.ii p.409
62 B.P.P.1874, Vol.ix p.497
63 ibid p.516
64 ibid pp.549 & 560
65 ibid p.521
66 ibid
67 ibid
68 ibid p.543
69 ibid
70 ibid
71 B.P.P.1874, Vol.ix p.477 pp.(ii) and (iv)
72 B.P.P.1878-9, Vol.xx p.169
73 ibid p.270
74 ibid
75 Stated in the marginal note to section 185
76 B.P.P.1880, Vol.ii pp.408 & 409

77   B.P.P.1908, Vol.ii p.74; B.P.P. 1909, Vol.iii p.426
78   B.P.Deb.1908, Vol.195 p.1178
79   ibid
80   B.P.Deb.1908, Vol.196 p.485
81   ibid
82   B.P.Deb.1908, Vol.195 p.1179
83   B.P.Deb.1908, Vol.196 p.486
84   B.P.Deb.1908, Vol.195 p.1179
85   B.P.Deb.1909, Vol.196 p.486
86   ibid p.487
87   N.Walker op cit p.130
88   H.L.Deb.1909, Vol.1 p.638
89   ibid p.725
90   ibid
91   ibid
92   ibid
93   ibid p.727
94   ibid p.957
95   ibid p.959
96   ibid p.960
97   ibid pp.961 & 962
98   ibid p.963
99   ibid pp.962 & 963
100 D.Seaborne Davies op cit p.279
101 N.Walker op cit p.130
102 H.C.Deb.1922, Vol.150 pp.615 & 616
103 H.L.Deb.1922, Vol.50 p.438
104 ibid pp.438 & 439
105 N.Walker op cit p.130
106 H.L.Deb.1922, Vol.50 p.760
107 ibid p.440
108 ibid pp.440 & 441
109 ibid p.441
110 ibid p.758
111 ibid pp.762-764
112 ibid p.766
113 *R v O'Donoghue* [1927] 20 Cr.App.R.132
114 N.Walker op cit p.132
115 H.C.Deb.1936-7, Vol.318 p.236
116 H.C.Deb.1937, Vol.322 p.1165
117 H.L.Deb.1937-8, Vol.108 p.295
118 D.Seaborne Davies op cit p.281
119 N.Walker op cit p.125
120 ibid p.134

121 J.Ll.J.Edwards "Diminished Responsibility: A Withering Away of the Concept of Criminal Responsibility" in G.O.Mueller *Essays in Criminal Science* (London, 1961) p.302

122 D.Seaborne Davies op cit p.220

123 J.Fitzjames Stephen *A History of the Criminal Law of England* Vol.ii (London, 1883) p.175

124 N.Walker op cit p.147

125 Report of the Royal Commission on Capital Punishment [1949-53] op cit para.407

126 ibid

127 ibid para.408

128 ibid para.409

129 Evidence from the Scottish Crown Agent to the Royal Commission on Capital Punishment [1949-53] Cmd 8932 op cit para.383

130 ibid para.410

131 N.Walker op cit p.148

132 Report of the Royal Commission on Capital Punishment [1949-53] op cit para.285

133 ibid para.411

134 ibid para.412

135 ibid p.276

136 ibid para.413

137 ibid

138 eg.T.B.Smith "Diminished Responsibility" [1957] Crim.L.R.354 p.355 and D.W.Elliott "The Homicide Act, 1957" [1957] Crim.L.R.282 p.283

139 N.Walker op cit p.149

140 C.Hollis *The Homicide Act* (London, 1964) p.21

141 H.C.Deb.1955-6, Vol.545 written answers p.219

142 *Murder: Some Suggestions for the Reform of the law Relating to Murder in England* (London, 1956)

143 N.Walker op cit p.149

144 ibid

145 Report of the Heald Committee *Murder: Some Suggestions for the Reform of the law Relating to Murder in England* (London, 1956) p.15

146 ibid p.17

147 ibid p.19

148 C.Hollis op cit p.49

149 E.Griew "The Future of Diminished Responsibility" [1988] Crim.L.R.75 p.77

150 N.Walker op cit p.150

151 ibid

152 ibid

153 C.Hollis op cit p.22

154 H.C.Deb.1956, Vol.561 p.314

155 ibid p.316

156 eg.Mr.Rees-Davies ibid pp.324 & 330

157 ibid pp.320 & 321

158 ibid p.321

159 Mr Paget, ibid p.353

160 Report of the (Butler) Committee on Mentally Abnormal Offenders Cmnd 6244 (London, 1975) paras.18.39-18.41
161 Criminal Law Revision Committee 14th Report *Offences Against the Person* Cmnd 7844 (London, 1980) para.914
162 H.C.Deb.1956, Vol.561 p.354
163 ibid p.407
164 ibid p.408
165 ibid p.417
166 p.410
167 ibid p.415
168 ibid p.416
169 ibid p.453
170 ibid p.455
171 ibid p.456
172 eg Mr Silverman ibid p.469
173 ibid p.489
174 ibid
175 F.Boland "Diminished Responsibility as a Defence in Irish Law: Past English Mistakes and Future Irish Directions" [1996] 6 I.C.L.J. 19 p.21
176 H.C.Deb., 1956 Vol.561 p.489
177 ibid p.442
178 ibid
179 F.Boland op cit p.221
180 An observation by Mr Hale H.C.Deb., 1956 Vol.561p.425
181 H.L.Deb.1956-7, Vol.201 Lord Silkin pp.1176 & 1177 and Lord Chorley p.1207
182 H.L.Deb.1956-7, Vol.202 p.255
183 ibid pp.356 & 357
184 ibid p.358
185 ibid p.362
186 ibid p.362
187 ibid p.365
188 ibid p.366
189 ibid p.368
190 H.C.Deb.1956-7, Vol.564 pp.454-457
191 C.Hollis op cit p.55
192 ibid pp.55 & 56
193 ibid p.56
194 H.L.Deb.1956-7, Vol.201 p.1196
195 C.Hollis op cit p.56
196 ibid

6 The Defence of Diminished Responsibility in English Law

As shown in Chapter Five, the introduction of diminished responsibility into English Law was a half-hearted response by the Government of 1956 to the growing pressure for abolition of the death penalty. The perfunctory discussion of the defence's terms and the haste with which the bill was rushed through were later to lead to uncertainty as to the precise scope of the defence. As a result, it fell on the Judiciary to imbue the words of the defence with meaning (impaired mental responsibility, for example, is not a term of art in law or psychiatry) and to delineate its precise scope. By tracing the development of the defence I will show that the introduction of diminished responsibility into English law has, nonetheless, abated the controversy surrounding the insanity defence and led to a resolution of the medico-legal conflict. This will be illustrated by discussing the range of mental abnormalities encompassed by the defence and the operation of diminished responsibility in practice.

The Operation of the Defence of Diminished Responsibility

At first it was unclear whether the Crown could accept the plea of diminished responsibility where the psychiatric evidence was unanimous or whether the issue had to be left to the jury. The early cases[1] indicate that the courts initially favoured the second option[2] and insisted that the prosecution was obliged to probe the soundness of the psychiatric evidence in cross examination.[3] Then in *Cox,*[4] the Court of Appeal approved the procedure whereby the plea of diminished responsibility could be accepted at the discretion of the trial judge where the medical evidence was uncontested. Now if at a diminished responsibility manslaughter trial there is unanimous psychiatric evidence from both sides or uncontradicted medical testimony (likely to come from the defence only)[5] that the defendant was of diminished responsibility, either the case must not go to the jury or the trial judge must direct the jury to find a manslaughter verdict under section 2 of the Homicide Act unless there "be *some evidence* arising from other testimonyor the circumstances of the case upon which [the jury] can properly act" to convict of murder.[6]

Walker found that as long ago as 1964, there was no prosecution rebuttal of the psychiatric evidence for the defence in 75% of section 2 manslaughter cases.[7] Dell's research has shown that for the period of 1976/1977, the plea not guilty to murder but guilty to section 2 manslaughter was accepted by the prosecution in 86.5% of such cases,[8] the result was that 80% of diminished responsibility cases were dealt with by guilty pleas.[9] More recent figures suggest that during 1986-8, while 178 diminished responsibility pleas were accepted by the prosecution (85%) a mere 31 (15%) were the subject of jury verdicts.[10] Thus, in the majority of diminished responsibility cases, the prosecution and the court accord deference to the medical view of abnormality of mind and impaired mental responsibility. Deference to the medical view of abnormality of mind can also be seen in the wide array of abnormalities covered by section 2, discussed *below*.

There is no compulsion on the jury, despite medical concurrence, to find that responsibility is diminished, since the jury has to reach its verdict on all the facts and circumstances of the case, not just the medical evidence.[11] In *R v Dix*[12] it was argued that by the same token upon which a jury could overturn medical evidence if there was sufficient evidence to convict of murder, a jury could be asked to convict of section 2 manslaughter without medical evidence if there was sufficient outside evidence of substantial mental abnormality.

Shaw L.J., while finding counsel's argument attractive and that the terms of section 2(1) of the Homicide Act, 1957 do not require that medical evidence be adduced in support of a defence of diminished responsibility, nevertheless upheld the trial judge's ruling that section 2(1) makes it a practical necessity.[13] Counsel's argument it was ruled, could hold up, only if the parenthesis in the subsection ("whether arising from a condition of arrested or retarded development of mind or any inherent causes or induced by disease or injury") was descriptive of *all* forms of abnormality of mind so that psychiatric evidence as to what sort was unnecessary.[14] However, Lord Parker in *Byrne*[15] had made it clear that the defendant must show not only the existence of abnormality of mind but also that it falls within the above parenthesis and is substantial.[16] Shaw L.J's. view was that what emerges from Lord Parker's statement is that scientific evidence of a medical kind "is essential" to establish what is referred to in the above parenthesis.[17] Hence a section 2 manslaughter defence without psychiatric evidence seems impossible.[18]

A considerable proportion of this Chapter will be dedicated to discussing those abnormalities of mind which the psychiatric witnesses testify to and which lead to diminished responsibility manslaughter verdicts.[19] In this manner I will outline the parameters of the defence (which have taken a considerable length of time to be settled), with reference to several criminal law principles and defences. This will reveal the evolution of a happy partnership between law and medicine on the issue of diminished responsibility and the success of the defence in dealing with cases of abnormality of mind which are regarded as falling outside the ambit of the McNaghten Rules but which nevertheless merit some form of excuse.

Abnormality of Mind

Irresistible Impulse

Firstly, I will focus on the plea of irresistible impulse which, as I have shown in Chapter Two, was frequently offered in cases of volitional and moral insanity during the nineteenth and early twentieth centuries. After 1910, however, the Court of Appeal came down heavy-handedly against any attempt to alter the McNaghten Rules and pronounced very firmly that irresistible impulses due to insanity would not be recognised by the English courts as a legal defence. Contemporaneous with the steadfast opposition shown by the English courts, a movement to recognise irresistible impulse as part of the test of insanity was initiated in Irish law. This eventually culminated in its approval by the Irish Supreme Court in *Doyle v Wicklow County Council*,[20] a decision which mirrored earlier acceptance of the plea in the United States. In contrast with the Irish position from the 1930's, pleas of irresistible impulse became less frequent in England, until eventually irresistible impulse was no longer offered as evidence of insanity. That the judicial opposition to irresistible impulse stemmed in large part from a conflict over the distribution of power between the legal and medical professions emerges from a lecture delivered by Lord Hewart in 1927 before the Medical Society of London where he said of the defence of irresistible impulse

> If the law were relaxed in the way which has been suggested..the result might be to transfer to a section of the medical profession the question whether a great number of ordinary criminals should be held responsible to the law.[21]

By the 1950's the medical categories of moral and volitional insanity had gone out of vogue and been replaced by the "psychopathic personality". Similarities between moral insanity and psychopathy can be discerned from the report of the Royal Commission on the Law Relating to Mental Illness and Mental Deficiency (1954-57), which described psychopaths as persons whose

> Daily behaviour shows a want of social responsibility and of consideration for others, of prudence and foresight and of ability to act in their own best interests. Their persistent anti-social mode of conduct may include inefficiency and lack of interest in any form of occupation; pathological lying, swindling, and slandering; alcoholism and drug addiction; sexual offences, and violent actions with little motivation and an entire absence of self-restraint, which may go as far as homicide. Punishment or the threat of punishment influences their behaviour only momentarily, and its more lasting effect is to intensify their vindictiveness and anti-social attitude.[22]

It was unclear at first whether the psychopath (ie. the characteristic victim of irresistible impulses[23]) would be embraced by the diminished responsibility defence in the absence of some other recognised form of abnormality, such as mental subnormality (as in *Matheson*[24]) or drunkenness (*Di Duca*).[25] After all, psychopathy is a personality disorder and the Homicide Act stressed *abnormality of mind*. Furthermore, the Scottish defence of diminished responsibility had by now become much more restrictive. In *Carraher v H.M. Advocate*[26] it was held by a Full Bench that "the plea of diminished responsibility, which is anomalous in our law, should not be extended or given wider scope than has hitherto been accorded to it in the decisions"[27] and that psychopathic personality disorder should henceforth, not be regarded as a species of diminished responsibility.[28]

As early as 1909 Lord Guthrie in *H.M. Advocate v Edmonstone*[29] had stated, although *obiter*, that "[t]he law has never countenanced the idea that persons with a diminished moral sense in consequence of having been brought up in bad surroundings can be dealt with differently from others".[30] More recently Lord Cooper in *H.M. Advocate v Braithwaite* stated "it will *not* suffice in law, for the purpose of this defence of diminished responsibility merely to show that an accused person has a very short temper, or is unusually excitable and lacking in self-control. The world would be a very convenient place for criminals and a very dangerous place for other people, if that were the law. It must be much more than that"[31] whilst the Lord Justice-General in *Caldwell v H.M. Advocate* asserted that "[e]vidence of ruthlessness, of callousness and of disregard for others is evidence rather of a criminal disposition than of diminished responsibility".[32] These words were still being quoted with approval in 1963 by Lord Wheatley in the case of *Burnett,*[33] a psychopathically hot-tempered man who murderously attacked both his mistress and her husband when they showed signs of becoming reconciled.[34]

It seemed likely that the English defence of diminished responsibility would follow the course pre-ordained for it by the Scottish case-law. The Attorney General had stipulated in the Parliamentary debates on the Homicide Bill, that the chosen wording of section 2 was intended "to bring English law into line with the Scottish doctrine, and not to go further than that".[35] *Spriggs*[36] gave the Court of Appeal its first opportunity to settle the issue. There prosecuting counsel contended that because the defendant had a high intelligence quotient he could not be suffering from an abnormality of mind despite medical evidence that the defendant lacked ability to control his emotions. In summing up, the judge gave no ruling on these conflicting submissions but simply left it to the jury to say whether they were satisfied that the accused came within the statutory definition. It is quite likely that the jury were influenced by prosecuting counsel's contention when they convicted the accused. Nonetheless, the Court of Appeal, pursuing a course of non-interference as regards the terms of the Act, held that the trial judge had taken a proper course of action.

In *Byrne* the trial judge directed the jury as to the meaning of section 2 in substantially the same terms as those urged by counsel for the prosecution in *Spriggs*; that is, that difficulty or even inability of an accused person to exercise will-power to control his physical acts could not amount to such abnormality of mind as substantially impaired his mental responsibility. The accused was a sexual psychopath who had strangled a young woman and then mutilated her body. On appeal, Lord Parker in the Court of Criminal Appeal ruled that "abnormality of mind" means

> A state of mind so different from that of ordinary human beings that the reasonable man would term it abnormal. It appears to us to be wide enough to cover the mind's activities in all its aspects, not only the perception of physical acts and matters and the ability to form a rational judgment as to whether an act is right or wrong, but also the ability to exercise will-power to control physical acts in accordance with that rational judgment. The expression "mental responsibility for his acts" points to a consideration of the extent to which the accused's mind is answerable for his physical acts which must include a consideration of the extent of his ability to exercise will-power to control his physical acts".[37]

At last irresistible impulse was admitted into English law although *via* the defence of diminished responsibility. This route has led to one important difference. It is not necessary that the impulse on which the defendant acted should be found by the jury to be irresistible; it is sufficient if the difficulty which the defendant experienced in controlling it was substantially greater than would be experienced in like circumstances by an ordinary man, not suffering from mental abnormality.[38] This view has been approved in *Simcox*[39] and *Lloyd*.[40] The result in *Byrne* is in keeping with modern psychiatric knowledge[41] and with the opinion of the Royal Commission on Capital Punishment (1949-53) which found[42] that

> Since a psychopath would not ordinarily be held to suffer from a disease of the mind, or..from mental deficiency, it would not be open to the courts to find them irresponsible, either under the McNaghten Rules in their present form or if the law were amended in the way we have suggested..In our view, however, the available evidence justifies the conclusion that *in many cases the responsibility of psychopaths can properly be regarded as diminished*.[43]

Aware of the philosophical conundrum on which the defence of irresistible impulse had foundered, Lord Parker in *Byrne* acknowledged that

> There is no scientific measurement of the degree of difficulty which an abnormal person finds in controlling his impulses. These problems, which in the present state of medical knowledge are scientifically insoluble, the jury can only approach in a broad, common-sense way.[44]

Criticism on this ground quickly followed on the heels of *Byrne*, Lady Wooton arguing that it is not possible to get inside another man's skin to assess the strength of his impulses or his ability to have acted otherwise than as he did.[45] Wooton is of the view that the state of a man's knowledge or intellect is much more easily tested than the state of his will[46] but as Hart points out[47]

> A man's knowledge is surely as much, or as little, locked in his breast as his capacity for self control. Questions about the latter indeed may often be more difficult to answer than questions about a man's knowledge; yet in favourable circumstances if we know a man well and can trust what he says about his efforts or his struggles to control himself we may have just as good ground for saying 'Well he just could not do it though he tried' as we have for saying 'He didn't know that the pistol was loaded'. And we sometimes may have good general evidence that in certain conditions, eg. infancy or a clinically definable state, such as depression after childbirth, human beings are unable or less able than the normal adult to master certain impulses.

Hart asserts that the philosophical arguments pitch the case too high: they are supposed to show that the question whether a man could have acted differently is in principle unanswerable and not merely that in law courts we do not usually have clear enough evidence.[48] In any event, the law's concern is with establishing "moral certainty" and not metaphysical certainty.[49] The difficulties arise from the nature of psychopathy which the Gowers Commission described as "one of the most obscure and intractable problems we have to consider".[50] Although the Royal Commission felt "that the concept of psychopathic personality is a necessary and legitimate one"[51] it acknowledged that "the question whether a psychopath should be regarded as criminally responsible for his actions is one of great difficulty".52

This view is seconded by Lady Wooton who says that

The psychopath is a critical case for those who would retain a distinction between the responsible and the irresponsible..[and that]..the psychopath makes nonsense of every attempt to distinguish the sick from the healthy delinquent by the presence or absence of a psychiatric syndrome, or by symptoms of mental disorder which are independent of his objectionable behaviour.53

Surely this is an argument in favour of dealing with the psychopath *via* the defence of diminished responsibility which indicates reduced culpability, as opposed to through the medium of the insanity defence which signifies blamelessness and whose outcome is a technical acquittal. Further arguments in favour of this course of action are firstly, the fact that most psychiatrists view psychopathy as a personality disorder rather than as a mental illness and secondly, the fact that the Butler Committee has taken the view that it is non-curable54 and therefore, that prison is a preferable receptacle to a mental hospital.55

After a brief flurry of discussion following *Byrne*, criticism of the admission of irresistible impulse waned. Over a century's conflict about the recognition of irresistible impulse as a species of insanity ended with one judgment. The Homicide Act and particularly the decision in *Byrne* appear to have effected a reconciliation between the legal and psychiatric conceptions of insanity. Norrie describes the acceptance of irresistible impulse as "an intellectual fudge between the legal and the psychiatric categories".56 The end result was "the partial acceptance of the psychiatric concept with regard to murder through the 1957 Act, albeit on the law's terms".57

States of Automatism

In Chapter One I have examined the widening of the concept of disease of the mind in the McNaghten Rules in the interest of public protection and the concomitant erosion of the defence of automatism by the English judiciary. The recognition of epilepsy (*Sullivan*),[58] sleep-walking (*Burgess*)[59] and hyperglycaemia (*Hennessy*)[60] as species of insanity has been most controversial. As Mackay has stated "[t]here is an argument that the Rules were never intended to encompass cases of automatism".[61] Furthermore, it is plainly an affront to common sense to label the diabetic, the sleep-walker and the epileptic as insane. A combination of stigma and the mandatory indefinite hospitalisation which followed a finding of insanity has led many of these defendants to plead guilty rather than be labelled insane.[62] In the case of murder, diminished responsibility with its wide powers of disposal has, since 1957, acted as a safeguard in these cases. In the recent case of *Campbell* [63] a retrial was ordered after medical evidence was given that the defendant would suffer seizures when excited or aroused, which were capable of founding a diminished responsibility defence. The Defendant had been convicted of murdering a female hitch-hiker. Morris and Blom-Cooper[64] cite the cases of *Brian George Candy,*[65] *William Reynolds,*[66] *William Henry Abernathy,*[67] *Rodney William Bailey*[68] and *Stanley Lister*[69] as instances where epileptics succeeded in raising the defence of diminished responsibility. The sentence imposed in these cases varied from life imprisonment to a hospital order. They also describe the case of *Richard William Bryant* (age 79), a Naval pensioner, who strangled his wife with a dressing gown cord at home. They were devoted to each other. On 23/3/1961 at Hampshire Assizes, Bryant was found not guilty of murder but guilty of manslaughter under section 2, after doctors testified that he suffered from arteriosclerosis. Mr Justice Elwes made a hospital order with restrictions for twelve months under sections 60 and 65 of the Mental Health Act, 1959.[70] It is interesting to compare the outcome of this case with that of *Kemp* whose arteriosclerosis led to a finding of insanity (rather than automatism). The indefinite committal which followed is the equivalent of a hospital order with restrictions without limit of time.[71] The decision in *Rabey*[72] that the defendant's dissociative state caused by the ordinary stresses and strains of life, merited a finding of insanity, has been somewhat less controversial (this case is discussed in more detail in Chapter One). Although not described as "dissociation" similar states have, in the past, also led to successful diminished responsibility defences. Morris and Blom-Cooper recount the cases of *Rosalia Garofalo,*[73] *Albert Houghton,*[74] *Alec Taylor Lawrence,*[75] *Edmund William Barber*[76] and

Reginald James Bruce[77] where emotional stress led to a successful diminished responsibility plea. More recently in *Eeles* the terminology of dissociation was deployed[78] when a 36-year-old man was tried for shooting dead a family of three who had made his life a living hell. The family, two of them with a history of mental trouble, were said to have tormented neighbours for years with insults, arguments, late-night record playing and banging on doors. *Eeles* was jailed for three years after a jury found him not guilty of murder but guilty of manslaughter by reason of diminished responsibility.[79]

The harsh result in *Burgess* has been ameliorated in England by the Criminal Procedure (Insanity and Unfitness to Plead) Act 1991, which provides for discretionary disposal of the criminally insane. However there is no possibility of discretionary disposal for insane murderers. Undoubtedly therefore, there is a continuing need for the discretionary disposal consequences which accompany the diminished responsibility defence, to protect the epileptic, the diabetic and the sleep-walker[80] who kill, from the "double-edged acquittal"[81] which follows a finding of insanity in the case of murder. Clearly the defence of diminished responsibility has, in these cases, bridged the gap between a verdict of murder (resulting in either the death penalty or today, the mandatory life sentence) and an insanity verdict (whose consequence in murder is mandatory indefinite committal). With the restriction of the defence of automatism due to the expansion of "disease of the mind", the diminished responsibility defence has availed those murderers who wished to avoid the stigma of an insanity verdict and its inflexible disposal consequences. As the above cases illustrate, the wide disposal consequences associated with diminished responsibility have permitted a more just and humane outcome in cases where indeterminate hospitalisation might not be perceived to be necessary or deserved. For this reason it may be concluded that diminished responsibility has remedied several defects in the McNaghten Rules: Not only abnormalities that fail to reach the standard of McNaghten madness have come within the defence of diminished responsibility, but the defence has attracted defendants who *do* fall within the Rules, as a result of its ability to respond more accurately to their individual needs.

By giving expression to the medical view of epilepsy, arteriosclerosis and dissociation (these are not regarded as amounting to medical insanity nor as needing indefinite hospitalisation) it is tempting to infer the evolution of a happy partnership between law and medicine, exemplified in the above cases. This has also arisen because the defence is propitious to psychiatric testimony on almost any abnormality of mind that might substantially impair responsibility. The defence's potential as a forum for psychiatric testimony will now be addressed.

Premenstrual Tension

Attempts to have premenstrual tension (P.M.T.) recognised as a complete defence to criminal charges have been unsuccessful in both England[82] and the United States.[83] In English law, therefore, P.M.T. is only relevant to mitigation of sentence. In murder cases, where there is no discretion as to sentence, P.M.T. has been held to amount to an abnormality of mind for the purpose of the diminished responsibility defence. Treating the condition as a mental abnormality that may lead to a diminished responsibility verdict if responsibility is substantially impaired, has bridged the wide gulf between a conviction of murder and the defence of insanity. It has also paved the way for the reception of medical evidence on abnormalities of mind produced by bodily malfunctions and provided a just disposition for the defendant whose abnormality has produced an alien character or proclivities.

      The premenstrual syndrome (P.M.S.) has a variety of symptoms including headache, breast swelling and tenderness, abdominal bloating, weight gain, acne, asthma, constipation, cravings for sweet or salty foods, tension, irritability, aggressiveness, lethargy, anxiety and depression,[84] which occur in the same phase in each menstrual cycle, followed by a symptom-free phase.[85] These symptoms appear several days before the onset of menstruation and reach peak intensity during the last four days of the pre-menstruation period or the first four days of actual menstruation, the paramenstruum.[86] Despite disagreement amongst the medical profession about the definition of P.M.S.[87] (particularly what symptoms it embraces and the precise limit of the paramenstruum), its aetiology[88] and treatment[89], the evidence advanced in favour of the condition is convincing. As Bancroft observes "behind this controversy is a clinical problem of some magnitude".[90]

As well as increased propensity to recidivism during the paramenstruum,[91] Dalton has discovered that psychiatric disabilities have been exacerbated by P.M.S.. An analysis of hospital admissions for acute psychiatric illness showed that 46% of female patients were admitted during their paramenstruum. Women suffering from P.M.T. constituted 53% of the attempted suicides, 47% of those admitted for acute depression and 45% of those admitted for schizophrenia.[92]

P.M.S. has now been accepted as being an abnormality of mind within section 2 of the Homicide Act, in three English cases. In *R v Craddock*,[93] a woman of thirty years stabbed to death a barmaid after a fight broke out in the pub where she worked. She was convicted of manslaughter due to diminished responsibility brought on by P.M.S., after medical evidence was tendered that her uncontrolled disruptive behaviour, which had resulted in thirty previous convictions, could be treated by daily injections of progesterone. The case was set back to allow a period of treatment, during which the defendant's behaviour improved considerably. Mr James Miskin, Recorder of London, made a probation order of three years (the maximum possible), with a condition that Craddock should receive such treatment as prescribed.

In *R v English*[94] a thirty seven year old woman was convicted of diminished responsibility manslaughter owing to P.M.S., after she killed her lover by crushing him against a lamp post with her car. English had no previous convictions and no history of uncontrolled violence. Psychiatric evidence was offered to the effect that P.M.S. follows from post natal depression in about 90% of cases. English had suffered from this condition in 1966. Evidence was given that the defendant's sterilisation in 1971 had increased the severity of P.M.S.. P.M.S. combined with a long period of food abstinence was apparently responsible for her violent, irritable and impulsive behaviour. Dr Katharina Dalton, who had also found Craddock to be suffering from P.M.S., gave evidence that P.M.S. is a disease of the body and therefore a disease of the mind because the upset bodily metabolism upsets the mental processes. She was supported in this by Dr Hamilton, a consultant psychiatrist at Broadmoor. English was banned from driving for one year and given a conditional discharge for a year. Her "treatment" was to see that she ate regularly and avoided alcohol.

In 1988 the Court of Appeal substituted a verdict of manslaughter on the grounds of diminished responsibility, after Dr Dalton tendered evidence that the defendant had been suffering from a conjunction of premenstrual tension and post-natal depression when she had killed her mother.[95]

A recent commentator has advocated treating P.M.S. as a condition justifying an acquittal on the grounds of automatism.[96] Because P.M.S. arises from a condition *internal* to the sufferer this approach is unlikely to commend itself to the courts. (In *Burgess* and *Hennessy* sleep-walking and hyperglycaemia were held to amount to a disease of the mind because of their internal origin). Nevertheless, he has proposed that there should be an acquittal on the grounds of automatism where the effect of the state of disequilibrium is to create an alien character or proclivities and he lists involuntary intoxication, post traumatic stress disorder, battered woman's syndrome, severe premenstrual tension, hyperglycaemia, hypoglycaemia and epilepsy, as conditions which should exclude liability on these grounds.[97] However, the law's position is that automatism is limited to *unconscious* involuntary action. (On the other hand it cannot be asserted with confidence that much of the purposive automatic behaviour which has led to a verdict of automatism can be viewed as being unconscious. As Fingarette has noted "'unconsciousness.' 'automatic,' and 'involuntary' - often are plainly inaccurate as descriptions of the crucially relevant features of the behaviour. These terms are usually used, in effect, as mere code words to trigger a desired legal outcome").[98] The diminished responsibility defence can be used, as it has been in the case of P.M.T., as a medium for dealing with those cases where *mens rea* is present, sparing the defendant from a verdict of murder and the mandatory life sentence. Even where *mens rea* is absent "the plea of diminished responsibility..is a more appropriate vehicle for consideration of questions surrounding volition and the exercise of will-power than any newly formulated defense giving rise to a special verdict".[99]

Because of social defence considerations Mackay is loath to see all cases of automatism qualify for an outright acquittal, irrespective of cause.[100] The writer would agree. The implications of treating P.M.S. as a species of automatism should be obvious: If one is to classify *any* bodily disease where the metabolism upsets the mental processes as meriting an acquittal on the ground of automatism then the floodgates are likely to be opened. There are probably many cases where high testosterone levels in men account for outbursts of violence. The implications of P.M.T. as a complete defence are evident from Dalton's discovery that 49% of 156 newly committed London prisoners had committed their crime in the paramenstruum (i.e. four days before and the first four days of menstruation).[101] As is evident from the discussion of the defence of automatism in Chapter One, the courts have been anxious to impose constraints on the numbers who can plead it.

The feminist objection to recognition of P.M.T. as a legal excuse is that, while on the surface, appearing to give recognition to the real and painful experience of an individual woman, P.M.T. as a legal defence simply replicates traditional male stereotypes of women as "victims of their biology"[102] or as likely to commit offences during the paramenstruum.[103] There is also a danger that the existence of the insanity defence leads to the stereotyping of all mentally ill persons as a threat to public safety yet this is not a valid reason for abolishing the insanity defence. A second feminist argument is that the *law* is more predisposed to explore psychiatric explanations for women's behaviour.[104] However this objection is not one which can be levied at the diminished responsibility defence itself. This is not a gender specific defence but focuses on mental abnormality in both sexes. (The connection between P.M.T. and psychiatric ill-health has been documented by Clare).[105] In the context of the diminished responsibility defence, which has emerged as a forum for psychiatric testimony, it cannot be said that the courts are any less disposed to explore psychiatric explanations for men's behaviour.

Taylor and Dalton concede that science may never be able to say that a criminal act was actually *determined* by an individual's hormonal condition rather than merely influenced by it and that it is presently impossible to determine precisely, to what degree conduct may be influenced by the premenstrual syndrome.[106] This is not a stumbling block to recognition of P.M.T. within the defence of diminished responsibility, as causation is not a feature of the diminished responsibility defence. Rather, diminished responsibility *per se* is a status that reduces liability to punishment. Admittedly, large numbers might have to be excused full liability to punishment (Dalton estimates that the incidence of P.M.T. may be as high as 40%)[107] but surely a diminished responsibility defence is more appropriate than an acquittal on the grounds of automatism. Through a diminished responsibility verdict treatment can be provided *via* a hospital order and if it is felt that there is some measure of blameworthiness involved a prison sentence can be imposed to reflect that level of culpability.

Allowing medical testimony on P.M.T. has paved the way for the reception of medical evidence on bodily malfunctions which affect normal mental processes. Despite a century's reluctance to listen to medical developments on insanity, they are now deferred to in the context of the diminished responsibility plea. Nowhere is this more obvious than in the recent case of *Hobson*[108] where the murder conviction of a battered woman was quashed. She had stabbed her abusive and alcoholic partner to death during an argument. A retrial was ordered on the grounds that there was fresh evidence that she might have been suffering from battered woman syndrome which had, since the time of the trial, entered the standard British classification of mental diseases and which was thus capable of founding the defence of diminished responsibility. The inference is irresistible from *Hobson* that if the psychiatric profession describes a condition as a mental abnormality then it must be a mental abnormality. However it has taken a considerable length of time for this position to become settled.

The Medical Viewpoint

R v Walden,[109] a case decided in the early years of the defence, revealed initial uncertainty regarding the scope of abnormality of mind and a judicial reluctance to recognise the medical view of mental abnormality. There Hilberry asked[110]

> Suppose the jury ask what they are to understand by abnormality of mind. If the judge can't tell them we are getting very near to trial by doctor. What on earth does 'substantially impaired his mental responsibility' mean? Does anyone know?
> Counsel: No except for the medical men.

It was not until *Byrne's* case that the Court of Appeal at last delivered a considered interpretation.[111] There the meaning of "abnormality of mind" was clarified by Lord Parker who held that it meant

A state of mind so different from that of ordinary human beings that the reasonable man would term it abnormal. It appears to us to be wide enough to cover the mind's activities in all its aspects, not only the perception of physical acts and matters and the ability to form a rational judgment as to whether an act is right or wrong, but also the ability to exercise will-power to control physical acts in accordance with that rational judgment.[112]

By recognising more than the merely cognitive impairments embraced by the McNaghten Rules, this decision suggested that the medical view of abnormality of mind would prevail. However, what kinds of causes are "inherent", what kinds of trauma will count as "injury", and what is meant by "disease" remain somewhat unclear.[113] It has been said that variations in the weight given to the parenthetic limitation on "abnormality of mind" have been able to continue throughout the history of the section because of the courts' failure to elucidate the meaning of the parenthesis.[114]   As late as 1975, the Butler Committee on Mentally Abnormal Offenders described "abnormality of mind" as "an extremely imprecise phrase", even as limited by the parenthesis and defined by the Court of Appeal in *Byrne*.[115] They found that evidence is often stretched due to the humanity of the medical profession so that psychopathic personality, reactive depressions and dissociated states are testified to arise from "inherent causes" within the section.[116] Although some psychiatrists have used section 2 creatively, it seems that others have been less aware of the section's potential for flexible reading.[117] Thus the fate of a number of people charged with murder since 1957, has turned on the robustness and sophistication of their expert witness.[118]

Ambitious witnesses, like Dr Katherina Dalton who has testified to the existence of P.M.T. in a number of killings, have widened the ambit of the defence and permitted a more humane outcome in deserving circumstances. According deference to the medical view of abnormality of mind has led to the evolution of a happy partnership between the legal and medical professions on the issue of diminished responsibility. This is exemplified by the general practice of accepting the plea of guilty to diminished responsibility manslaughter, where unanimous medical evidence is forthcoming[119] thus saving a considerable amount of court time and expense and avoiding unnecessary distress to the defendant and relatives of the deceased.

Although the Butler Committee's preference was for abolition of the mandatory life sentence and the defence of diminished responsibility,[120] in the event of retention of the mandatory life sentence they wished to keep section 2 *in its essentials* but with an improvement in the wording.[121] They proposed substituting "abnormality of mind (whether arising from a condition of arrested or retarded development of mind or any inherent causes or induced by disease or injury)" with a requirement of mental disorder as defined in section 4 of the Mental Health Act 1959. The Butler Committee was concerned to reconcile the meaning of mental abnormality with the meaning of mental disorder in civil committal procedures. Simplifying the psychiatrist's function was therefore a concern, although the inference seems irresistible that they desired to retain the present position which allows the medical view of mental abnormality to prevail. However the Criminal Law Revision Committee was concerned that section 4 might be more restrictive of medical testimony than section 2(1). The Committee was concerned about cases such as the depressed father who kills a severely handicapped subnormal child or a morbidly jealous person who kills his or her spouse[122] and consulted the medical advisers to the Department of Health and Social Security who did not share these concerns.[123] Section 4 of the Mental Health Act 1959 defines mental disorder as "mental illness, arrested or incomplete development of mind, psychopathic disorder, and any other disorder or disability of mind". "[A]ny other disorder or disability of mind" in section 4 is extremely wide and like mental disorder, has no limiting parenthesis akin to section 2 of the Homicide Act, 1957.[124] One concern is that some psychiatrists might be emboldened to identify transient disorders of mind for the purpose of diminished responsibility defences, that because of anxious respect for the language of the parenthesis, they would not formerly have felt able to advance as relevant.[125] Some prosecutors and judges might feel similarly liberated.[126] However, given that according the medical profession autonomy in the working of section 2 has proved satisfactory, it should not be assumed that this change in the wording of the diminished responsibility defence would lead to an unsavoury redefinition of the boundary between murder and manslaughter by medical witnesses.[127] It might, however, lead to inconsistency in the operation of the defence.

The requirement of "medical or other evidence" of a mental disorder within section 4(1) of the Mental Health Act, 1959 may mean that medical evidence would not always be necessary.[128] This would threaten to undermine the medical profession's authority in the working of the diminished responsibility defence.[129] Medical evidence should always be a pre-requisite to a finding of diminished responsibility if the McNaghten conflict is to be resolved.

Intoxication

The application of the diminished responsibility defence to an abnormality of mind caused partly by intoxication has been much less satisfactory than its application to the conditions described above. In the case of a combined diminished responsibility/intoxication defence the rules on diminished responsibility are swept aside and the policy considerations that underlie the law on intoxication take precedence. These considerations, as stated in the Law Commission's Consultation Paper on Intoxication,[130] are that it would be

> Too dangerous, or too unjust, in terms of unmerited acquittals or failure to control drunkards who threaten their fellow citizens, to allow evidence of intoxication to be taken into account in determining mens rea.

Although the diminished responsibility plea was frequently allowed in cases of drunkenness in nineteenth century Scotland, often in the absence of any evident mental abnormality other than the state of intoxication itself, this approach was abandoned in 1921 in favour of the rule in *Beard's*[131] case. This rule, which has been approved more recently in *Majewski,*[132] allows intoxication to negate *mens rea* only in crimes requiring a specific intent. The introduction of diminished responsibility into English law brought with it a new challenge: how to deal with the offender who pleaded both diminished responsibility and intoxication at the time of the offence. Was the Scottish approach to be followed or could a more lenient formula be worked out? The legal position where diminished responsibility and intoxication combine has only recently been settled by the judiciary and its evolution has been lengthy and fraught.

In Scotland following *H.M. Advocate v Dingwall*,[133] an abnormal mental state falling short of legal insanity which was induced by intoxication was capable of giving rise to a verdict of diminished responsibility. There Lord Deas treated the defendant's repeated attacks of *delirium tremens* as one of the relevant considerations in allowing the jury to return a verdict of culpable homicide instead of murder. Lord Deas took the same course of action in *H.M. Advocate v Granger*[134] where the defendant was charged with the murder of a police constable while suffering from *delirium tremens*, directing the jury that

> Although the jury might not consider the panel in the present case to have been insane, it did not follow that they must convict him of the capital offence. He would say to them, as he said to the jury in Dingwall's case at Aberdeen, that a weak or diseased state of mind, not amounting to insanity, might competently form an element to be considered in the question between murder and culpable homicide.[135]

A succession of nineteenth century Scottish cases showed that henceforth, intoxication by itself could reduce a verdict of murder to one of culpable homicide: In *H.M. Advocate v Margaret Roberts or Brown*[136] an old woman was charged with the murder of two infant grandchildren by placing them on a fire of live coals after having taken a considerable quantity of alcohol. The medical evidence negatived the defence of insanity. It was established that she was of intemperate habits and became violent when intoxicated, although she was fond of her grandchildren. She told the doctor who saw her after the occurrence that she thought something had entered the house, and that she had struggled with it. Lord McLaren directed the jury that if they were of the opinion that the accused was watching the children with no evil intention, and that under the influence of some momentary hallucination induced by drunkenness she had placed the children on the fire, they were entitled to return a verdict of culpable homicide. This they did (unanimously) and a sentence of ten years' penal servitude was pronounced upon the accused.

However in the case of *Thomas Ferguson*,[137] there was evidence of weakness of mind caused by previous intemperance. The accused was, in fact, sober at the time he had stabbed his wife. Although Lord Deas referred to *Dingwall* and to the principle adumbrated therein, he pointed out that this was a much more difficult case to which to apply that principle and law. *Dingwall* was habitually a much kinder husband than the prisoner, and there was neither the deliberate preparation for the act, nor the ferocity in its execution which the prisoner's act manifested here.[138] The jury duly found the accused guilty of murder, although with a recommendation to mercy on account of being a man of weak mind.

John McDonald[139] had killed his wife and another man by beating them with a piece of wood and a piece of iron. The defence pleaded temporary insanity brought on by alcoholism and further submitted that at the highest, the jury could only place the crime within the category of culpable homicide. The Lord Justice Clerk held that

> While drunkenness is no excuse, yet if the means adopted were not of themselves likely to lead to bad results, and if there was no malice aforethought here, then the fact that the man was in a drunken state may be considered in determining the question between murder and culpable homicide. I should have had great difficulty in saying that, but for the fact that I see from the full and clear citation of authorities which we have had, that some of my brethren have taken that view in some similar cases. I have some doubts whether or not it is consistent with principle, but if you will keep clearly in view that drunkenness is no excuse for what occurred here, then I am not inclined to set my own opinion against that of the experienced Judges to whom I have referred, and to debar you from considering whether a crime committed in this drunken state, without motive and without preconceived malice, although murder, in the strict sense of the law, may not be viewed by you as falling within the category of a case of aimless violence not absolutely murderous.[140]

Again in *H.M. Advocate v David Kane,*[141] the jury were told by the same Lord Justice Clerk that they could take the accused's intoxicated condition into account in considering whether the killing of his wife was murder or culpable homicide.

H.M. Advocate v John Graham[142] involved the trial of a defendant who had shot his wife after a bout of drinking. Evidence was led of his devotion to her, that he was a man of soft temperament and that he was subject at times to fits which left him unconscious as a result of having been struck by lightning when a young man. The Lord Justice Clerk left the issue of culpable homicide to the jury, illustrating the comparisons with

Dingwall's case.

In England the old and rigid rule that voluntary drunkenness cannot be taken into account if it does not produce a state of insanity (albeit temporary[143]), was gradually relaxed in a series of cases spanning the nineteenth century, culminating with *D.P.P. v Beard*. Here the House of Lords ruled that drunkenness is a defence to crimes of specific intent only (as distinct from crimes of basic intent), provided it prevents the accused from having that intent. *Beard* has since been followed in *R v Majewski*. However, in the case of murder an alternative charge of manslaughter (a crime of basic intent) will lie, to which intoxication is no defence. The similarities between the *Beard* approach and the Scottish approach are so striking that it is arguable that *Beard* was yet another case where diminished responsibility was partially accepted in English law. One may look at the English approach to intoxication as creating a defence in cases of murder (a crime of specific intent) which will result in a verdict of manslaughter (a basic intent crime) where the accused was so intoxicated as to be incapable of forming the specific intent required for murder. *Beard* was yet another example of judicial legislation intended to mitigate the severity of the law on murder. However I have failed to treat this as a precursor to the English defence of diminished responsibility as the "defence" component was not limited to murder but to all crimes of specific intent. Furthermore, *Beard* involves substantially more than simply whether the defendant had the specific intent required for his crime. The major part of the law propounded in *Beard* is taken up with constructing rules to ensure that the jury do not take intoxication into account in determining whether the defendant had the *mens rea* required for crimes of basic intent.[144] For identical reasons I treat the Californian diminished capacity defence (abolished in 1983[145]) as falling outside the remit of my discussion of diminished responsibility. The Californian diminished capacity defence was used to negate a *mens rea* element required by the definition of the offence,[146] allowing conviction for any lesser-included offence which does not require a particular mental element.[147] It was not aimed at establishing reduced responsibility as a ground for mitigation and it was not restricted to cases of murder.[148]

In the early years of the twentieth century the Scottish defence of diminished responsibility was restricted considerably, especially where intoxication formed part of the defence and the English approach to intoxication, as stated in *Beard*, seems to have found more favour with the Scottish judges. In *H.M. Advocate v Nicholas Page Campbell*[149] the accused was charged with the murder of his wife by beating her to death while in a state of intoxication. The medical evidence was to the effect that he was not insane but that he had at one time been injured in the head, and as a result he was abnormally susceptible to alcohol and abnormally violent when under its influence. The defence contended that the intoxicated condition of the accused at the time of the assault reduced the crime from murder to culpable homicide. The Lord Justice Clerk, Scott Dickson, approving *D.P.P. v Beard* as part of Scottish law, ruled that the accused was guilty of murder unless at the time of the assault he was, owing to drunkenness, in such a condition that he had not the intention and could not form the intention of doing serious injury to his wife. The jury found the accused guilty of culpable homicide rather than murder and he was sentenced to penal servitude for twelve years.

The Scottish defence of diminished responsibility was restricted further in *H.M. Advocate v Savage.*[150] The defendant was tried for the murder of a woman by cutting her throat with a razor. Evidence was led on behalf of the accused that at one time he had received an injury to his head and instances were given of his eccentric conduct on several occasions. Evidence was also led to the effect that he was in the habit of indulging to excess in alcohol and was constantly under its influence and that at times he also drank methylated spirits and that when under their influence he was violent and irresponsible. Witnesses also spoke of his being under the influence of methylated spirits or alcohol on the night of the murder.

The Lord Justice-Clerk, Alness, first stated that the Scottish doctrine of diminished responsibility must be applied with care and he then proceeded to delimit its precise scope

> There must be aberration or weakness of mind; that there must be some form of mental unsoundness; that there must be a state of mind which is bordering on, though not amounting to insanity; that there must be a mind so affected that responsibility is diminished from full responsibility to partial responsibility..And I think one can see running through the cases that there is implied..that there must be some form of mental disease.[151]

Not surprisingly the jury unanimously found the accused guilty of capital murder.

Beard and *Campbell* were approved some years later by Lord Justice General Normand who ruled that the crime of murder is not reduced to the crime of culpable homicide by the drunkenness of the accused, unless the drunkenness is such as to render the accused incapable of forming the intent to kill or to do serious injury at the time when the crime is committed.[152]

Carraher v H.M. Advocate[153] concerned a psychopathic man tried for murder by stabbing when drunk. The medical evidence stated that his psychopathy would be aggravated when intoxicated. In this case it seems that drunkenness was considered in isolation from the defendant's psychopathic personality, rather than in association with it, and the defendant was convicted of murder. On appeal, Lord Normand gave the same direction as he had given in *Kennedy*. As neither psychopathic personality nor intoxication short of negativing intention was sufficient to reduce a charge of murder to manslaughter, the defendant's appeal was dismissed.

When diminished responsibility was introduced in England, therefore, it seemed that intoxication would not afford a defence if Scottish law was followed. The case of *Di Duca*[154] gave the Court of Appeal its first opportunity to settle the issue. The defendant who was convicted of capital murder relied on the defence of diminished responsibility, arguing that the toxic effect of drink substantially impaired his responsibility. The judge directed the jury on the effect of drink on intent, without any reference to the effect of drink on diminished responsibility. On appeal the Court of Appeal held that it is "very doubtful" if the transient effect of drink, even if it does produce such a toxic effect on the brain, can amount to an "injury" within section 2 and evaded coming to a definite decision by ruling that in this case there was no evidence of abnormality of mind.

Not long after in *R v Dowdall*,[155] Donovan J. stated that if a normal person got drunk or drank to excess it would be no defence to say that he lost his self-control or that his self-control was diminished. The section in the Homicide Act dealing with diminished responsibility was not intended to be, nor was it, a charter for drunkards. He also directed the jury that if they accepted that the defendant was suffering from an abnormality of mind which substantially impaired his responsibility for the killing then they should find him guilty of manslaughter instead of murder. Two doctors had expressed the view that even if the defendant did not drink at all he would still suffer from an abnormality of mind, and the jury duly found him guilty of manslaughter under section 2.

Again in *R v Clarke and King,*[156] the Court of Appeal, although *obiter,* asserted that their substitution of a manslaughter verdict

> Must not be taken to be ruling that any abnormality of mind however slight and producing however little impairment will constitute a defence when that slight impairment is increased substantially by drink: that was a matter which remained to be considered on another occasion.[157]

The first authoritative pronouncement on the law where diminished responsibility and intoxication combine did not arrive until the decision of *Fenton*[158] where five medical witnesses agreed that the defendant was suffering from an abnormality of mind by virtue of his psychopathic personality, which had been aggravated by drink on the night of the killings. The jury later disclosed in response to an observation of the trial judge that they were unanimously of the view that the killings would not have occurred if the appellant had not had so much to drink. The judge, however, ruled that the effect of the alcohol consumed by the defendant was to be ignored since the effect of the alcohol did not amount to an abnormality of mind due to inherent causes. Accordingly, he directed the jury that they must convict of murder if satisfied that the combined effect of the factors other than alcohol was insufficient to amount to a substantial impairment in the mental responsibility of the defendant.

On appeal, the Court of Appeal held that self-induced intoxication cannot of itself produce an abnormality of mind due to inherent causes and that the trial judge was not guilty of a misdirection when he told the jury to ignore the effect of alcohol. It did, however, hold that a case may arise where the defendant proves such a craving for drink or drugs as to produce in itself an abnormality of mind within the meaning of section 2(1). Undoubtedly, the court had in mind the case of the alcoholic who cannot resist alcohol, as falling within the diminished responsibility defence. This issue was to recur some years later in *Tandy.*[159]

Not long afterwards *Turnbull,*[160] charged with murder by stabbing, was convicted of murder after the jury was directed that it was for them to decide, weighing the evidence, which was the main factor for the killing, the defendant's inherent defect of mind (due to psychopathy) or the effect of alcohol. This is an entirely different direction to that given by the trial judge in *Fenton* since it requires a causal connection between the defendant's abnormality of mind and the killing.[161] This is not a requirement of section 2 of the Homicide Act. On this view diminished responsibility *per se* would no longer be an exculpatory state as it is where intoxication is not in issue, unless the jury is satisfied that it caused the killing.[162] The trial judge also asked the jury "[h]ave the defence satisfied you that it is more probable than not that Turnbull would have acted as he had on this night even had he not taken drink?" thus abandoning the requirement of causation and asking a question which is by its very nature, unanswerable.

On appeal it was held that the jury had been properly directed, but then the Court of Appeal went on to hold that the defendant must show that his abnormality of mind substantially impaired his mental responsibility for his acts and omissions notwithstanding the effect of the alcohol in causing loss of self-control, which is the direction that was given in *Fenton*. On this approach the jury would have to be directed that the defence is made out only if the defendant has proved that he would have been of diminished responsibility in the absence of intoxicants.

Disregarding evidence of intoxication when deciding the issue of diminished responsibility gives expression to the principle underlying *Beard* and *Majewski* that a person who voluntarily chooses to take an intoxicant which causes him to cast off the restraints of reason, conscience and volition should not afterwards be permitted to rely on his self-induced incapacitation when harm is caused to others. The concern underlying *Turnbull* and *Fenton* is that it would be only too easy for a defendant both to claim and to succeed in a claim that his responsibility was diminished because of intoxication.[163] The result of giving effect to these policy considerations through the medium of the diminished responsibility defence is that juries will have to be directed to take intoxication into account for the purpose of deciding whether the defendant had the specific intent required for murder (in accordance with *Beard* and *Majewski*) and to exclude intoxication from consideration in deciding whether his responsibility was diminished. This approach is both inconsistent and unprincipled as it treats intoxication as relevant to one aspect of *mens rea* but not relevant to another (that of diminished responsibility).[164]

Further objections to the *Fenton* approach are the complexity that a hypothetical issue of this nature creates and the accompanying substantial risk of confusion and error on the jury's part. Although speaking of *Majewski*, the observations of the Law Commission that "it is difficult to think that it operates in practice other than by its detailed rules being substantially ignored"[165] and "[t]he strong possibility is, therefore, that the *Majewski* rule works only because it is not properly applied; and that juries deal with cases not by applying the full complexities of the rule, and asking the hypothetical questions that it seems to demand, but by a more simple approach"[166] are reservations that apply with equal force to a combined defence of intoxication and diminished responsibility. On a philosophical level one may object on the ground that an inquiry into the subjective mental state of a defendant can only be into his actual mental state and not into what that state might or would have been in different circumstances.[167]

In *Gittens*[168] the defendant who had been suffering from depression and had taken alcohol and drugs, murdered his wife and then raped and murdered his step-daughter. He sought to raise the defence of diminished responsibility. The jury were directed that they must decide whether the substantial cause of the appellant's conduct was due to abnormality of mind due to inherent causes or whether it was due to drink or drugs. On appeal, defence counsel contended that that was not the problem which the jury were required to decide under section 2(1) of the Homicide Act, 1957. Doubting whether *Turnbull* went as far as asking the jury to decide what was the substantial cause of the defendant's behaviour, the Court of Appeal held that the direction approved in *Turnbull*, taken as a whole, was correct but was not a direction which should be followed in the future. Instead the Court of Appeal approved the approach in *Fenton*, saying that since abnormality of mind induced by drink or drugs was not, generally speaking, due to inherent causes and was not, therefore, within section 2(1), the jury should consider whether the combined effect of other matters which did fall within the subsection amounted to such abnormality of mind as substantially impaired the defendant's mental responsibility.

So far the decision appears straightforward but Professor Smith's commentary on the case has added another layer of complexity to this area of the law when he claimed that

> If the jury are to ignore the effect of drink or drugs they necessarily have to answer a hypothetical question, or perhaps two such questions. If the defendant had not taken drink and killed would he, because of the inherent causes have been under diminished responsibility? It may be, however that the jury will be of the opinion that, if the defendant had not taken drink or drugs, he would not have killed at all. In that case, it appears that the defence would not be open.[169]

He concludes that the two questions for the jury in logical sequence are

> Have the defence satisfied you on the balance of probabilities that, if the defendant had not taken drink-
> (i) He would have killed as he in fact did? And
> (ii) He would have been under diminished responsibility when he did so?[170]

The requirement that the defendant prove that he would have killed in the absence of intoxicants formed no part of the *ratio* in *Gittens*. Presumably, it is the fact that diminished responsibility only arises as a defence where there has been a killing which has led Professor Smith to ask this question. Unfortunately, the true answer to Professor Smith's hypothetical question can never be conclusively proved as this is a situation that has never happened.[171] Its result is that the risk of jury confusion is compounded even further than under the *Fenton* approach.[172]

Admittedly the question may be relevant in the case of irresistible impulses, to the issue of the defendant's abnormality of mind in the absence of intoxicants and an inquiry into whether the defendant would have had an irresistible impulse to kill had he not taken drink or drugs may shed light on his probable mental condition in the absence of intoxicants.[173] However, in other cases such as mental illness or mental retardation this question gives us no insight into the defendant's likely state of mind in the absence of intoxicants and the jury is likely to answer it in the negative, denying the defence of diminished responsibility to an otherwise abnormal defendant with substantially impaired mental responsibility.[174]   Professor Smith's approach may thus involve the suspension of the diminished responsibility defence when a defendant cannot prove to the satisfaction of the jury that he would have killed in the absence of intoxicants.[175]

Nevertheless, Professor Smith's approach has been approved by the Court of Appeal in *R v Atkinson*.[176] In his commentary to this case Professor Smith acknowledges that the task of the jury in answering two hypothetical questions is far from simple and that the answers given must be somewhat speculative, but he concludes that the present policy of the law of ignoring evidence of voluntary intoxication renders hypothetical questions inevitable.

Professor Smith's commentary has arisen again for consideration in *Egan*. There the trial judge invited the jury to consider whether

> (1) Drink or abnormality was the cause of the killing
> (2) Drink produced a disinhibiting effect upon the defendant which caused him to kill when otherwise he might not have.

The defendant appealed *inter alia* on the ground that the judge erred in directing the jury that if they thought no one could tell whether the murder would have happened without the intoxication then the defendant had failed in his defence of diminished responsibility. Defence counsel contended that the approval in *Atkinson* of Professor J.C.Smith's commentary on *Gittens* was *obiter* and misguided and that his suggestions were irreconcilable with the ratio of *Gittens* itself, which was that the issue for the jury was not one of choice between causes or substantial causes of the killing but whether the abnormality of mind substantially impaired the defendant's mental responsibility.

The Court of Appeal in *Egan* held that far from being *obiter*, Professor Smith's questions were central to the court's decision in *Atkinson*. Furthermore, the court felt that his questions were "most appropriate and ought to be applied generally".[177] The court held that there was no misdirection by the trial judge and concluded that the judgments in *Gittens* and *Atkinson* should be regarded together as "representing the high authority on the troublesome subject of diminished responsibility where drink is a factor".[178] Unfortunately, words such as these fail to emphasise the responsibility of the law on intoxication for producing the present unsatisfactory state of affairs and one may be forgiven for thinking that the blame lies with the defence of diminished responsibility.[179]

It appears from *Tandy* that in the case of abnormality of mind arising from alcoholism alone, if the defendant has voluntarily chosen to take his first drink of the day he cannot maintain that the resulting abnormality is due to disease. In support of this view the trial judge asserted

> The choice [of the appellant whether to drink or not to drink on Wed March 5 1986] may not have been easy but..if it was there at all it is fatal to this defence, because the law simply will not allow a drug-user, whether the drug be alcohol or any other, to shelter behind the toxic effects of the drug which he or she need not have used.[180]

and later

> But clearly she did take drink on March 5, and if she did that as a matter of choice, she cannot say in law or in common sense that the abnormality of mind which resulted was induced by disease.[181]

The Court of Appeal approved this direction and stated that section 2(1) would not be available unless the defendant was a "chronic alcoholic" either with gross impairment of her judgement and emotional responses or where her drinking had become involuntary so that she was no longer able to resist the impulse to drink. Dismissing the appeal, the Court of Appeal noted that the defendant had chosen to drink vodka rather than her customary drink of cinzano and that she had been able to stop drinking although her supply of vodka was not exhausted.

McAuley describes as "suspect" the exclusion of individuals suffering from abnormality of mind due to drinking, where the initial consumption was voluntary.[182] He argues that if the logic of the analogous insanity rule is that the defendant has a good defence because his defect of reason was caused by a supervening illness, rather than the drinking that gave rise to the illness, it seems to follow that a *Tandy*-type defendant, whose abnormality of mind was similarly induced, should have a good defence of diminished responsibility notwithstanding the fact that the supervening illness was brought on by the voluntary consumption of alcohol.[183] Since it is clear that a defendant who drinks in order to get himself into a state in which he knows he will kill is guilty of murder if he kills in that state,[184] McAuley submits that there is no need for a special rule barring the defence in cases where the defendant's illness was triggered by voluntary intoxication.[185] It appears harsh to exclude alcoholics like *Tandy* since they will usually consume alcohol before withdrawal symptoms arise or become distressing.[186] The alcoholic who waits until they became intolerable, leading to involuntary drinking is arguably no less culpable and therefore no more entitled to a diminished responsibility defence than the alcoholic who drinks before the onset of withdrawal symptoms in order to avoid their effect.[187]

The judgment of the Court of Appeal in *Tandy* sets a very high standard for a diminished responsibility defendant to meet. As shown *above*, the psychopath is entitled to a diminished responsibility defence if he had substantial difficulty controlling his sadistic impulses. Why, therefore, should an alcoholic not be entitled to a defence of diminished responsibility if he had substantial difficulty controlling his impulse to drink?

The Criminal Law Revision Committee's 14th Report on Offences Against the Person[188] has recommended that "evidence of voluntary intoxication adduced in relation to a defence should be treated in the same way as evidence of voluntary intoxication adduced to negative the mental element", in order to rectify the difficulties occasioned by the present law on intoxication. The C.L.R.C. was, however, assuming the continued existence of the *Majewski* rule, so that by virtue of their recommendation, intoxication could be taken into account in determining whether the defendant was of diminished responsibility (which only applies to murder, a crime of specific intent) but could not be taken into account in relation to defences applying to an offence of basic intent. This would lead to unsatisfactory and inconsistent results, thus perpetuating the difficulties which at present pervade the law on intoxication and a preferable solution would be to follow the approach adopted by the High Court of Australia in *O'Connor*[189] whereby evidence of intoxication is treated like any other evidence in deciding whether a defendant had *mens rea*. A logical extension of this principle would be to treat intoxication as part of the relevant evidence in deciding the issue of diminished responsibility or any other criminal law defence.[190] The *O'Connor* approach which also applies in New Zealand, Hawaii and Indiana has proved satisfactory and its application in Australia has shown that the fears on which *Majewski* is based are unfounded.[191] However, this would not alter the Court of Appeal's requirement that an alcoholic defendant's initial consumption of alcohol be involuntary.

Arguably, the *Majewski* principle filters out the most deserving cases of an intoxication defence, and the assurance of a manslaughter conviction to those who kill without specific intent has the same practical result as a successful plea of diminished responsibility, making the criticisms voiced above merely academic. Theoretically, the difficulty which arises when hospitalisation is necessary may be overcome by transfer to hospital from prison of those in need of psychiatric treatment. In reality however, the waiting list is long and transfer may take years.[192] Furthermore, there are, undoubtedly, mentally abnormal murderers who, although intoxicated at the time of the killing, are deserving of a defence of diminished responsibility and who *do* have the specific intent required for murder when they kill.

The legal position of a defendant who is surreptitiously administered drink or drugs and who kills while suffering from diminished responsibility due to a combination of intoxicants and another abnormality of mind has yet to be settled. Will the defendant be required to prove that he would have killed in the absence of intoxicants or will he have the slightly less onerous burden of proving that he would have been of diminished responsibility without the influence of drink or drugs? The recent decision of the House of Lords in *Kingston* which has signalled a return to common law principles,[193] suggests that the principle underlying the defence of diminished responsibility may be given expression where involuntary intoxication has contributed in part to the defendant's abnormality of mind.

Because of the Legislature's failure to delimit the scope of the defence of diminished responsibility and the law's antagonism to evidence of intoxication, the elucidation of the law where intoxication and diminished responsibility occur concomitantly has been slow. The present position, requiring a defendant to prove that he would have killed even in the absence of intoxicants and that he would have been suffering from diminished responsibility regardless of their effect, is unsatisfactory for its complexity and the impossible question that it asks the jury. The requirement in the case of alcoholism alone, that the initial consumption of alcohol be involuntary, sets a very high standard for the defendant in a diminished responsibility trial to meet and is inconsistent with the standard of control expected of the psychopath. The problems discussed above arise from the nature of the present law on intoxication and the law's antagonism to the defendant who mounts a defence based on intoxication. These problems do *not* stem from any defect in the diminished responsibility defence, which works well in cases where intoxication is not involved. As the *Majewski* principle is accorded precedence where intoxication and diminished responsibility occur together, whatever solution is adopted to remedy the difficulties of a joint diminished responsibility/intoxication defence must have its origin in the law of intoxication.[194]

The above discussion reveals that, despite its hasty introduction, the operation of the diminished responsibility defence has been successful in all cases except where intoxication and diminished responsibility combine - where its only failing is that it is sacrificed to the supposed lesser evil of excluding evidence of intoxication or treating a defendant under its effects more harshly. In the course of demonstrating the merits of the defence, this Chapter has examined the diminished responsibility defence in relation to the other criminal law defences of automatism and insanity. In reality, however, the defence applies across a vast spectrum of human behaviour.

> An "abnormal state of despair" induced by the need to care for an imbecile child or by a diagnosis of cancer in a beloved relative, leading in each case to a "mercy killing"; "a reactive depressed state" associated with the breaking of an engagement or the discovery of unfaithfulness in a spouse; "mixed emotions of depression, disappointment or exasperation" causing a "lack of control" over the defendant' actions in similar circumstances; inability to hold down a job; even an attempt at suicide *after* the commission of the offence charged - all of these have been adduced as at least contributory evidence of diminished responsibility.[195]

Substantially Impaired Mental Responsibility

An aspect of the diminished responsibility defence which has not gone without criticism is the requirement of substantial impairment of mental responsibility. This requirement has led to a wealth of academic commentary, most of which has done nothing to elucidate its meaning.[196] This difficulty of interpretation stems from the fact that section 2 is elliptical "almost to the point of nonsense".[197] If as suggested by Griew,[198] the irreconcilable words "impaired..mental" and "responsibility" are forced apart, the section begins to make sense: He had an abnormality of mind (of appropriate origin). This had a substantial adverse effect upon one or more relevant functions or capacities (of perception, judgment, feeling, control).[199] In the context of the case this justifies the view that culpability is substantially reduced. The outcome is diminished liability: manslaughter.[200] Its elliptical nature explains the confusion in the House of Commons during the debates on the Homicide Bill and such expressions of discomfort as: "the Bill is just as far from clear to many of us who have been considering it for that considerable length of time".[201] Haste in passing this legislation undoubtedly hindered clarification of section 2 in Parliament, and is discussed in detail in Chapter Five *above*.

If the words are compacted together in a different form we end up with: his abnormality of mind is of such consequence in the context of this offence, that his legal liability for it ought to be reduced.[202] This is almost identical to what the judges who gave evidence to the Butler Committee, gleaned from the section:

> The defendant has shown recognisably abnormal mental symptoms and..in all the circumstances it would not be right to regard his act as murder in the ordinary sense; so it is open to the jury to bring in a verdict of manslaughter.[203]

If "mental responsibility" is a legal or a moral question then it follows that substantially impaired mental responsibility is for the jury to determine. This is what the Court of Appeal decided in *Byrne*. However in practice the psychiatric profession testify time and time again on the issue of substantial impairment of mental responsibility. According to Dell[204] defence counsel will not raise section 2 unless they have received positive testimony on this issue from one or more psychiatrists. Her study revealed not one case in which the defence lawyers were without a pre-trial report in which a psychiatrist said he thought responsibility was substantially diminished.[205]   Mitchell's recent survey has disclosed the criteria used by forensic psychiatrists in assessing responsibility. Some of these are cause for concern, such as the requirement of a link between abnormality and the killing (not a requirement of the defence) by some doctors. Furthermore he found that some doctors are influenced by the likely sentence imposed by the court, or the public interest.[206]   Although Mitchell gives no indication of how many, it seems that some psychiatrists are rewriting section 2 so as to require additional criteria to substantial impairment of responsibility. This was also evident in cases of battered spouse syndrome where some doctors considered the proportionality between the killer's response and the abuse suffered, although it is not clear whether this was treated as a pre-requisite to finding impairment of responsibility or abnormality of mind.

In practice therefore, it is the doctors who decide whether the defence can be attempted.[207]   It is also the doctors who decide whether the defence will succeed in the 85% of diminished responsibility cases where the medical evidence of diminished responsibility is unanimous or unchallenged by the prosecution and the court accepts the plea. And it is the doctors who dictate the success of the defence in those cases that reach the courts, by their undoubted influence on the jury's conclusion when they testify on the ultimate issue of substantially impaired mental responsibility.

Undoubtedly the "nonsensical quality of the statutory language"[208] (especially the requirement of substantial impairment of "mental responsibility") has created difficulty for the psychiatrist, a view endorsed by the Butler Committee on Mentally Abnormal Offenders.[209]   Similarly, Dell has found that "although the presence or absence of mental responsibility is not a medical matter, doctors grapple with it".[210]

Rather than devoting their attention exclusively to rewording the requirement of substantially impaired mental responsibility, the Butler Committee opted to reinforce the line between expert witness and jury. As said above, in the event of retention of the mandatory life sentence they wished to keep section 2 *in its essentials* but with an improvement in the wording. The wording they proposed[211] was

Where a person kills or is party to the killing of another he shall not be convicted of murder if there is medical or other evidence that he was suffering from a form of mental disorder as defined in s4 of the Mental Health Act 1959 and if, in the opinion of the jury, the mental disorder was such as to be an extenuating circumstance which ought to reduce the offence to manslaughter.

The Criminal Law Revision Committee, when reporting in 1980, agreed that the wording of section 2 is unsatisfactory.[212] However they expressed the reservation that the Butler Committee's rewording may in one respect be too lax.[213] Seeing as the judge would have to give some guidance to the jury as to what extenuating circumstances ought to reduce the offence, and in practice that means that the mental disorder has to be substantial enough to reduce the offence to manslaughter, they considered that the definition should be tightened up so as to include that ingredient upon which the jury would have to be directed to give them the necessary guidance.[214] Hence they suggested that "the mental disorder [should be] such as to be a substantial enough reason to reduce the offence to manslaughter".[215] Whether this would provide adequate guidance for a jury deciding a diminished responsibility case, will be discussed further *below*.

However a flaw in the wording is the words "in the opinion of the jury". Figures for 1986-8 suggest that 85% of diminished pleas are accepted by the prosecution and that a mere 15% are the subject of jury verdicts.[216] Hence it must be the case that judges in practice accept unanimous or unchallenged psychiatric evidence and do not allow such cases to go before the jury. Some provision allowing the judge to decide if the mental disorder is "a substantial enough reason to reduce the offence to manslaughter", is therefore necessary.[217] This has been embodied in Clause 56 of the Law Commission's Draft Criminal Code Bill:

(1) A person who, but for this section, would be guilty of murder is not guilty of murder if, at the time of his act, he is suffering from such abnormality as is a substantial enough reason to reduce his offence to manslaughter.
(2) In this section "mental abnormality" means mental illness, arrested or incomplete development of mind, psychopathic disorder, and any other disorder or disability of mind, except intoxication

(3) Where a person suffering from mental abnormality is also intoxicated, this section applies only where it would apply if he were not intoxicated.

The Butler Committee's reformulation has the effect of bringing "into sharper focus" the "true functions of the judge, the expert witness and the jury in the criminal trial".[218]   The jury would have to decide if the disorder should reduce the offence to manslaughter, a task akin to that suggested by the Royal Commission on Capital Punishment in 1953 in relation to the insanity defence and which was rejected by the D.C. Court of Appeals in *U.S. v Brawner*.[219]   Although the Butler reformulation has manifested a far superior mastery of the English language than the draftsmen of 1957, Professor Griew predicted that judges, having to operate the law in the revised form, would quickly become embarrassed by a difficulty in it that has, up to now, been kept partially concealed by the working of the section[220] - its failure to provide adequate guidance for the jury. Under the Homicide Act the jury is provided with no criterion for determining whether or not responsibility is substantially impaired. But as it stands, section 2 is so badly worded that it can be made to work better than its framers intended.[221]   This is because of "a benevolent conspiracy between the psychiatrist and the trial judge"[222] in the operation of the defence, which permits the psychiatrists to testify on the issue of impaired responsibility. The difficulty of the jury's task explains the courts' indulgent attitude to such testimony. This attitude was carried to extremes in the relatively recent Court of Appeal decision of *Campbell* where it was said that there was no *prima facie* evidence of diminished responsibility because the psychiatric witness "never addressed himself in his evidence to the final matter which would have to be proved by the defence..namely that the abnormality of mind was such as substantially to impair the mental responsibility of the appellant for his acts".[223]

The Law Commission's reformulation is to be preferred to that of Butler because of its failure to limit the expert's role. However, medical evidence should be a pre-requisite. Not only should the requirement of mental disorder give recognition to the psychiatric viewpoint but the issue of impaired responsibility should be framed so as to enable psychiatric testimony on this issue. Undoubtedly, it is the failure of the English Legislature to differentiate the roles of jury and expert witness which has contributed to the evolution of a successful partnership between legal and medical professions in the working of the diminished responsibility defence.

By remedying the limitations of the criminal law defences of automatism and insanity, diminished responsibility has emerged as a vehicle for humanely dealing with murderers when the circumstances surrounding the killing arouse strong feelings of sympathy and the defendant is not felt to merit the mandatory life sentence and the stigma of a murder conviction. The defence has also alleviated the pressure on the criminal law to recognise conditions like P.M.T. and Battered Woman Syndrome as exculpatory excuses resulting in an outright acquittal. There is a limit to the law's ability to recognise social and emotional pressures without denying its own rationale as a punitive mechanism relying on individual responsibility.[224] By siphoning off infanticide, killing during domestic strife and mercy killing into a category of crime with a less severe penalty than for murder and by presenting the issue in medical terms, the law has been able to maintain a punitive stance to the social problem, laced with an unthreatening show of compassion.[225] Undoubtedly the pragmatic manner in which section 2 operates can be regarded as one of its major strengths.[226]

The defence has also remedied several shortcomings of the McNaghten Rules. Its discretionary disposal consequences which provide a vehicle for responding to the individual defendant's needs has meant that defendants have chosen to plead diminished responsibility over insanity in order to avoid mandatory indefinite hospitalisation. The defence has also dealt with abnormalities of mind which failed to meet the standard of McNaghten madness and which would otherwise have led to the mandatory life sentence (or formerly capital punishment) because of the law's failure to recognise the abnormality in question as a wholly excusing condition.

The recognition of irresistible impulses as a species of diminished responsibility has ended more than a century of controversy over the McNaghten Rules and resolved the medico-legal conflict that pervaded discussions of the insanity defence. The resolution of this conflict stems from the deference that the diminished responsibility defence shows to the medical view of abnormality of mind. The psychiatrist's view is accepted in the 85% of cases where the judge accepts the medical testimony outright and the case does not go to trial. In the 15% of cases which are the subject of jury trial the defence has emerged as a forum for psychiatric testimony which is given greater credence than previously under the Rules. At the same time the court retains its seisin of the case.[227] In exceptional circumstances the case may still be sent to trial despite unanimous psychiatric evidence of mental abnormality.[228]   Dell found that 1.5% of cases went to trial because the judge or prosecution thought it appropriate for the issue to be decided by a jury, even though the medical evidence was unanimously in favour of a diminished responsibility finding.[229] The result has been the emergence of the legal and medical professions from a state of cold war to an entente cordiale. It is therefore not surprising that academics, lawyers and even the judiciary have called for the introduction of this defence into Irish law.[230] Yet an attempt to have diminished responsibility recognised by the judiciary as part of Irish law failed in *the People (DPP) v Joseph O'Mahony* [231] when the Irish Supreme Court held that the Homicide Act, 1957 was not declaratory of a common law principle. It seems likely that a defence of diminished responsibility may soon be introduced into Irish law [232] by the Government's Criminal Justice (Mental Disorder) Bill 1996 which has been discussed by the writer elsewhere.[233] Section 5 of the 1996 bill requires that the Jury/Special Criminal Court find that the accused

> Committed the act alleged against him
> was suffering at the time from a mental disorder and
> the mental disorder was not such as to justify a finding of not guilty by reason of mental disorder but was such as to substantially diminish his responsibility for the act.

Unlike the Butler Committee's proposed reformulation the proposed Irish diminished responsibility defence does not sharply delineate the expert and jury's functions. The definition of mental disorder in section 1 appears to be the psychiatrist's domain, but it would have been preferable if medical evidence had been stated as being a pre-requisite.[234]

Satisfaction with the English diminished responsibility defence has been such that it has entirely usurped the McNaghten Rules. Figures for 1993 show that while one homicide defendant was found insane, sixty two were found guilty of diminished responsibility manslaughter.[235] In 1994 no homicide defendant was found insane but sixty one were found guilty of diminished responsibility manslaughter.[236] This has led to almost a disappearance of the old McNaghten debate. As Hart has commented

> The change made by the introduction of diminished responsibility was both meagre and half-hearted. Nonetheless it marked the end of an era in the criticism of the law concerning the criminal responsibility of the mentally abnormal.[237]

Notes

1   In *Matheson* [1958] 42 Cr.App.R.116 the Court of Appeal decided that pleas of guilty to manslaughter under section 2 of the Homicide Act were not to be accepted by trial judges and that the issue had to be put to the jury even if the prosecution agreed that the defendant's responsibility was diminished and had no rebutting evidence to offer.

2   F.McAuley *Insanity, Psychiatry and Criminal Responsibility* [Dublin, 1993] p.160

3   *R v Din* [1962] 42 Cr.App.R.116

4   [1968] 1 All.E.R.386 at p.387

5   S.Spencer "Homicide, Mental Abnormality and Offence" in *Mentally Abnormal Offenders* [Toronto, 1984] p.97

6   *R v Vernage* [1982] Crim.L.R.598 p.599

7   N.Walker *Crime and Insanity in England*, Vol 1 [Edinburgh, 1968] p.161

8   S.Dell *Murder into Manslaughter* [Oxford, 1984] p.26

9   ibid p.28

10 House of Lords, *Report of the Select Committee on Murder and Life Imprisonment Vol. ii - Oral Evidence* part i, p.115

11 *Walton v R* [1978] 1 All E.R.542 p.543

12 [1982] 74 Cr.App.R.306

13 ibid p.311

14 ibid

15 [1960] 3 All E.R.1

16 ibid p.4

17 *R v Dix* [1982] 74 Cr.App.R.306 p.311

18 S.Spencer op cit p.96

19 For an illustration of the medical conditions which typically give rise to diminished responsibility verdicts see Power "Diminished Responsibility" [1967] 7 Med. Sci.& L.185 p.187

20 [1974] I.R.55

21 Excerpts of this lecture have been published by the Law Times [1927] Vol.164 p.384

22 Report and Minutes of Evidence, 8th day, p.287, quoted by Wooton *Social Science and Social Pathology* (London, 1959) p.249

23   J.Ll.J. Edwards "Social Defence and Control of the Dangerous Offender" [1968] C.L.P.23 p.48 instances this as one of the most frequently recorded symptoms of psychopathy.
24   [1958] Cr.App.R.145
25   [1959] Cr.App.R.167
26   [1946] J.C.108
27   ibid p.118
28   ibid p.117
29   [1909] 2 S.L.T.223
30   ibid p.224
31   [1945] J.C.55 pp.57 & 58
32   [1946] S.L.T.9
33   The Proceedings were reported only in the press
34   Details are given by N.Walker op cit p.156
35   H.C.deb 1956, Vol.561 p.321
36   [1958] 1 All E.R.300
37   [1960] 3 All E.R.1 p.4
38   Smith and Hogan (7th ed) (London, 1992) p.213
39   [1964] Crim.L.R.402 p.403
40   [1966] 1 All E.R.107 p.109
41   Insanity Defense Work Group "American Psychiatric Association Statement on the Insanity Defense" [1983] 140 Am.J.Psych.681 p.685
42   Report of the Royal Commission on Capital Punishment [1949-53] Cmd 8932 (London, 1953) para.401
43   Emphasis added
44   3 All E.R.1 p.5
45   Lady Wooton *Crime and the Criminal Law* (2nd ed) (London, 1981) p.78
46   Lady Wooton *Social Science and Social Pathology*, op cit p.230
47   H.L.A.Hart *Punishment and Responsibility* (Oxford ,1968) p.203
48   ibid
49   H.Fingarette *The Meaning of Criminal Insanity* (Berkley, 1972) p.83
50   Report of the Royal Commission on Capital Punishment 1949-53 op cit para.394
51   ibid
52   ibid para.398
53   Lady Wooton *Social Science and Social Pathology* op cit p.250
54   Report of the (Butler) Committee on Mentally Abnormal Offenders, Cmnd 6244 (London, 1975) para.5.34
55   ibid para.5.38
56   A. Norrie *Crime, Reason and History: A Critical Introduction to Criminal Law* (London, 1993) p.182
57   ibid
58   *R v Sullivan* [1983] 2 All E.R.673
59   *R v Burgess* [1991] 2 All E.R.769
60   *R v Hennessy* [1989] 2 All E.R.9
61   R.D.Mackay *Mental Condition Defences in the Criminal Law* (Oxford, 1995) p.66
62   Eg. Sullivan and Quick

63   *unreported* 25 Oct.1996, lexis
64   *A Calender of Murder: Criminal Homicide in England since 1957* (London, 1964)
65   ibid p.41
66   ibid p.83
67   ibid p.171
68   ibid p.173
69   ibid p.247
70   ibid p.178
71   S.Dell "Wanted: an Insanity Defence That can be Used" [1983] Crim.L.R.431 p.432
72   54 C.C.C.3d.1
73   Morris and Blom-Cooper op cit p.51
74   ibid p.54
75   ibid p.60
76   ibid p.80
77   ibid p.128
78   Glanville Williams *Textbook of the Criminal Law* (2nd ed) (London, 1983) p.674
79   See *The Times* 22 Nov 1978
80   The *obiter dictum* of Lord Lane in *R v Smith* [1979] 1 W.L.R.1445 suggests that
      sleep-walking will qualify for the defence of diminished responsibility
81   Described in these terms by Celia Wells "Whither Insanity?" [1983] Crim.L.R.787
      p.788
82   *R v Smith (Sandie)* [1982] Crim.L.R.531
83   *People v Santos* No.1KO46229 Crim.C.T., N.Y., Nov 3 1982
84   R.A.Diliberto "Premenstrual Stress Syndrome Defence: Legal, Medical and Social
      Aspects" 33 Med.Trial Tech.Q.351 at p.352
85   Taylor and Dalton "Premenstrual Syndrome: A New Criminal Defense?" (1983) 19
      Calif.W.L.Rev.269 pp.271 & 272
86   ibid p.272
87   J. Bancroft *The Premenstrual Syndrome - a Reappraisal of the Concept and the
      Evidence* (Cambridge, 1992) pp.3-7
88   See W.R.Keye, Jr. *The Premenstrual Syndrome* (Philadelphia, 1988)
89   ibid
90   J.Bancroft op cit p.3
91   Taylor and Dalton op cit pp.274 & 275
92   ibid p.275
93   Reported in *the Lancet* [1981] 25 Nov.1238
94   ibid
95   *R v Reynolds* [1988] Crim.L.R.679
96   G.R.Sullivan "Involuntary Intoxication and Beyond" [1994] Crim.L.R.272 p.274
97   ibid
98   H.Fingarette "Diminished Mental Capacity as a Criminal Law Defence" [1974] 37
      M.L.R.264 p.271
99   R.D.Mackay "McNaghten Rules OK? The Need for Revision of the Automatism and
      Insanity Defenses in English Criminal Law" [1987] 5 Dick.J.Int.L.167 p.191
100   R.D.Mackay *Mental Condition Defences in the Criminal Law* op cit p.67
101   Dalton and Taylor op cit p.274

102   David Fraser "Still Crazy After All These Years: A Critique of Diminished Responsibility" in Stanley Yeo *Partial Excuses to Murder* (Sydney, 1991) p.122

103   D'Orban [1983] 30 Br.J.Hosp.Med.404 p.409 notes "it would be unjustifiable to assume that women are generally more liable to commit offences during the paramenstuum; the association may only apply in a subgroup of female offenders who are also prone to psychological or behavioural disturbance at other times of the menstrual cycle"

104   Helena Kennedy *Eve was Framed* (London, 1992) p.104

105   A.W.Clare *Psychiatric and Social Aspects of Premenstrual Complaint* (Cambridge, 1983)

106   Taylor and Dalton op cit pp.282 & 283

107   ibid p.273

108   [1998] 1 Cr.App.R.31

109   [1959] 43 Cr.App.R.201

110   R.F.Sparks "'Diminished Responsibility' in Theory and Practice." [1964] 27 M.L.R.9 p.14, f.n.12

111   N.Walker op cit p.154

112   [1960] 3 All E.R.1 p.4

113   E.Griew "The Future of Diminished Responsibility" [1988] Crim.L.R.75 p.77

114   ibid p.78

115   Report of the (Butler) Committee on Mentally Abnormal Offenders Cmnd 6244 op cit para.19.5

116   ibid

117   E.Griew "The Future of Diminished Responsibility" op cit p.79

118   ibid

119   S.Dell *Murder into Manslaughter* op cit p.28 says that this occurs in 80% of cases but recent figures suggest that this figure is higher.

120   Report of the (Butler) Committee on Mentally Abnormal Offenders Cmnd 6244 op cit para.19.14

121   ibid para.19.17

122   Criminal Law Revision Committee 14th Report *Offences Against the Person* Cmnd 7844 (London, 1980) para.92

123   ibid

124   E.Griew "The Future of Diminished Responsibility" op cit p.79

125   ibid p.80

126   ibid

127   F.Boland "Diminished Responsibility as a Defence in Irish Law: Past English Mistakes and Future Irish Directions" (1996) 6 I.C.L.J.19 p.27

128   E.Griew "The Future of Diminished Responsibility" op cit p.80

129   F.Boland "Diminished Responsibility as a Defence in Irish Law: Past English Mistakes and Future Irish Directions" op cit p.26

130   *Intoxication and Criminal Liability* Consultation Paper No.127 (London, 1993) para.1.13

131   [1920] 14 Cr.App.R.159

132   [1976] 2 All E.R.142

133   [1867] 5 Irv.466

134 [1878] 4 Couper 86
135 ibid p.103
136 [1886] 1 White 103
137 *H.M. Advocate v Thomas Ferguson* [1887] 4 Couper 552
138 ibid p.558
139 *H.M. Advocate v John McDonald* [1890] 2 White 517
140 ibid pp.523 & 524
141 [1892] 2 White 386
142 [1906] 5 Adam 212
143 *R v Davis* [1881] 14 C.C.C.563
144 *Intoxication and Criminal Liability* Law Commission Consultation Paper No.127 op cit para.1.13
145 R.L.Sadoff "PMS: Political and Legal Perspectives" p.20 in W.R.Keye Jr. *The Premenstrual Syndrome* op cit
146 H.W.Wales "An Analysis of the Proposal to "Abolish" The Insanity Defense in S.1: Squeezing a Lemon" [1976] 124 Uni.Pa.L.Rev.687 p.708
147 J.R.Brady "Abolish the Insanity Defense? No!" (1971) 8 Houston L.Rev. 629 p.634
148 ibid
149 [1921] J.C.1
150 [1923] J.C.49
151 ibid p.51
152 *Kennedy v H.M. Advocate* [1944] J.C.171
153 [1946] J.C.108
154 [1959] Cr.App.R.167
155 *The Times* 22 Jan.1960
156 [1962] Crim.L.R.836
157 ibid p.838
158 [1975] 61 Cr.App.R.261
159 [1988] 87 Cr.App.R.45
160 [1977] 65 Cr.App.R.242
161 F.Boland "Intoxication and Criminal Liability" [1996] 60 J.C.L.100 p.101
162 ibid
163 ibid
164 Insanity is sometimes treated as connoting absence of *mens rea* presumably because although *mens rea* may be strictly present *mens rea* is viewed as requiring a guilty healthy mind. On this analysis diminished responsibility also connotes absent *mens rea*.
165 *Intoxication and Criminal Liability*, Consultation Paper No.127 op cit para.3.24
166 ibid para.4.6
167 *Intoxication and Criminal Liability*, Consultation Paper No.127 op cit para.3.20
168 [1984] 79 Cr.App.R.272
169 [1984] Crim.L.R.553 p.554
170 ibid
171 F.Boland "Intoxication and Criminal Liability" op cit p.103
172 ibid
173 ibid

174   See G.R.Sullivan "Intoxicants and Diminished Responsibility" [1994] Crim.L.R.156
175   F.Boland "Intoxication and Criminal Liability" op cit p.103
176   [1985] Crim.L.R.314
177   [1992] 95 Cr.App.R.278 p.286
178   ibid p.288
179   F.Boland "Intoxication and Criminal Liability" op cit p.103
180   [1988] 87 Cr.App.R.45 p.49
181   ibid
182   F.McAuley op cit p.164
183   ibid pp.164 & 165
184   *A.G. for Northern Ireland v Gallagher* [1963] A.C.340
185   F.McAuley op cit p.165
186   G.R.Sullivan "Intoxicants and Diminished Responsibility" op cit p.57
187   F.Boland "Intoxication and Criminal Liability" op cit p.103
188   Criminal Law Revision Committee 14th Report *Offences Against the Person* Cmnd 7844 op cit para.277
189   [1980] 54 A.L.J.R.349
190   F.Boland "Intoxication and Criminal Liability" op cit p.104
191   See The Law Commission *Intoxication and Criminal Liability* Consultation Paper No.127 op cit pp.59-61
192   Cf : S.Dell *Murder into Manslaughter* op cit pp.44 & 45 and A.Grounds "Transfer of Sentenced Prisoners to Hospital" [1990] Crim L.R.544
193   F.Boland "Involuntary Intoxication is Not a Defence" [1995] 4 Web J.C.L.I.
194   See F.Boland "Intoxication and Criminal Liability" op cit for a discussion of the Law Commission's recent proposals for reform of this area of the law.
195   Lady Wooton "Diminished Responsibility: a Layman's View" [1960] 76 L.Q.R.224 p.229
196   Cf: F.Boland "Diminished Responsibility as a Defence in Irish Law: Past English Mistakes and Future Irish Directions" op cit pp.28-30
197   E.Griew "Reducing Murder to Manslaughter: Whose Job?" [1986] 12 Journal of Medical Ethics 18 p.19
198   ibid p.20
199   ibid
200   ibid
201   Mr.A.Greenwood (M.P.for Rossendale) H.C.deb.1956, Vol.561, Col.489
202   E.Griew "Reducing Murder to Manslaughter: Whose Job?" op cit p.20
203   Report of the (Butler) Committee on Mentally Abnormal Offenders Cmnd 6244 op cit para 19.4
204   S.Dell "The Mandatory Sentence and Section 2" [1986] 12 Journal of Med.Ethics 28 p.30
205   ibid
206   B.Mitchell "Putting diminished responsibility law into practice: a forensic psychiatric perspective" [1997] 8 J.Forensic Psychiat.620 p.626
207   ibid
208   ibid p.87

209   Report of the (Butler) Committee on Mentally Abnormal Offenders Cmnd 6244 op cit para.19.5

210   S.Dell "Diminished Responsibility Reconsidered" [1982] Crim.L.R.809 p.813

211   Report of the (Butler) Committee on Mentally Abnormal Offenders Cmnd 6244 op cit para.19.17

212   Report of the Criminal Law Revision Committee 14th Report *Offences Against the Person* op cit para.92

213   ibid para.93

214   ibid

215   ibid

216   H.O.L. *Report of the Select Committee on Murder and Life Imprisonment, Vol.ii - Oral Evidence*, Part 1 op cit p.115

217   S.Dell "Diminished Responsibility Reconsidered" op cit p.817

218   E.Griew "The Future of Diminished Responsibility" op cit p.84

219   See Chapter Three *above.*

220   E.Griew "The Future of Diminished Responsibility" op cit p.86

221   ibid p.87

222   R.D.Mackay *Mental Condition Defences in the Criminal Law* op cit p.186

223   [1987] 84 Cr.App.R.255 p.259

224   A.Norrie op cit p.189

225   ibid

226   Mackay *Mental Condition Defences in the Criminal Law* op cit p.204

227   A.Norrie op cit p.190

228   An example is the case of *Peter Sutcliffe* discussed in H.A.Prins "Diminished Responsibility and the Sutcliffe Case: Legal, Psychiatric and Social Aspects (A 'Layman's View)'" [1983] 23 Med, Sci & L.17

229   S.Dell *Murder into Manslaughter* op cit p.26

230   See F.Boland "Diminished Responsibility as a Defence in Irish Law" (1995) 5 I.C.L.J.173 pp.181-193

231   [1986] I.L.R.M.244

232   See *Irish Times* 26 Feb.1998

233   F.Boland "The Criminal Justice (Mental Disorder) Bill 1996" [1997] 4 Web J.C.L.I.

234   ibid

235   Criminal Statistics, 1995, p.84

236   ibid

237   H.L.A. Hart op cit p.193

7 Conclusions

At the heart of the controversy surrounding the McNaghten Rules has been a conflict between the legal and psychiatric professions. By examining the development of the doctrine of irresistible impulse, the product test and the justly responsible test I have shown the impossibility of satisfactorily reformulating the insanity defence and the failure of insanity defence reforms to resolve the medico-legal conflict. This has been reinforced by the fate of the American Law Institute's test, the Butler Committee's proposed test and the abolitionists' proposal, each of which has added fuel to fire this controversy. Undoubtedly, it is the English diminished responsibility defence that has proven to be the most satisfactory solution to the Herculean challenge posed by reformulation of the insanity defence. The defence of diminished responsibility has resolved the controversy over where the boundary between responsibility and irresponsibility should be drawn and over which of the legal or medical professions should have the final say in drawing this line.

Although admitted as a fob to ward off the proponents advocating abolition of the death penalty, the diminished responsibility defence has done much more than spare undeserving murderers from a conviction of murder. The main source of the controversy over the insanity defence has been its treatment of responsibility as an all or nothing concept. The defence of diminished responsibility enables a more accurate assessment of the individual's *moral* culpability. In moral responsibility there are certainly grades of excuse:

> The question of an agent's responsibility for a particular act or effect of an act need not be 'either-or'; and because acts can be voluntary to a degree, and agents more or less responsible, some excuses can lessen, without eliminating, the agent's culpability.[1]

The diminished responsibility defence has answered the prayers of those who call for individualisation within the rule of law[2] and has stepped in to save mentally abnormal killers from a murder conviction where the defences of automatism or insanity would have failed them. It has also saved mentally abnormal murderers from an inappropriate finding of

170

insanity with consequent mandatory indefinite hospitalisation. The defence has also accorded legal recognition to irresistible impulses which were the forum for over 100 years' conflict between law and medicine over the insanity defence. The admission of irresistible impulse as a species of diminished responsibility signalled the beginning of a happy partnership between law and medicine in the working of the diminished responsibility defence. The creators of the defence could hardly have foreseen such co-operation. Evidence of this partnership can be seen in the willingness of the courts to listen to medical testimony on various mental abnormalities for the purpose of a diminished responsibility defence, thus legitimising the medical view of mental abnormality. It is also evident in the willingness of the courts to listen to medical testimony on the issue of substantially impaired mental responsibility. The partnership is revealed in the Crown's practice of accepting the plea where the medical evidence of diminished responsibility is unanimous and the ruling of the Court of Appeal requiring that in these cases the defendant should not go to trial, in the absence of outside evidence indicating normality. The Butler Committee's approach of sharply delineating the jury's function has, therefore, threatened to undermine the psychiatrist's special position in the operation of the defence and would affect the current satisfactory practice whereby the judge accepts the plea in uncontested cases and the case does not go before a jury. A paradigmatic example of the working of this medico-legal partnership is in the law's insistence on medical testimony, thus according special status to the medical profession in the operation of the defence, while at the same time retaining its right to try diminished responsibility cases where appropriate, despite unanimous medical evidence of mental abnormality. It is therefore important that any reformulation of the diminished responsibility defence should treat medical evidence as a pre-requisite to a successful defence.

The diminished responsibility defence's major triumph has been its resolution of the medico-legal controversy underpinning the McNaghten Rules since the time of their enactment. The most trenchant critics of the insanity defence were the psychiatric profession who felt that the law embraced an outdated test of insanity. Reforms in the United States were viewed as granting too much autonomy to the medical profession in criminal trials by entrusting psychiatrists with the determination of responsibility or irresponsibility. The diminished responsibility defence not only succeeds in giving recognition to the psychiatric view of mental illness but also satisfies those who would not have the psychiatric profession determine the issue of irresponsibility. The psychiatrist does not testify that the defendant should be wholly exculpated, rather, that he is less blameworthy than his mentally normal counterpart. The diminished responsibility defence recognises grades of responsibility consistent with the psychiatric view of gradations in mental abnormality:

> In reality..madness and sanity are but points on a continuum along which we are all inclined to move during difficult moments in our lives.[3]

Notes

1   S.Uniacke "What are Partial Excuses to Murder?" in Stanley Meng Heong Yeo *Partial Excuses to Murder* (Sydney, 1991) p.1 at p.11
2   J.Hall "Psychiatry and Criminal Responsibility" [1956] 65 Yale L.J.761 p.767
3   R.P.Bentall "Deconstructing the concept of 'schizophrenia'" [1993] 2 Journal of Mental Health 223 p.234

Bibliography

Arenella, P. The Diminished Capacity and Diminished Responsibility Defenses: Two Children of a Doomed Marriage [1977] 77 Columbia Law Review 827

Arrigo, B.A. Insanity Defense Reform and the Sign of Abolition: Re-Visiting Montana's Experience [1997] 10 International Journal for the Semiotics of Law 191

Ashworth, A. and Gostin, L. Mentally Disordered Offenders and the Sentencing Process [1984] Criminal Law Review 195

Ashworth, A. and Shapland, J. Psychopaths in the Criminal Process [1980] Criminal Law Review 628

Ashworth, A.J. Self-Defence and the Right to Life [1974] 23 Cambridge Law Journal 282

Ashworth, A.J. The Doctrine of Provocation [1976] 35 Cambridge Law Journal 292

Atkin L.J. Report of the Committee on Insanity and Crime [1924], Cmd 2005 H.M.S.O.

Baker, E. Human Rights, M'Naghten and the 1991 Act [1994] Criminal Law Review 84

Bancroft, J *The Premenstrual Syndrome - a Reappraisal of the Concept and the Evidence* Cambridge University Press, Cambridge, 1993

Barnes, H. A Century of the McNaghten Rules [1944] 8 Cambridge Law Journal 300

Barton, S. Criminal Law - Insanity in the Supreme Court [1991] 13 Dublin University Law Journal 127

Bazelon, D.L. Justice Stumbles on Science [1966] 1 Irish Jurist 272

Behlmer, G.K. Deadly Motherhood: Infanticide and Medical Opinion in Mid-Victorian England [1979] 34 Journal of the History of Medicine 403

Belli, M.M. Did McNaghten need a Psychiatrist, a Lawyer or a Definition? [1971] 11 Medicine, Science and the Law 25

Bennun, M. & Garener-Thorpe, C. McNaghten Rules Epilepsy - OK? [1984] 47 Modern Law Review 92

Bentall, R.P. Deconstructing the Concept of "Schizophrenia" [1993] 2 Journal of Mental Health 223

Beytagh, F.X. Individual Rights, Judicial Review and Written Constitutions in *Human Rights and Constitutional Law* Roundhall Press, Dublin, 1992

Binchy, W. Mental Retardation and the Criminal Law [1984] 2 Irish Law Times 111

Bluglass, R. Regional Secure Units and Interim Security for Psychiatric Patients [1978] 1 British Medical Journal 489

Bluglass, R., Psychiatry, the law and the Offender - Present Dilemmas and Future Prospects The 7th Denis Carroll Memorial Lecture, Institute for the Study and Treatment of Delinquency, Croydon, 1980

Boland, F. Diminished Responsibility as a Defence in Irish Law [1995] 5 Irish Criminal Law Journal 177

Boland, F. Involuntary Intoxication is Not a Defence [1995] 4 Web Journal of Current Legal Issues

Boland, F. Diminished Responsibility as a Defence in Irish Law: Past English Mistakes and Future Irish Directions [1996] 6 Irish Criminal Law Journal 19

Boland, F. Intoxication and Criminal Liability [1996] 60 Journal of Criminal Law 100

Boland, F. Insanity, the Irish Constitution and the European Convention on Human Rights [1996] 47 Northern Ireland Legal Quarterly 260

Boland, F. Intoxication and Criminal Liability (1996) 60 Journal of Criminal Law 100

Boland, F.*Diminished Responsibility as a Defence in Ireland Having Regard to the Law in England, Scotland and Wales* PhD Leeds, 1996

Bonnie, R.J. The Moral Basis of the Insanity Defense [1983] 69 American Bar Association Journal 194

Brahams, D. Pre-menstrual Syndrome: a Disease of the Mind? [1981] The Lancet 1238

Brahams, D. R v Sullivan: Epilepsy, Insanity and the Common Law (1983) 133 New Law Journal 137

Brahams, D. Criminal Behaviour and Medicinal Treatment-Iatrogenic crime [1987] 84 Law Society's Guardian Gazette 2175

Brett, P. Irresistible Impulse and the McNaghten Rules [1960] 23 Modern Law Review 545

Browne, N. *Against the Tide* Gill and Macmillan, Dublin, 1986

Browne, V. Hundreds of Citizens Sentenced to Squalor *Irish Times* 7 June 1995

Browne, V. Prisoners Degraded Instead of Helped at Mountjoy *Irish Times* 14 June 1995

Buck, W. and Walklate, S. Homicide and the Role of the Forensic Psychiatric Recommendations in Relation to Outcome in Cases of Diminished Responsibility in N.Clark and G.Stephenson eds. *Rights and Risks: The Application of Forensic Psychology, Issues in Criminological and Legal Psychology, No.21*, The British Psychological Society, Leicester, 1994

Bullogh, V. and Voght, M. Women Menstruation and Nineteenth Century Medicine [1973] 47 Bulletin of the History of Medicine 66

Butler Committee Report of the Committee on Mentally Abnormal Offenders, Cmnd 6244, H.M.S.O.,London, 1975

Butler Interim Report of the Committee on Mentally Abnormal Offenders Cmnd 5698, H.M.S.O., London, 1974

Byrne and McCutcheon *The Irish Legal System* (2nd ed.) Butterworth (Ireland) Ltd, Dublin, 1989

Byrne, R. Habeas Corpus and Conditions of Confinement in Prison (1979) 14 Irish Jurist 109

Callahan, Mayer and Steadman Insanity Defense Reforms in the U.S. - post Hinckley [1987] 2 Mental and Physical Disabilities Law Reporter 54

Card, Cross and Jones *Criminal Law* (12th ed.) Butterworths, London, 1992

Carney, P. Anachronism of our Criminal Insanity Laws *Irish Times* 13 January 1990

Carney, R.M. and Williams, B.D. Premenstrual Syndrome: A Criminal Defense [1983] 59 Notre Dame Law Review 253

Carson,D and Wexler, D.B. New Approaches to Mental Health Law: Will the UK Follow the US Lead, Again? [1994] Journal of Social Welfare and Family Law 79

Casey, J.P. The Judicial Power Under Irish Constitutional Law [1975] 24 International and Comparative Law Quarterly 305

Cassells Diminished Responsibility [1964] 7 Canadian Bar Journal 8

Charleton, P. *Offences against the Person* Roundhall Press, Dublin, 1992

Chubb, B. *The Politics of the Irish Constitution* Institute of Public Administration, Dublin, 1991

Clare, A.W. *Psychiatric and Social Aspects of Premenstrual Complaint* Cambridge University Press, Cambridge 1983

Clements, L.M. Epilepsy, Insanity and Automatism [1983] 133 New Law Journal 949

Coles, E.M. and Jang, D. A Psychological Perspective on the Legal Concepts of "Volition" and "Intent" [1996] 4 Journal of Law and Medicine 60

Cooter, R. Phrenology and the British Alienists ca. 1825-1845 in A Scull(ed.) *Madhouses, Maddoctors and Madmen* Edinburgh University Press, Edinburgh, 1981

Coulter, C. Changes in Insanity Legislation Delayed by Inaction *Irish Times* 5 May 1997

Coulter, C. Juries are Unlikely to Bring in "Guilty but Insane" Verdicts While law Remains as it is *Irish Times* 26 February 1998

Criminal Law Revision Committee 14th Report *Offences Against the Person* Cmnd

7844, H.M.S.O., London, 1980

Criminal Responsibility (Trials) Bill 1924 Debate on the Criminal Responsibility (Trials) Bill 1924, Volume 57 House of Lords Debates

D'Orban Medicolegal Aspects of the Premenstrual Syndrome [1983] 30 British Journal of Hospital Medicine 404

Dail Eireann Debate on Insanity Irish Parliamentary Debates 1991, Volume 405

Dalton, K. *The Premenstrual Syndrome and Progesterone Therapy* Heinemann Medical, London, 1984

De Breadun, D. Owen Will Change law on Criminal Insanity *Irish Times* 24 April 1996

De Grazia, E. The Distinction of Being Mad [1954] 22 University of Chicago Law Review 339

Debate on McNaghten's Case Hansards debates LXVII [1843] p288 and p714

Debate on The Child Murder (Record of Sentence of Death) Bill, 1909 House of Lords Debates. 1909 Volume 1

Debate on The Child Murder (Trial Bill), 1922 House of Commons Debates 1922, Volume 150, House of Lords Debates, 1922 Volume 50

Debate on The Children Bill, 1908, British Parliamentary Debates 1908, Volumes 195 and 196

Debate on The Infanticide Bill, 1936, House of Commons Debates 1936-7, Volume 318

Debate on The Infanticide Bill 1937 House of Commons Debates 1937-8, Volume 108

Debate on True's Reprieve [1922] British Parliamentary Papers Volume 155, pages 201 and 2421

Dell, S. and Smith, A. Changes in the Sentencing of Diminished Responsibility Homicides [1983] 142 British Journal of Psychiatry 20

Dell, S. Diminished Responsibility Reconsidered [1982] Criminal Law Review 809

Dell, S. The Detention of Diminished Responsibility Homicide Offenders [1983] 23 British Journal of Criminology 50

Dell, S. *Murder into Manslaughter The Diminished Responsibility Defence in Practice* University Press, Oxford 1984

Dell, S. The Mandatory Sentence and Section 2 (1986) 12 Journal of Medical Ethics 8

Dell, S. Wanted: An Insanity Defence That can be Used [1983] Criminal Law Review 43

Devlin, Lord Mental Abnormality and the Criminal Law in *Changing Legal Objectives* R. St. J. Macdonald (ed.) University of Toronto Press, Toronto, 1963

Devlin, P. Criminal Responsibility and Punishment: Functions of Judge and Jury [1954] Criminal Law Review 661

DiLiberto, R.A. Premenstrual Stress Syndrome Defence: Legal, Medical and Social Aspects 33 Medical Trial Technique Quarterly 351

Dix, G.E. Psychological Abnormality as a Factor in Grading Criminal Liability: Diminished Capacity, Diminished Responsibility, and the Like [1971] 62 Journal of Criminal Law, Criminology and Police Science 313

Doherty, E.F. Men Criminals and Responsibility [1966] 1 Irish Jurist 285

Dolan, M.C. and Campbell, A.A. The Criminal Procedure (Insanity and Unfitness to Plead) Act 1991: A Case Report and Selected Review of the Legal Reforms [1994] 34 Medicine, Science and the Law 155

Donnelly, M. Battered Women who Kill and the Criminal Law Defences [1993] 3 Irish Criminal Law Journal

D'Orban Women who Kill Their Children [1979] 134 British Journal of Psychiatry 560

Doub, C.E. Recent Trends in the Criminal Law [1960] 46 American Bar Association Journal 139

Dressler, J. Provocation: Partial Justification or Partial Excuse? [1988] 51 Modern Law Review 467

Eastman, N. Abused Women and Legal Excuses [1992] 142 New Law Journal 1549

Edwards, J.Ll.J. Diminished Responsibility - A Withering Away of the Concept of Criminal Responsibility? in G.O.Mueller *Essays in Criminal Science* Sweet and Maxwell, London, 1961

Edwards, J.Ll.J. Social Defence and Control of the Dangerous Offender [1968] 21 Current Legal Problems 23

Edwards, S. *Women on Trial: A Study of the Female Suspect, Defendant and Offender in the Criminal Law and Criminal Justice System* Chapter 3 Manchester University Press, Manchester, 1984

Edwards, S. Mad, Bad or Pre-Menstrual [1988] 138 New Law Journal 456

Edwards, S. Battered Women who Kill [1990] 140 New Law Journal 1380

Edwards, S. Battered Woman Syndrome [1992] 142 New Law Journal 1351

Elliott, D.W. The Homicide Act, 1957 [1957] Criminal Law Review 282

Elliott, D.W. The Interpretation of the Homicide Act, 1957 [1960] Criminal Law Review 5

Faigman, D.L. The Battered Woman Syndrome and Self-Defense: A Legal and Empirical Dissent [1986] 72 Virginia Law Review 619

Faulk, M. Mentally Disordered Offenders in an Interim Regional Medium Secure Unit [1979] Criminal Law Review 686

Fennell, P. Diversion of Mentally Disordered Offenders from Custody [1991]

Criminal Law Review 333

Fennell, P. The Criminal Procedure (Insanity and Unfitness to Plead) Act 1991 [1992] 55 Modern Law Review 547

Ferguson, P.W. *Crimes Against the Person* Butterworths, Edinburgh, 1990

Fingarette, H. *The Meaning of Criminal Insanity* University of California Press; Berkeley, Los Angeles, 1972

Fingarette, H. Diminished Mental Capacity as a Criminal Law Defence [1974] 37 Modern Law Review 264

Fingarette, H. Disabilities of Mind and Criminal Responsibility - A Unitary Doctrine [1976] 76 Columbia Law Review 236

Fitzgerald, G. Now Action is Needed to Cut Out Political Jobbery *Irish Times* 22 October 1994

Fitzjames Stephen, J. on the Policy of Maintaining the Limits at Present Imposed by the Law on the Criminal Responsibility of Madmen - Papers Read Before the Juridical Society, 1855-58 London, 1855

Fitzjames Stephen, J. *A General View of the Criminal Law of England* MacMillan & Co., London and Cambridge, 1863

Fitzjames Stephen, J. *A History of the Criminal Law of England* Volume ii, MacMillan & Co., London, 1883

Fletcher *Rethinking Criminal Law* Little Brown & Co, Boston, 1978

Fletcher, G.P. The Individualization of Excusing Conditions [1974] 47 Southern California Law Review 1269

Forde, M. *Constitutional Law of Ireland* The Mercier Press, Cork and Dublin, 1987

Fraser, D. Still Crazy After all These Years: A Critique of Diminished Responsibility in S.M.H.Yeo *Partial Excuses to Murder* Federation Press and Law Foundation of New South Wales, Sydney, 1991

Fridman, G.H.L., Moral Insanity & the McNaughten Rules [1953] 17 Journal of Criminal Law 370

Gannage, M. The Defence of Diminished Responsibility in Canadian Criminal Law [1981] 19 Osgoode Hall Law Journal 301

Gibb, A.D. Diminished Responsibililty for Crime [1959] Scots Law Times 85

Glanville Williams The Royal Commission and the Defence of Insanity [1954] 7 Current Legal Problems 16

Glanville Williams Diminished Responsibility [1961] 1 Medicine, Science and the Law 41

Glanville Williams *Textbook of the Criminal Law* (2nd ed.) Stevens and Sons, London, 1983

Glueck, S. *Mental Disorder and the Criminal Law* Little Brown and Co., Boston 1925

Glueck, S. *Law and Psychiatry* Tavistock Publications Ltd, London, 1963

Golding, S.B. Fault Lines [1994] 80 American Bar Association Journal 40

Goldstein, A. *The Insanity Defense* Yale University Press, New Haven and London, 1967

Goldstein, J. and Katz J. Abolish the "Insanity Defense"-Why Not? [1963] 72 Yale Law Journal 853

Goode, M. on Subjectivity and Objectivity in Denial of Criminal Responsibility: Reflections on Reading Radford [1987] 11 Australian Criminal Law Journal 131

Gordon, G.H. *The Criminal Law of Scotland* (2nd ed.) W.Green and Son Ltd., Edinburgh, 1978

Gostin, L. Human Rights, Judicial Review and the Mentally Disordered Offender [1982] Criminal Law Review 779

Gowers Ernest Report of the Royal Commission on Capital Punishment, 1949-1953 Cmd 8932

Griew, E. Diminished Responsibility and the Trial of Lunatics Act, 1883 [1957] Criminal Law Review 521

Griew, E. Another Nail for M'Naghten's Coffin? [1984] 134 New Law Journal 935

Griew, E. Let's Implement Butler on Mental Disorder and Crime! [1984] 37 Current Legal Problems 47

Griew, E. Reducing Murder to Manslaughter: Whose Job? [1986] 12 Journal of Medical Ethics 18

Griew, E. The Future of Diminished Responsibility [1988] Criminal Law Review 75

Grimes and Horgan *Introduction to Law: Ireland* Wolfhound Press, Dublin, 1981

Grounds, A. Transfer of Sentenced Prisoners to Hospital [1990] Criminal Law Review 544

Grounds, A. The Transfer of Sentenced Prisoners to Hospital 1960-1983 A Study in One Special Hospital [1991] 31 British Journal of Criminology 54

Grubin, D. What Constitutes Fitness to Plead [1993] Criminal Law Review 748

Hale, Sir M. *History of the Pleas of the Crown* Ch.4 Professional Books Ltd, London, 1971

Hall, J. Psychiatry and Criminal Responsibility [1956] 65 Yale Law Journal 761

Hall Williams, J.E. The Psychopath and the Defence of Diminished Responsibility (1958) 21 Modern Law Review 544

Hall Williams, J.E. Diminished Responsibility in Murder and the Role of the Judiciary [1960] 23 Modern Law Review 191

Hall Williams, J.E. Irresistible Impulse and Diminished Responsibility [1961] 24 Modern Law Review 164

Hall Williams, J.E. Diminished Responsibility-Satisfactory Developments [1962] 25 Modern Law Review 83

Halpern, A.L. Uncloseting the Conscience of the Jury – A Justly Acquitted Doctrine (1980) 52 Psychiatric Quarterly 144

Hamilton, J.R. Diminished Responsibility [1981] 138 British Journal of Psychiatry 434

Hamilton, J.R. Insanity Legislation [1986] 12 Journal of Medical Ethics 13

Harris, R. *Murders and Madness: Medicine, Law and Society in the Fin de Siecle* Clarendon Press, Oxford, 1989

Hart, H.L.A *Punishment and Responsibility* Clarendon Press, Oxford, 1968

Hayes, S.C. Diminished Responsibility: The Expert Witness' Viewpoint in S.M.H.Yeo *Partial Excuses to Murder* Federation Press and Law Foundation of New South Wales, Sydney 1991

Hayward, A.R. *Murder and Madness: A Social History of the Insanity Defence in Mid-Victorian England* M.Litt, Oxford, 1983

Heald Committee Report Murder: *Some Suggestions for the Reform of the Law Relating to Murder in England* The Inns of Court Conservative and Unionist' Society, Temple EC4, 1956

Henchy Committee Third Interim Report of the Interdepartmental Committee on Mentally Ill and Maladjusted Persons entitled *Treatment and Care of Persons Suffering from Mental Disorder who Appear Before the Courts on Criminal Charges* Prl.8275 Dublin, 1978

Hermann, D.H.J. *The Insanity Defense: Philosophical Historical and Legal Perspectives* Charles C Thomas, Springfield Illinois, 1983

Heuston, R.F.V. Personal Rights Under the Irish Constitution [1976] 11 Irish Jurist 205

Higgins, J. The Origins of the Homicide Act 1957 [1986] 12 Journal of Medical Ethics 8

Hilary Defence of Uncontrollable Impulse [1936] 2 Ir Jur 5

Hill, D. Character and Personality in Relatin to Criminal Responsibility [1962] 2 Medicine, Science and the Law 221

Hoffman, A.O. Defence of Insanity-Tests of Insanity [1931] 22 American Journal of Criminal law, Criminology and Police Science 437

Hogan, G.W. Irish Nationalism as a Legal Ideology [1986] 75 Studies 528

Hogan, G.W. Unenumerated Personal Rights: Ryan's Case Re-Evaluated [1990-2] Irish Jurist 95

Hogan, G.W. The Early Judgments of Mr Justice Brian Walsh in *Human Rights and Constitutional Law* Roundhall Press, Dublin, 1992

Hollis, C. *The Homicide Act* Victor Gollancz Ltd, London, 1964

Holtzman, E. Premenstrual Symptoms: No Legal Defense [1986] 60 St John's Law

Review 712

Homicide Bill 1956, Debate on the Homicide Bill 1956: 560, 561 and 563 House of Commons Debates; Volumes 201 and 202 House of Lords Debates

Horder, J. Sex, Violence and Sentencing in Domestic Provocation Cases [1989] Criminal Law Review 546

Horder, J. Provocation and Loss of Self-Control [1992] 108 Law Quarterly Review 191

Horder, J. *Provocation and Responsibility* Clarendon Press, Oxford, 1992

Horder, J. Pleading Involuntary Lack of Capacity [1993] 52 Cambridge Law Journal 298

Hughes, G. The English Homicide Act of 1957: The Capital Punishment Issue, and Various Reforms in the Law of Murder and Manslaughter [1959] 49 Journal of Criminal Law, Criminology, and Police Science 521

Hunter, J. and Bargen, J. Diminished Responsibility: 'Abnormal Minds', Abnormal Murderers and What the Doctor Said in S.M.H.Yeo *Partial Excuses to Murder* Federation Press and Law Foundation of New South Wales, Sydney, 1991

Jacobs, F.G. The Protection of Human Rights in the Member States of the European Community: The Impact of the Case Law of the Court of Justice in *Human Rights and Constitutional Law* (ed.James O'Reilly) Roundhall Press, Dublin, 1992

Jaconelli, J. The European Convention on Human Rights as Irish Municipal law (1987) 22 Irish Jurist 13

Jones, A. *Women who Kill, 1937- 1991* Victor Gollanz Ltd, London, 1991

Kadish, S.H.The Decline of Innocence [1968] 26 Cambridge Law Journal 273

Katz, W.C. Law, Psychiatry and Free Will [1954 22 University of Chicago Law Review 397

Keane, R. Fundamental Rights in Irish Law: A Note on the Historical Background in *Human Rights and Constitutional Law* Roundhall Press, Dublin, 1992

Keedy, Edwin R. Insanity and Criminal Responsibility [1917] 30 Harvard Law Review pp.535 and 724

Keedy, Edwin R. Irresistible Impulse as a Defense in the Criminal Law [1952] 100 University of Pennsylvania Law Review 956

Keeton, G.W. *Guilty but Insane* London, 1961

Keith of Avonholm Some Observations on Diminished Responsibility [1959] 4 Juridical Review 109

Kelly, J.M. *The Irish Constitution* (2nd ed.) Jurist Publishing Co Ltd, Dublin, 1984

Kelly, D. and O'Regan, M. Owen Promises Bill to Amend law on Criminal Insanity *Irish Times* 24 April 1996

Kenison, F.R. Pioneers in Criminology XII Charles Doe [1830-1896] [1956] 47

The Journal of Criminal Law, Criminology and Police Science 277

Kennedy, H. *Eve was Framed: Women and British Justice* Chatto and Windus Ltd,. London, 1992

Kenny, A. *Freewill and Responsibility* Routledge and Kegan Paul, London, 1978

Kenny, A. The Expert in Court in *The Ivory Tower Essays in Philosophy and Public Policy* Basil Blackwell, Oxford, 1985

Kenny, A. Anomalies of Section 2 of the Homicide Act 1957 [1986] 12 Journal of Medical Ethics 24

Keye, W.R.Jr. *The Premenstrual Syndrome* W.B.Saunders Co., Philadelphia, 1988

Kodwo, B.J. Homicide and Elements of Diminished Responsibility [1983] 127 Solicitors' Journal 590

La Fave, W.R. and Scott, A.W.Jr. Substantive Criminal Law Volume 1 Chapter 4 West Publishing Co, St Paul, Minnesota, 1986

LaFond, J.Q. and Durham, M.L. *Back to the Asylum: The Future of Mental Health Law and Policy in the United States* Oxford University Press, New York, 1992

Laurie, G.T. Automatism and Insanity in the Laws of England and Scotland [1995] 40 Juridical Review 253

Law Commission Consultation Paper No. 127 Intoxication and Criminal Liability H.M.S.O. London, 1993

Law Commission No.229 Intoxication and Criminal Liability (Legislating the Criminal Code) H.M.S.O., London, 1995

Leader-Elliott, I.D. Intoxication Defences: The Australian Perspective in S.M.H.Yeo *Partial Excuses to Murder* Federation Press and Law Foundation of New South Wales, Sydney, 1991

Lee, J. Constitutional Review may Prove to be Another Irish Solution *Irish Times* 20 April 1995

Loizidou, E. A Phantasmatic Moment: The Defence of Insanity [1997] 8 Law and Critique 115

Longford Lord *Prisoner or Patient* Chapmans Publishers Ltd, London, 1992

Louisell, D.W. and Hazard, G.C. Jr. Insanity as a Defense: The Bifurcated Trial [1961] 49 California Law Review 2

Low, Jeffries and Bonnie *The Trial of John W.Hinckley Jr: A Case Study in the Insanity Defense* Foundation Press, New York, 1986

Mackay, I. The Sleepwalker is not Insane [1992] 55 Modern Law Review 714

Mackay, R.D. Non-Organic Automatism [1980] Criminal Law Review 350

Mackay, R.D. The Automatism Defence - What Price Rejection? (1983) 34 Northern Ireland Legal Quarterly 81

Mackay, R.D. Diminished Responsibility - Some Observations Arising From Three Case Studies (1986) 26 Medicine, Science and the Law 60

Mackay, R.D. Pleading Provocation and Diminished Responsibililty Together [1988] Criminal Law Review 411

Mackay, R.D. Post-Hinckley Insanity in the U.S.A. [1988] Criminal Law Review 88

Mackay, R.D. Fact and Fiction About the Insanity Defence [1990] Criminal Law Review 247

Mackay, R.D. The Decline of Disability in Relation to the Trial [1991] Criminal Law Review 86

Mackay, R.D. The Consequences of Killing Very Young Children [1993] Criminal Law Review 21

Mackay, R.D. *Mental Condition Defences in the Criminal Law* Clarendon Press, Oxford, 1995

Mackay, R.D. and Kearns, G. The Continued Underuse of Unfitness to Plead and the Insanity Defence [1994] Criminal Law Review 576

Mackay, R.D. and Kearns, G. The Trial of the Facts and Unfitness to Plead [1997] Criminal Law Review 644

Magee, A. Strike Action by Nurses at St.Brendan's Approved by Union Chiefs *Irish Times* 7 April 1994

Maier-Katkin, D. and Ogle, R.A. Rationale for Infanticide Laws [1993] Criminal Law Review 903

McAuley, F. Anticipating the Past: The Defence of Provocation in Irish Law [1987] 50 Modern Law Review 133

McAuley, F. The Civilian Experience of the Insanity Defence [1989] 24 Irish Jurist 227

McAuley, F. *Insanity Psychiatry and Criminal Responsibility* Roundhall Press, Dublin, 1993

McAuley, F. "Legal Insanity" a key Issue in Case *Irish Times* 3 April 1996

McCall, Smith & Sheldon *Scots Criminal Law* Butterworths, Edinburgh, 1992

McDowell, M. Time for Change *Irish Independent* 13 February 1991

Meakin, R.G. Diminished Responsibility: Some Arguments for a General Defence (1988) 52 Journal of Criminal Law 406

Mercier, C. *Criminal Responsibility* Clarendon Press, Oxford, 1905

Mercier, C. *Crime and Insanity* Williams and Norgate, London, 1911

Mitchell, B. Diminished Responsibility Manslaughter: (1997) 8 The Journal of Forensic Psychiatry 101

Mitchell, B. Putting diminished responsibility into practice: a forensic psychiatric perspective (1997) 8 The Journal of Forensic Psychiatry 620

Montrose, J.L. The McNaghten Rules (1954) 17 Modern Law Review 383

Montrose, J.L. The McNaghten Rules (1955) 18 Modern Law Review 505

Moore, M. S. *Law and Psychiatry: Rethinking the Relationship* Cambridge

University Press, London, 1984

Morgan, D.G. *Constitutional Law of Ireland* (2nd ed.) Roundhall Press ltd., Dublin, 1990

Morgan, D.G. Selection of Candidates for Higher Judiciary Can no Longer be Left to Government Whim *Irish Times* 19 September 1994

Morgan, D.G. O'Hanlon Has Undermined the Collective Reputation of the Judiciary *Irish Times* 2 March 1995

Morris, N. Insanity and Responsibility [1950] 13 Modern Law Review 372

Morris, N. Wrong in the McNaghten Rules [1953] 16 Modern Law Review 435

Morris, N. Psychiatry and the Dangerous Criminal [1968] 41 Southern California Law Review 514

Morris, N. *Madness and the Criminal Law* University of Chicago, Chicago, 1982

Morris, T. & Blom-Cooper, L. *A Calendar of Murder: Criminal Homicide in England since 1957* Michael Joseph Ltd, London, 1964

Morse, S.J. Diminished Capacity: A Moral and Legal Conundrum [1979] 2 International Journal of Law and Psychiatry 271

Morse, S.J. Excusing the Crazy: The Insanity Defense Reconsidered [1985] 58 Southern California Law Review 779

Neustatter Psychiatric Aspects of Diminished Responsibility in Murder [1960] 28 Medico-Legal Journal 92

Nicolson, D. and Sanghvi, R. Battered Women and Provocation: The Implications of R v Ahluwalia [1993] Criminal Law Review 728

Norrie, A. *Crime Reason and History A Critical Introduction to Criminal Law* Ch.9 Weidenfeld and Nicolson, London, 1993

Nuttall, C. Courts Regard Female Killers as no Deadlier than the Male *Sunday Times*, 9 May 1993

O'Donovan, K. Defences for Battered Women who Kill [1991] 18 Journal of Law and Society 219

O'Donovan, K. The Medicalisation of Infanticide [1984] Criminal Law Review 259

O'Hanlon, R.J. Not Guilty Because of Insanity [1968] 3 Irish Jurist 61

O'Loughlin, E. and MacDubhghaill, U. Army Called in to Relieve Psychiatric Nurses: Medical Orderlies and Other Soldiers are Ordered to St.Brendan's *Irish Times* 8 April 1994

O'Morain, P. Prisoners With Mental Illness Join Waiting List *Irish Times* 27 July 1992

Orchard, G. Surviving Without Majewski-A View from Down Under [1993] Criminal Law Review 426

O'Regan, E. "Insane" Plea no let-off for killer-Experts *Irish Independent* 8 April 1996

Osborough, N. McNaghten Revisited, [1974] 9 Irish Jurist 76

Parker, G. The Decline of Daniel McNaghten [1967] Criminal Law Review 327

Peay, J. Mental Health Review Tribunals and the Mental Health (Amendment) Act [1982] Criminal Law Review 794

Perkins, R.M. & Boyce, R.N. *Criminal Law* (3rd ed.) New York, 1982

Perlin, M.L. Back to the Past: Why Mental Disability Law "Reforms" Don't Work (1993) 4 Criminal Law Forum 403

Pollak, A. Report on Gallagher "Recovery" Withdrawn Family of Sligo Murder Victims Fear Release *Irish Times* 26 April 1995

Power, D.J. Diminished Responsibility [1967] 7 Medicine, Science and the Law 185

Power, D.J. & Selwood, D.H.D. *Criminal Law and Psychiatry* Barry Rose Books, London, 1987

Prevezer, S. Automatism. ii A Question of Law [1962] 25 Modern Law Review 227

Prevezer, S. Criminal Homicides other than Murder [1980] Criminal Law Review 530

Prins, H.A. Diminished Responsibility and the Sutcliffe Case: Legal Psychiatric and Social Aspects (A Layman's View) [1983] 23 Medicine, Science and the Law 17

Quinn, S.E. *Criminal Law in Ireland* Magh Itha Teoranta, Wicklow, 1988

Radford, J. and Russell, D. eds. *Femicide: The Politics of Woman Killing* Open University Press, 1992

Redlich, P. The 17 Year Delay That Made our Insanity Laws a Time Bomb *Sunday Independent* 21 July 1996

Reid, J. The Working of the New Hampshire Doctrine of Criminal Insanity [1960] 15 University of Miami Law Review 14

Reid, J. Understanding the New Hampshire Doctrine of Criminal Insanity [1960] 69 Yale Law Journal 367

Reid, J. The Companion of the New Hampshire Doctrine of Criminal Insanity [1962] 15 Vanderbilt Law Review 721

Reik, L.E. The Doe-Ray Correspondence: A Pioneer Collaboration in the Jurisprudence of Mental Disease [1953] 63 Yale Law Journal 183

Report of The Select Committee on Codification of The Criminal Law 1878 British Parliamentary Papers Volume 2; 1878-9 British Parliamentary Papers Volume 20

Report of the Select Committee on Murder and Life Imprisonment 1988-89 House of Lords Paper 78 Vol ii, Oral Evidence, part 19

Report of The Select Committee on The Law of Homicide Amendment Bill 1872 British Parliamentary Papers Volume 2; 1874 British Parliamentary Papers

Volumes 2 and 9

Rodriquez, J.H., Lewinn, L.M. and Perlin, M.L. The Insanity Defense Under Siege: Legislative Assaults and Legal Rejoinders [1983] 14 Rutgers Law Journal 397

Royal Commission on Capital Punishment 1864-6 Report and Minutes of Evidence before the Royal Commission on Capital Punishment 1864-6 in British Sessional Papers 1866, XXI

Sandes, R.L. *Criminal Law and Procedure in the Republic of Ireland* Sweet and Maxwell Ltd., Dublin, 1951

Schopp, R.F. Returning to McNaghten to Avoid Moral Mistakes: [1988] 30 Arizona Law Review 135

Schopp, R.F. *Automatism, Insanity and the Psychology of Criminal Responsibility*, Cambridge University Press, Cambridge, 1991

Scott, P.D. Has Psychiatry Failed? In the Treatment of Offenders The Fifth Denis Carroll Memorial Lecture Institute for the Study and Treatment of Delinquency

Scull, A. The Social History of Psychiatry in the Victorian Era in A Scull (ed.) *Madhouses, Maddoctors and Madmen* Edinburgh University Press, Edinburgh, 1981

Seaborne Davies, D. Child Killing in English Law [1937] 1 Modern Law Review 203

Seaborne Davies, D. Irresistible Impulse in English law [1939] 17 Canadian Bar Review 147

Sheehan, P.A. *The Criminal Law of Ireland* Alex Thom and Co.Ltd, Dublin, 1952

Showalter, E. and Showalter, E. Victorian Women and Menstruation [1970-1] 14 Victorian Studies

Showalter, E.Victorian Women and Insanity [1980] 23 Victorian Studies 157

Slovenko, R. Surveying the Attacks on Psychiatry in the Legal Process (1996) 1 Journal of Evidence and Proof 48

Slovenko, R. The Insanity Defense in the Wake of the Hinckley Trial (1983) 14 Rutgers Law Journal 373

Smith and Hogan *Criminal law* (7th ed.) Butterworths, London, 1992

Smith, R. The Boundary Between Insanity and Criminal Responsibility in Nineteenth Century England in A Scull (ed.) *Madhouses, Maddoctors and Madmen* Edinburgh University Press, Edinburgh, 1981

Smith, R. *Trial by Medicine; Insanity and Responsibility in Victorian Trials* Edinburgh University Press, Edinburgh, 1981

Smith, T.B. Diminished Responsibility [1957] Criminal Law Review 354

Smith, T.B. *British Justice; The Scottish Contribution* Stevens & Sons Ltd, London, 1961

Sparks, R.F. 'Diminished Responsibility' in Theory and Practice [1964] 27 Modern Law Review 9

Sparrow, G. *Women who Murder* Arthur Barker Ltd, London, 1970

Special Report on Criminal Code (Indictable Offences Procedure) and Court of Criminal Appeal Bills, Procs 1883 (225) XI 319

Spencer, S. Homicide, Mental Abnormality and Offence in *Mentally Abnormal Offenders* Craft M.et al Bailliere Tindall Eastbourne, Philadelphia, Toronto, 1984

Spirer, J. The Psychology of Irresistible Impulse [1943] 33 Journal of Criminal Law 457

St.John-Stevas, N. A new Test of Criminal Responsibility in Cases of Insanity [1955] 18 Modern Law Review 391

Steadman, H.J. Et Al *Before and After Hinckley: Evaluating Insanity Defense Reform* The Guildford Press, London, 1993

Stockley, E.W. Mental Disorders and Criminal Responsibility: The Recommendations of the Royal Commission on Capital Punishment. [1955] 33 Texas Law Review 482

Stone, N. The Decline and Fall of the Psychiatric Probation Order [1994] 158 Justice of the Peace 380, 402

Sullivan, G.R. Intoxicants and Diminished Responsibility [1994] Criminal Law Review 156

Sullivan, G.R. Involuntary Intoxication and Beyond [1994] Criminal Law Review 272

Sullivan, W.C. *Crime and Insanity* Edward Arnold and Co., London, 1924

Sutherland, P.J. and Gearty, C.A. Insanity and the European Court of Human Rights [1992] Criminal Law Review 418

Taylor, Lawrence and Dalton Premenstrual Syndrome: A New Criminal Defense? [1983] 19 California Western Law Review 269

Temkin, J. Automatism and Proper Precautions [1974] 37 Modern Law Review 199

Tolmie, J. Provocation or Self-Defence for Battered Women who Kill? in S.M.H.Yeo *Partial Excuses to Murder* Federation Press and Law Foundation of New South Wales, Sydney, 1991

Tomison, A. Case Report: McNaughton today [1993] 4 Journal of Forensic Psychiatry 360

Tynan, M.M. Independence of Judges Raised *Irish Times* 11 March 1994

Uniacke, S. What are Partial Excuses to Murder? in S.M.H.Yeo *Partial Excuses to Murder* Federation Press and Law Foundation of New South Wales, Sydney, 1991

Virgo, G. Sanitising Insanity - Sleep-walking and statutory Reform [1991] 50

Cambridge Law Journal 386

Virgo, G. (The Law Commission Consultation Paper on Intoxication and Criminal Liability) Reconciling Principle and Policy [1993] Criminal Law Review 415

Walker, N. 1883 and all that; An historical note on the Criminal Procedure (Insanity) Act 1964 (c.84) [1966] Criminal Law Review 17

Walker, N. *Crime and Insanity in England, Vol 1: The Historical Perspective* Edinburgh University Press, Edinburgh, 1968

Walker, N. *Crime and Insanity in England Vol 2: New Solutions and New Problems* Edinburgh University Press, Edinburgh, 1973

Walker, N. Butler v C.L.R.C. and Others [1981] Criminal Law Review 596

Walker, N. McNaughtan's Innings: a Century and a Half Not Out (1993) 4 Journal of Forensic Psychiatry 207

Walsh, J.J. The Concepts of Diminished Responsibility and Cumulative Intent: A Practical Perspective [1991] 33 Criminal Law Quarterly 229

Ward, T. Law, Common Sense and the Authority of Science: Expert Witnesses and Criminal Insanity in England, Ca.1840-1940 [1997] 6 Social and Legal Studies 343

Wasik, M. Cumulative Provocation and Domestic Killing [1982] Criminal Law Review 29

Wasik, M. Partial Excuses in the Criminal Law [1982] 45 Modern Law Review 516

Wechsler, H. The Criteria of Criminal Responsibility [1954] 22 University of Chicago Law Review 367

Weihofen, H. The Flowering of New Hampshire (1954) 22 University of Chicago Law Review 356

Weihofen, H. and Overhoser, W. Mental Disorder Affecting the Degree of a Crime (1947) 56 Yale Law Journal 959

Wells, C. Whither Insanity [1983] Criminal Law Review 787

Wells, C. Domestic Violence and Self-Defence [1990] 140 New Law Journal 127

Wells, C. Battered Woman Syndrome and Defences to Homicide: Where Now? (1994) 14 Legal Studies 266

Wertham, F. Psychoauthoritarianism and the Law [1954] 22 University of Chicago Law Review 336

West, D.J. and Walk, A.(eds.) *Daniel McNaghten; His trial and the Aftermath* Gaskell Books, London, 1977

Wexler, D.B. Redefining the Insanity Problem [1985] 53 George Washington Law Review 528

White, S. Insanity Defences and Magistrates' Courts [1991] Criminal Law Review 207

White, S. The Criminal Procedure (Insanity and Unfitness to Plead) Act [1992]

Criminal Law Review 4

White, S. and Bowen, P. Insanity Defences in Summary Trials [1997] 61 Journal of Criminal Law 198

Wilczynski, A. and Morris, A. Parents who Kill Their Children [1993] Criminal Law Review 31

Winslade, W.J. and Ross, J.W. The *Insanity Plea* Charles Scribner's sons, New York, 1983

Wooton, B.. *Social Science and Social Pathology* Allen and Unwin Ltd, London, 1959

Wooton, B.. Diminished Responsibility: A Layman's View [1960] 76 Law Quarterly Review 224

Wooton, B. *Crime and the Criminal Law* (2nd ed.) Stevens and Sons, London, 1981

Wright, D.R. *The Development of Legal Responsibility in the Criminal Law of Scotland* PhD, University of Aberdeen, 1954

Yeates, P. Concern at Man's Detention *Irish Times* 11 January 1993

Zeegers, M. Diminished Responsibility: A Logical, Workable and Essential Concept [1981] 4 International Journal of Law and Psychiatry 433

Zilboorg, G.A. Step Toward more Enlightened Justice [1954] 22 University of Chicago Law Review 331

Index